2001 CATALOGUE OF
ERRORS
ON U.S. POSTAGE STAMPS

Stephen R. Datz

© 2000 by
Krause Publications, Inc.

All rights reserved under the Universal Pan American Conventions. No portion of this publication may be reproduced or transmitted in any form or by any means, electronic or mechanical, including photocopy, recording, or any information storage and retrieval systems, without permission in writing from the publisher, except by a reviewer who may quote brief passages in a critical article or review to be printed in a magazine or newspaper, or electronically transmitted on radio or television.

Copyright infringement is a criminal offense, and infringers are subject to criminal and civil penalties under Title 17 of the United States Code.

The publisher is neither in the market to buy nor sell error stamps and cannot respond to inquiries about the identification, genuineness, or value of an error stamp.

Every effort has been made to insure accuracy in the information contained herein, however, typographical errors may exist.

This catalog is intended as a reference based on the best information available at press time. Readers are advised that prices for errors are normally subject to fluctuation and should contact stamp dealers active in the market for timely quotes when buying or selling. Please refer to introduction section for more information on pricing.

Advertising appearing in this book has been accepted in good faith by the publisher. The publisher neither endorses nor accepts any liability for the contents of any advertising appearing herein.

Published by

700 E. State Street • Iola, WI 54990-0001
Telephone: 715/445-2214

Please call or write for our free catalog of numismatic publications.
Our toll-free number to place an order or obtain a free catalog is 800-258-0929
or please use our regular business telephone 715-445-2214
for editorial comment and further information.

Library of Congress Catalog Number: 97-80544
ISBN: 0-87341-942-1

Printed in the United States of America

CONTENTS

Introduction	1
Printer Abbreviations	8
Numbering Changes	8
Imperforates	9
Air Mail Imperforates	103
Special Delivery Imperforates	107
Postage Due Imperforates	107
Official Stamp Imperforates	108
Migratory Bird Imperforates	109
Color Omitted Errors	110
Color Omitted Air Mail Stamps	147
Color Omitted Migratory Bird Stamps	149
Color Omitted Postage Due Stamps	150
Color Omitted Stamped Envelopes	151
Color Omitted Aerogrammes	156
Color Omitted Postal Cards	157
Color Omitted Airmail Postal Cards	159
Inverts	160
Postal Card Inverts	162
Reverse Inscription Omitted	163
Reverse Inscription Inverted	164
Census of Plate Number Coil Strips	165
EFOs & Other Unusual Stamps	169

ACKNOWLEDGMENTS

Many individuals generously assisted in the preparation of this book. Sincere thanks are extended to all who contributed. Special thanks are due Jacques C. Schiff, Jr. for his encouragement and resources in making this book a reality. Sincere thanks also to Marvin Frey for his help and guidance in editing the section on EFOs. Among those who have helped with this or previous editions (including the late *) are:

Ken Beiner	John Greenwood	James B. Peterson
Larry Bustillo	Herman Herst Jr. *	D. James Samuelson
Mike Charles *	John Hotchner	Robert A. Siegel *
Robert Dowiot	William S. Langs	John Tison
Bob Dumaine	James McDevitt	Wm. Wallerstein *
Marvin Frey	Bruce H. Mosher	Martin Wilkinson
Howard P. Gates Jr. *	Jack S. Molesworth	Wayne Youngblood
Stan Goldfarb	Jack Nalbandian	

Our sincere appreciation to the following firms for their assistance in providing auction catalogues and prices realized, or retail price lists for this edition.

Matthew Bennett, Inc.
Richard E. Drews Philatelic Auctions
EFO Collectors Club
Ivy & Mader Auctions, Inc.
Jack Nalbandian, Inc.
Regency Stamps, Ltd.
Robert A. Siegel Auction Galleries, Inc.
Sam Houston Philatelics
Jacques C. Schiff Jr. Inc.
Shreves Philatelic Galleries, Inc.
Superior Stamp & Coin Co., Inc.
Weiss Philatelics

INTRODUCTION

The present scope of this work is three categories of major errors: stamps lacking perforations; multicolored stamps and postal stationery lacking one or more colors that would normally be present; and stamps and postal stationery of two or more colors in which one of the design elements was inverted during printing. Certain other stamps that resemble errors are included and described under **Error-Like Stamps** or in the **EFOs & Other Unusual Stamps** section. Other categories of errors exist, but are not presently within the scope of this catalogue.

Imperforates. To be considered an imperforate error, all traces of perforations (or die cuts) between two complete, adjacent stamps must be absent. The presence of even one perforation between stamps disqualifies it from being considered an imperforate error. The presence of incompletely impressed perforations or die cuts also disqualifies a stamp as an imperforate error. Refer to **Blind Perforations.**

The presence of a row of perforations completely within the design of one of the stamps of a pair and parallel to the row of omitted perforations, disqualifies the pair from being considered imperforate between, imperforate horizontally, or imperforate vertically, as the case may be. Perforations touching or cutting a design do not disqualify an error. Only when perforations are completely inside the border of a design does disqualification occur.

It is generally accepted that a single stray perforation hole (not part of a row) within a design does not affect an error's status as an error. An example is **IM 263**.

Some imperforates are the result of foldovers on booklets or sheet stamps. Some feel that such items should be regarded as freaks or oddities. However, our policy is to judge items on their physical appearance. If they meet the criteria set forth in a definition, they are listed without regard to how they may have been created, which in many cases cannot be known with certainty anyway.

At present, some controversy exists over whether a folding crease disqualifies an imperforate pair as a major error. In our opinion, the presence of a folding crease does not disqualify a stamp as an error because it is not material to the fundamental condition that defines the error: the complete omission of perfs between adjacent stamps. Since the presence of creases (or other faults) does not disqualify other major errors, it is illogical to conclude that they should disqualify foldovers from being major errors.

Where the chance for confusion exists, our policy is to describe errors according to the empirical evidence provided by their appearance. A case in point is the description of imperforate errors arising from booklets. Pairs from booklets with natural straight edges on two opposing exterior sides are best described as imperforate vertically or horizontally (whichever the case may be) in order to distinguish them from true imperforate betweens, which possess perforations on all exterior sides, and which may arise from foldovers. In some cases, both forms of errors exist for the same issue, and confusion arises where descriptions are not specific.

Stamps with perforations omitted between the stamp and the selvage are not listed because the omitted perforations do not occur between two adjacent stamps and, therefore, do not fall within the definition of an imperforate error. Their omission is not a reflection on their desirability or collectibility.

Color-Omitted Errors. To be considered a color-omitted error, 100 percent of the affected color(s) must be absent from the design. The presence of even one dot of color disqualifies a stamp. The stamp must be able to pass scrutiny under 30-power magnification. Colors absent from a design due to a perforation shift are not color-omitted errors.

Albinos, stamps with all color(s) omitted, exist for a few issues but are not included in this work. Their omission is not a reflection on their desirability or collectibility.

Tagging is applied by a separate printing plate and, although invisible to the naked eye, is considered by some to be a "color" for purposes of defining what constitutes a properly prepared stamp. Stamps with tagging omitted are not considered major errors and are not separately listed. In some cases, the omission of tagging is mentioned because it helps to authenticate the error.

Error-Like Stamps. Traditionally, to be regarded as a "legitimate" error, a stamp must have found its way into public hands by being sold at a post office. Several kinds of stamps, usually imperforates, have found their way into the philatelic domain by other means. While not errors in the traditional sense, they are similar in appearance.

Because it is the purpose of this catalogue to be used as a reference, to aid in identification, and to foster knowledge, certain of these stamps are included herein. They are identified by one of the following references.

PRF. *(Proof)*. Some early imperforates are arguably proofs, prepared in issued colors on stamp paper, either gummed or ungummed. Where the prevailing opinion is that an imperforate item was actually a stamp-like proof, the listing is identified by the symbol **PRF**.

NRI. *(Not Regularly Issued)*. Some imperforates were not regularly issued. Imperforate stamps have, on occasion, been traded for services or rare items (such as the 1869 pictorial inverts) needed for the National Museum's collection. Typically, they are identical to their perforated counterparts, except for the lack of perforations. They were intentionally allowed to leave government hands, although not made available to the general public. They are identified by the symbol **NRI**.

PW. *(Printer's Waste)*. In printer's terminology "make-readies" or "set-ups" is paper used to get presses up and running smoothly. It is usually discarded as waste, but occasionally finds its way into philatelic hands. On occasion, printer's waste—even after having been marked for destruction by quality control inspectors—has found its way into philatelic hands, inadvertently included in regular shipments of stamps. Most often, however, printer's waste reaches the market via a dishonest employee whose has stolen it from a printing plant or wastepaper destruction facility.

The term "printer's waste," has taken on a pejorative connotation in philately—purloined stamps. Generally, printer's waste is neither recognized nor esteemed by the philatelic community and many collectors prefer not to include printer's waste in their collections.

In some cases it is not clear how imperfect stamps (either marked for destruction or generally faulty) reached public hands. Some legitimate errors are known with destruction marks. And in some cases, printer's waste has the appearance of a perfectly legitimate error, but is known to have reached the market by having been misappropriated by someone inside a printing plant or destruction facility. In this catalogue, the term printer's waste takes the traditional connotation, that of stamps having reached the market by suspect means. It is identified by the symbol **PW**.

Errors purchased over a post office counter are perfectly legal to own. However, misappropriated stamps remain the property of the United States Government and are not legal to own. Stamps that could not have been purchased at a post office, such as full uncut sheets of booklet panes, should be avoided, as they remain government property.

Freaks and Oddities. A multitude of stamps exists containing irregularities such as perforation or color shifts, overinking or underinking, folding or other factors that make them strange in appearance. They are commonly referred to as EFOs (errors, freaks and oddities). Their value is usually, but not always, much less than that of major errors. Refer to the section on **EFOs & Other Unusual Stamps**.

FAKES

Fakes. Fakes exist for some errors. While many are crude, some are excellent and difficult to detect. Cautionary notes appear in the listings where appropriate. From a practical standpoint, the collector's best protection is dealing with knowledgeable, reputable dealers, or requiring, at least for items of high value, that an expert certificate from a recognized expertizing body be furnished.

Imperforate Singles. Generally, imperforate singles should be avoided. Some nineteenth century issues are known as error singles. However, many nineteenth and twentieth century stamps exist with huge margins that can be trimmed to resemble imperforates. An expert certificate is necessary for imperforate singles.

Blind Perforations. Blind perforations can be ironed out and made invisible to the naked eye. This is especially true of stamps with gum soaked off. Ungummed imperforates should be examined closely under magnification. The barest trace of even one perforation, even though not punched through, disqualifies the stamp from being imperforate. Pairs of stamps offered as imperforate should be carefully checked by a knowledgeable authority.

Colors Omitted. Certain dyes used in printing are susceptible to removal or alteration by exposure to light, heat or chemicals. Many, such as the Copernicus yellow-omitted error, are easily created, therefore, expertizing is recommended. Be suspicious of "newly discovered" color-omitted errors on 20- or 30-year-old stamps for which only a single copy is purportedly known.

Erasers have been used to remove colors from stamps, occasionally with treacherously deceptive results. Lithographed and gravure printed stamps are especially susceptible to this kind of tampering.

Because used stamps are particularly susceptible to tampering, our policy is not to list used color-omitted errors unless mint examples are also known.

Inverts. Clever fakes exist created by cutting a center design and inverting it in relation to its frame. The most clever of these do not cut entirely through the stamp's paper, so when viewed from the back, gum and paper are intact.

Used Errors. Used errors should be checked carefully. Blind perfs can be ironed out and chemical treatments or other operations performed to remove colors without having to worry about disturbing original gum, tagging, or the pristineness of the stamp. Use caution.

Expertizing. The publisher cannot give opinions regarding the genuineness of errors. The American Philatelic Expertizing Service (APEX), P.O. Box 8000, State College, PA 16803, and the Philatelic Foundation, 501 Fifth Avenue, Room 1901, New York, NY 10017, expertize error stamps. Contact them directly for information about their services before submitting a stamp for an opinion.

HOW TO USE THE CATALOGUE

Listings are divided into sections according to type of error: imperforates, colors omitted, and inverts. Listings are arranged as follows:

①

Zip Code. January 24, 1974. Photogravure. BEP.
  10c black, yellow, magenta & blue — ③
CO 57   yellow omitted — ⑥   40.00
  ＼   plate block of 8   ⑨   350.00
  ⑤ ⑧ —Quantity: 1,000+

☛ Caution. Extremely dangerous fakes, including color changelings, exist. Certificate of authenticity essential.

1. Illustration. Illustrations bordered in black are those of actual error stamps. Illustrations of actual error stamps are used wherever possible. Where an error illustration was not available, the illustration of a normal stamp—not bordered in black—is substituted. Illustrations of normal stamps are also used in cases where black and white reproduction does not adequately reveal a color-omitted error.

2. Description. Each error is described by the subject of the stamp, date of issue, form (se-tenant, souvenir sheet, etc.), method of printing, perforation, watermark, and type. *Watermark, perforation, and type are given only when necessary to distinguish one stamp from another of similar design.* Printers are listed for stamps issued after 1980.

3. Description. Denomination and color(s) are given. Only color information necessary to identify the stamp is given for imperforate errors. For color-omitted errors, individual colors and the printing process used to apply them are given.

4. Designs. Where multiple stamp designs are contained se-tenant in an error, each individual design is identified.

5. Numbering. Errors are classified by category. Individual types within a category are identified by a prefix and number.

IM prefix identifies imperforate errors.
CO prefix identifies color(s)-omitted errors.
IV prefix identifies invert errors.

A separate catalogue number is assigned to each error or variety. Multiples, such as plate blocks, Zip blocks, etc., are not separately numbered; they are regarded as varieties in form of the basic type.

Gaps in the sequence of catalogue numbers occur from time to time in order to accommodate possible future listings.

6. Form. Following the catalogue number is a listing of the error in its basic or most commonly encountered form. Other forms of the error (such as plate blocks, used copies, covers, etc.) are listed where known. The omission of a form does not necessarily imply that it does not exist, but only that it has not come to the attention of the publisher.

7. Price. Catalogue prices are based on the best information available at press time. Auction prices, advertised retail prices, and editors' judgments have been weighed and blended in an attempt to reflect a reasonable idea of value. **Prices are intended to reflect net retail prices, the price a consumer would expect to pay a dealer for stocking an item and making it available on demand.** Retail prices reflect a dealer's cost of overhead and investment in inventory.

Auction prices can be either higher or lower than listed prices, and vary from sale to sale. In general, auction prices tend to be lower than retail prices for plentiful items or items sold in bulk. And they tend to be higher than listed prices for items that rarely come to market, especially classic errors of premium quality.

In any case, there are no absolutes, and listed prices are not intended as such. They are intended—at best—to be a general guide to value. Note well, that because the market determines values, prices for individual items may vary—up or down—from those listed in the catalogue. This is especially true for newly discovered errors. Actual market prices also vary according to condition.

Condition. Prices are for sound stamps except where noted. Damaged or faulty copies usually sell for less, especially modern issues. Hinging is to be expected on issues before 1940, and prices are for hinged copies in fine to very fine (F-VF) condition. Better copies or never hinged (NH) copies often command a premium—often substantial. After 1940, prices are for NH copies in F-VF condition.

LRS. For rare, infrequently traded items, the Last Reported Sale (where known) is indicated by the initials **LRS**, followed by the date in parentheses and the transaction price.

Italics. Prices in italics are the editors' estimates where no precise information is available, such as newly discovered errors or infrequently traded errors. They should be regarded as tentative and subject to fluctuation. Actual market prices for these items may be either higher or lower.

Dash. (—). A dash indicates that insufficient pricing information exists, e.g. infrequently traded items or varieties such as plate blocks, etc. *Use of this symbol does not necessarily imply rarity.*

Covers. Prices for used modern errors on cover are for timely usage. *Philatelically inspired covers are usually worth much less.*

Pricing anomalies. Many errors exist in similar quantities but have different prices. *Do not assume that there is a dependable ratio of quantity to price. There is none.* Classic errors, such as the 1869 inverts or the inverted Jenny, sell for much more than modern errors of similar quantity. This, because values for classic rarities have been established over time.

Modern errors, as a group, are more plentiful. Generally, for modern errors—other factors being equal—the greater the eye appeal, the more dramatic and visually interesting the error, the greater the price. Those with topical appeal also tend to sell for more. In many cases, plate or position error blocks do not command the premium that their normal counterparts do. That is because error plate or position multiples are generally not as much in demand among error collectors as their normal counterparts are among the general collecting population. Also, pressure often exists to break multiples, even plate blocks, because they may be more salable as individual stamps, pairs, etc.

8. Quantity. Quantities known or reliably reported to exist are listed. The number listed under quantity is for the number of error stamps irrespective of form (pairs, blocks, etc.) unless otherwise stated. A quantity of 100 listed for in imperforate error means that 50 pairs could exist, or 25 blocks of 4, or some combination. In many cases the exact quantity existing is not ascertainable and, therefore, not given. Quantities given in italics are tentative and reflect the best information available at press time, which is often sketchy. The word "new" is used to indicate that the error appeared on the market just prior to press time. It appears together with an initial reported quantity, which should be considered tentative and subject to change.

Ranges are given, e.g. 50 to 100 pairs, where the general order of magnitude, but not the specific quantity, is acknowledged.

The term "reported" is used to indicate the quantity initially reported to exist. This number, especially for recently discovered errors, is subject to change. In addition, several general terms are used to indicate quantity believed to exist where exact information is not available.

Unique. Only one copy known.
Very Rare. Fewer than 10 copies.
Rare. Fewer than 25 copies.
Very Scarce. Fewer than 50 copies.
Scarce. Fewer than 100 copies.
Few Hundred. Generally, 100-300 copies.
Several Hundred. More than 300 copies.
Few Thousand. Generally, 1,000-3,000 copies.
Several Thousand. More than 3,000 copies.
N/a. Not available. No information available.

9. Notes. Information of interest to the reader. Cautionary notes, for fakes and other potential problems, are given where appropriate and indicated by the symbol ☛.

DEFINITIONS

Blind Perforations. Incompletely or partially impressed perforations, often barely indented into the paper and giving stamps the appearance of being imperforate, and perforations incompletely cut (visible on one side of a pane of stamps but not visible on the other side) by the new grinding technology.

Block. Four or more unseparated stamps arranged in a rectangle.

Booklet Pane. Small sheetlets of stamps bound into booklets between card-stock covers by staples, thread or glue. More recently, panes containing self-adhesive stamps have been issued without separate covers. They can be folded and inserted into wallet or purse, and are referred to as booklet panes.

Color Changeling. A stamp whose color(s) have been altered or eliminated by physical or chemical tampering. Certain stamp dyes are susceptible to alteration, especially bleaching by sunlight, heat, or chemicals. Color changelings are of no philatelic value.

EE Bars. Electric eye bars. Bars printed on margins of press sheets to guide them into position for perforating. These markings are normally trimmed off finished coil stamps.

EFO. See **EFOs & Other Unusual Stamps**.

Engraving. Also known as intaglio. A method of printing in which the design is engraved (recessed) into a metal plate. Ink fills the recesses and when printed, forms small ridges on the paper. Engraving can be identified by magnifying glass or by running your finger over the surface of the stamp and feeling the ridges.

Flat Press. A printing press that utilizes flat plates and prints paper one sheet at a time.

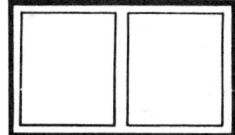

Imperforate. Lacking perforations. When used to describe a pair or multiple, imperforate means completely lacking perforations between stamps and on all sides. Stamps lacking die cuts are referred to as "die cut omitted."

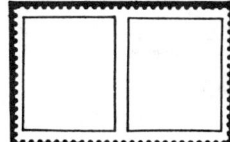

Imperforate Between. Lacking perforations

between two stamps, but with perforations present on all outer sides. Pairs or multiples may be either horizontal or vertical. In the case of booklet panes, this description is applied only to those having perforations on all outer sides (as often result from foldovers). Booklet pane pairs having natural straight edges on two opposing exterior sides are described as imperforate vertically or horizontally in order to distinguish them from true imperforate betweens, i.e. possessing perforations on all outer sides. Those with a natural straight edge at bottom can be described using the criteria set forth in **Imperforates—Other Configurations.**

Vertical Pair, Imperforate Horizontally. A pair of stamps, one atop the other vertically, lacking horizontal perforations between stamps and with horizontal straight edges at top and bottom. Perforations are present all across left and right sides.

Horizontal Pair, Imperforate Vertically. A pair of stamps, side by side horizontally, lacking vertical perforations between stamps and with vertical straight edges at either side. Perforations are present all across top and bottom.

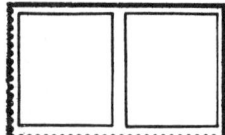

Imperforates—Other Configurations. Imperforates that do not conveniently fall into the above categories are described according to their appearance. The illustrated example is an imperforate horizontal pair with perforations at bottom and left, and straight edges at top and right.

The initial reference "imperforate" refers only to the omission of perforations between two stamps. Exterior sides are described according to the position and presence of perforations or straight edges. An item could have perforations on three sides and a straight edge on the fourth, or vice versa. This style is also appropriate for blocks or multiples, and for items imperforate horizontally or vertically on which perforations appear only part way across the exterior top or bottom or sides.

Whether each of these possible combinations constitutes a separate listing category, rather than mere sub-variety status, is not clear.

Imprint. A marginal inscription such as "American Bank Note Company." On modern issues "Use Zip Code," "Mail Early in the Day," and "Copyright USPS" often appear in margins.

Line Pair. On engraved, rotary-press coil stamps, a line is created by ink that fills the small space where the curved plates join and is printed in the same fashion as ink from the recessed stamp design.

Lithography. Also known as planographic or surface printing. This process is based on the antipathy of water and oil. A photographic image is exposed to a photosensitive plate. The area exposed becomes water insoluble. The unexposed, water-soluble area is washed away leaving an image that is receptive to ink. In some cases the inked image on the plate is transferred to a rubber-like blanket before being impressed on paper, hence the term offset printing.

Images are broken up into a series of dots in order to achieve tonal gradation. Color lithography involves the mingling of areas of dots from several plates, each printing a separate color, in order to achieve the effect of full color. Because each printing plate lays down only a single color, passes beneath several plates are necessary in order to achieve the final, full-color result. These passes may occur in several press runs or in a single press run through a large press capable of mounting and running multiple plates. Stamp production typically involves from four to seven plates (colors).

Color-omitted errors are produced when one or more plate impressions are omitted. You can observe the dot structure of lithography by examining any black-and-white or color printing, e.g. from a magazine or stamp, under a 10-power or stronger glass. You will see how the dots are used to yield tonal gradations and blend to make a variety of colors. In commercial printing four plates (colors) are typically used to achieve the full color effect: black, yellow, magenta (red) and cyan (blue). Stamp printing often employs additional plates, with a variety of specially mixed inks, in order to achieve a higher quality result.

Miscut. Cut abnormally so that portions of adjoining stamps appear together in the area normally occupied by a single design.

Pair. Two unseparated stamps.

Pane. A separate section of stamps, variously a quarter, half, or one-sixth sheet, as cut for retail sale from a press sheet.

Photogravure. Like lithography, the gravure plate is made by a photosensitive process; however, unlike lithography, the ink lies in small recesses and is very thinly applied. Tones are achieved by varying the depth of the recesses and thickness of the ink. The image is broken up into a series of fine points that keep the paper from being pressed into the recesses. The dot structure in photogravure is usually much finer than that used in lithography. You can see the difference by comparing a magazine illustration with a photogravure stamp under a 10 power magnifying glass.

Plate Number. A serial number usually appearing in the margin of a pane of stamps and, infrequently, on miscut coil or booklet stamps. Since about 1981, small plate numbers have appeared at the bottom of every nth stamp on most coil issues. Multicolored stamps usually, but not always, have a separate plate number for each color used in printing.

Rotary Press. A printing press on which the plates are curved in the form of a cylinder to facilitate continuous printing on a web of paper.

Se-tenant. Two or more different designs printed next to one another on a regular pane of stamps, a souvenir sheet, a booklet or a coil.

Splice. The splicing or joining of paper by glue or tape during stamp manufacture, typically in web-fed rotary printing. Tape splices are known in a variety of colors and types of tape, including paper and plastic. Splices are often referred to as paste-ups, a term originating from a time when most splices were made using glue or paste. At present, most, but not all, splices are made with tape. Splices on modern issues are usually the result of two webs of paper being joined during the printing process.

Strip. Three or more unseparated stamps arranged side-by-side or end-to-end.

Tagging. A luminescent coating, applied during printing, used to facilitate the facing and handling of mail by automated machinery. Usually invisible to the naked eye, it can be observed under ultraviolet light. Tagging may cover all or part of a stamp.

Transition Multiple. A pair, strip or block containing one or more color-omitted error stamps, one or more normal stamps, and in many cases, one or more stamps with color(s) partially omitted. Transition multiples are also known for some imperforate errors, where part of a pane, coil or booklet contains perforations and part does not. Transition multiples usually sell for a premium.

𝕌 𝕊 ℙ 𝕊
Double Line Watermark

U S P S
Single Line Watermark

Watermark. Letters impressed on paper during manufacture to discourage counterfeiting. Paper is thinner where the watermark has been impressed and, therefore, appears lighter when immersed in watermark detecting fluid.

PRINTERS

Abbreviations for printers appearing in the listings. Before 1980 most stamps were printed by the Bureau of Engraving & Printing. Printers are listed for stamps issued after 1980. Listings for twentieth century stamps not mentioning a printer were printed by the Bureau of Engraving & Printing.

ABN	American Bank Note Company
APU	Ashton-Potter (USA) Ltd.
AVR	Avery Dennison
BCA	Banknote Corporation of America
BEP	Bureau of Engraving & Printing
DBF	Dittler Brothers
GGI	Guilford Gravure Inc.
JWF	J.W. Fergusson & Sons
KCS	KCS Industries
NBC	National Bank Note Company
SSP	Sennett Security Products
SVS	Stamp Venturers
UBN	United Bank Note Co.
UCC	Union Camp Corporation
USB	U.S. Bank Note
3M	3M Corporation

NUMBERING CHANGES

The new catalogue number appears in bold at left followed by the old catalogue number or reason for change at right. In the case of delisted stamps, the former catalogue number appears.

IM 591	open
IM 592	a new listing
IM 594	IM 591
IM 596	IM 593
IM 597	a new listing
IM 600	IM 596
IM 602	a new listing
CO 204	a new listing
CO 205	CO 202
CO 206	CO 203
CO 208	CO 205
RIWF 1	a new listing
RIWF 2	RIWF 1
RIWF 3	RIWF 2

IMPERFORATE ERRORS

SERIES OF 1857/61

Benjamin Franklin. July 1857. Engraved.

1c blue, type IIIa

IM 1 used hz pair, imperf between   4,750.00
      Quantity: very rare

Benjamin Franklin. 1857. Engraved.

1c blue, type V

IM 2 used vrt strip of 5, imperf hz   —
      Quantity: unique

Typically, nineteenth century stamps are heavily hinged, contain only partial original gum and often, small faults. Prices are for stamps in such condition unless otherwise indicated. Sound stamps, stamps with full original gum, and lightly hinged copies sell for a premium.

3c WASHINGTON DESIGNS OF THE 1857/61 SERIES

Type I. The outer frame line intact all around.
Type II. The outer frame line is removed at the top and bottom. The side frame lines form a continuous line from stamp to stamp and extend beyond the design of the stamp.
Type III. The outer frame line is removed at top and bottom. The side frame lines extend only to the top and bottom of the stamp design.

George Washington. 1857. Engraved.

3c rose, type I

IM 3 used hz pair, imperf vrt   —
      Quantity: very rare

☛ Caution. Fakes exist.

IM 4 used vrt pair, imperf hz   —
      used single on cover **LRS**   6,600.00
      Quantity: 1 pair and one single on cover reported

IM 3 and IM 4 were printed from the same plates as the imperforate 1851 series. Regularly issued imperforate stamps of the 1851 series should not be confused with errors of the 1857 series. Also, proofs of the 1851 series in issued colors were printed on bond paper very similar in appearance to stamp paper. The two are so similar that it is very difficult, especially for the unpracticed eye, to distinguish one from another.

3c dull red, type II

IM 5 hz pair, imperf vrt   —
      as above, used   —
      Quantity: very rare

IM 6 vrt pair, imperf hz   —
      used vrt pair, imperf hz   —
      used strip of 3, imperf hz, on cover   —
      Quantity: very rare

IM 7 used hz pair, imperf between   —
      Quantity: very rare

3c dull red, type III

IM 7A hz strip of 3, imperf vrt, on cover
LRS (5/97) 8,250.00
single, imperf vrt —
Quantity: the two items as listed

The copy listed on cover is postmarked "Boston, Ms. Apr. 20, 1859," in red, contains two black grid cancels, and is addressed to St. Louis. The left stamp in the strip has a closed tear.

George Washington. 1857. Engraved.

12c black

IM 8 used hz pair, imperf between 11,000.00
Quantity: very rare

George Washington. 1860. Engraved.

24c gray or gray lilac

IM 9 imperf pair 16,000.00
single, imperf 1,250.00
Quantity: 2 pairs reported, singles very rare

In his book *Postage Stamps of the United States*, John Luff claims to "have seen 2 copies used on original envelopes." He thinks perhaps a pane got out. Lester Brookman claims these (24c-30c-90c) were trial printings submitted by Toppan, Carpenter & Co. to the Postmaster General and, therefore, not regularly issued.

Benjamin Franklin. 1860. Engraved.

30c orange

IM 10 imperf pair 7,500.00
single, imperf 2,500.00
used imperf pair 1,250.00
Quantity: 3 unused pairs and 1 used pair reported; singles very rare

Refer to note following **IM 9**. Luff states that a used single, printed in the brown orange shade peculiar to imperfs, exists on cover to France.

George Washington. August 1860. Engraved.

90c blue

IM 11 imperf pair —
single, imperf 3,000.00
Quantity: 1 pair reported; singles very rare

According to Lester Brookman a used single, with "good margins," appeared in the Pelander sale of February 1943. A set of **IM 9—IM 11**, including the unique 90c pair, sold at auction for $55,000 in May 2000.

SERIES OF 1857/1860
SPECIAL PRINTING OF 1875

Engraved. Printed by the Continental Bank Note Co. on bright, white paper, without gum. Imperforates are varieties of the perforated stamps issued for the Centennial Exposition of 1876. They vary in color from **IM 9**, **IM 10** and **IM 11** and can thus be distinguished.

IM 12 1c Franklin, bright blue
IM 13 3c Washington, scarlet
IM 14 5c Jefferson, orange brown
IM 15 10c Washington, blue green
IM 16 12c Washington, greenish black
IM 17 24c Washington, blackish violet
IM 18 30c Franklin, yellow orange
IM 19 90c Washington, deep blue

set of 8 pairs, imperf LRS (89) 71,500.00
set of 8 imperf margin singles LRS (85) 41,250.00
Quantity: singles very rare; one set of pairs reported; plus two pairs of the 1c, one pair of the 10c, and one pair of the 12c

SERIES OF 1861/1862

Benjamin Franklin. August 17, 1861. Engraved

1c blue

IM 20	used vrt pair, imperf hz Quantity: very rare	—

George Washington. August 17, 1861. Engraved.

3c rose red or various shades

IM 21	imperf pair, ungummed **PRF** block of 4, imperf block of 8, imprint & plate No. 11, imperf **LRS (12/99)** Quantity: scarce	600.00 — 1,897.50

IM 21 typically occurs with mottled paper.

IM 22	vrt pair, imperf hz used vrt pair, imperf hz Quantity: rare	*2,500.00* *750.00*

3c lake or carmine lake

IM 23	imperf pair strip of 4, imprint & plate No. 52, imperf **LRS (5/00)** bottom block of 8, imprint & plate No. 52, imperf **LRS (4/98)** Quantity: scarce; 3 imprint blocks	1,750.00 2,970.00 12,100.00

Trial color proofs were printed from Plate No. 34. Imprint blocks or strips are from Plate No. 52.

George Washington. August 17, 1861. Engraved.

10c green

IM 24	used vrt pair, imperf hz Quantity: very rare, possibly unique	—

George Washington. February 20, 1863. Engraved.

24c dark gray

IM 29	vrt pair, imperf **NRI** used single, imperf Quantity: 1-3 pairs known	— —

STAMPS WITH GRILLS

Grills, waffle-like in appearance, were impressed on stamps to break their paper fibers and permit better ink absorption, preventing washing and reuse. Several types of grills exist.

A grill: points up, grill covers entire stamp.
C grill: points up, grill measures about 13x16 mm.
F grill: points down, grill measures about 9x13 mm.

George Washington. 1867. Engraved.

3c rose, A grill

IM 30	imperf pair **PRF NRI** bottom imprint block of 8, imperf **LRS (12/99)** Quantity: rare	1,500.00 6,037.50

3c rose, C grill

IM 31	imperf pair **PRF NRI** imperf margin single with selvage Quantity: n/a	1,750.00 *1,000.00*

☞ 19th Century stamps often occur with large margins that can be trimmed to resemble imperforates. Single stamps, even margin copies, should be regarded with suspicion. Imperforate singles without expert certificate should be avoided.

3c red or rose red, F grill

IM 32	imperf pair **NRI** Quantity: very rare	1,000.00
IM 33	vrt pair, imperf hz Quantity: very rare	*1,000.00*

SERIES OF 1869
SPECIAL PRINTING OF 1875

Columbus. 1875. Engraved. National Bank Note Co.

15c brown & blue

IM 35	single, imperf hz Quantity: 5-10	*3,000.00*

A gem copy sold for $6,600 at auction in October 1998. No multiples exist.

A unique partial set of imperforate singles of the 1869 issue exists printed on gummed stamp paper that, unlike the regularly issued stamps of the series, lacks grills. The center of the 24c denomination is inverted. They were not regularly issued. The set includes the 1c, 3c, 12c, 15c (type I), 24c, 30c and 90c denominations. This group of seven sold for $94,600 in 1989.

SERIES OF 1870/1871

George Washington. April 1870. Engraved.

3c green, with grill

IM 36	imperf pair **NRI** block of 16 with plate No. 44, imperf Quantity: very scarce	1,250.00 —

3c green, without grill

IM 37	imperf pair **NRI** block of 10 with bottom imprint & plate No. 11, imperf Quantity: rare	750.00 *5,500.00*

SERIES OF 1873

Benjamin Franklin. 1873. Engraved. Secret mark.

1c ultramarine

IM 38	imperf pair **LRS (3/97)** used imperf pair Quantity: *approx 15 pairs, including 2 mint pairs*	1,155.00 *600.00*

Many are toned and creased. Price is for toned and creased pair.

Andrew Jackson. 1873. Engraved. Secret mark. White wove paper.

2c brown

IM 39	imperf pair Quantity: very rare	—

Andrew Jackson. June 21, 1875. Engraved. Secret mark. Yellowish wove paper.

2c vermilion

IM 40	imperf pair **PRF** imperf block of 4 imperf block of 16 with inscription & plate No. 161 **LRS (4/98)** Quantity: *scarce; 2 plate blocks*	800.00 — 5,225.00

George Washington. 1873. Engraved. Secret mark.

3c green

IM 41	imperf pair **PRF** Quantity: n/a	850.00

IM 42 used hz pair, imperf vrt —
Quantity: n/a

IM 43 used hz pair, imperf between 1,250.00
Quantity: rare

3c green, with grill

IM 44 imperf pair PRF 750.00
Quantity: n/a

Thomas Jefferson. 1873. Engraved. Secret mark.

10c brown

IM 45 hz pair, imperf between —
used imperf pair 2,750.00
Quantity: 2 pairs reported

SERIES OF 1879

George Washington. 1879. Engraved.

3c green

IM 46 imperf pair PRF 550.00
Quantity: rare

Thomas Jefferson. 1879. Engraved. Secret mark.

10c brown

IM 47 used vrt pair, imperf between —
Quantity: rare

Commodore O.H. Perry. 1879. Engraved.

90c carmine

IM 48 imperf pair PRF 2,250.00
imperf block of four —
Quantity: rare

Often contains faults. Price is for a sound copy.

George Washington. 1883. Engraved.

2c red brown

IM 49 imperf pair NRI —
Quantity: rare

SPECIAL PRINTING OF 1883

George Washington. 1883. Engraved. Soft porous paper.

2c pale red brown

IM 50 hz pair, imperf between NRI 2,000.00
top margin inscription strip of 6, center
pair imperf between LRS (6/96) 6,325.00
part sheet of 66 with right six pairs
imperf between - affixed to
cardboard LRS (87) 17,600.00
Quantity: at least 20 pairs

Price is for a sound copy.

Typically, nineteenth century stamps are heavily hinged, contain only partial original gum and often, small faults. Prices are for stamps in such condition unless otherwise indicated. Sound stamps, stamps with full original gum, and lightly hinged copies sell for a premium.

Andrew Jackson. October 1, 1883. Engraved.

4c blue green

IM 51 imperf pair PRF —
Quantity: scarce

Benjamin Franklin. June 11, 1887. Engraved.

1c ultramarine

IM 52	imperf pair	1,000.00
	used pair, imperf	525.00
	used strip of 3 on piece	—
	Quantity: rare	

A horizontal strip of 3 on piece postmarked Hoboken, New Jersey, March 25, 1890 (with toning on the left pair) and a horizontal strip on cover postmarked Hoboken, New Jersey, have been reported.

George Washington. September 10, 1887. Engraved.

2c green

IM 54	imperf pair	1,000.00
	used pair, imperf	1,000.00
	used strip of 3, imperf	—
	pair on cover, imperf	—
	Quantity: rare unused; one used pair, and one used strip of 3 reported.	

James A. Garfield. February 10, 1888. Engraved.

5c indigo

IM 55 imperf pair PRF   1,250.00
Quantity: rare

Alexander Hamilton. January 3, 1888. Engraved.

30c orange brown

IM 56 imperf pair PRF   1,500.00
Quantity: rare

Often contains faults.

Commodore O.H. Perry. February 28, 1888. Engraved.

90c purple

IM 57 imperf pair PRF   3,000.00
Quantity: rare

Usually contains faults.

Typically, nineteenth century stamps are heavily hinged, contain only partial original gum and often, small faults. Prices are for stamps in such condition unless otherwise indicated. Sound stamps, stamps with full original gum, and lightly hinged copies sell for a premium.

ISSUES OF THE AMERICAN BANKNOTE COMPANY SMALL FORMAT 1890/1893

In order to acquire rare stamps for the official collection at the National Museum, imperforate stamps, identical to their perforated counterparts, were exchanged for acquisitions, such as the 1869 inverts. A total of 56 imperforate sets, mostly in pairs or blocks of four, were released. Imperforate postage due stamps, series of 1891, were simultaneously released and appear in the postage due section.

Some regard these stamps as proofs, however, we regard them as stamps not regularly issued and refer to them as such (NRI).

In addition to the imperforate stamps, proofs of the 2c, 4c, and 5c denominations in various shades similar to the issued colors exist on gummed stamp paper. The 2c denomination reportedly exists in 5 shades; the 4c, in 11 shades; and the 5c, in 13 shades. They should not be confused with the imperforate stamps listed below.

Benjamin Franklin. February 22, 1890. Engraved.

1c dull blue

IM 58	imperf pair NRI	150.00
	block of 4, imperf	320.00
	plate block of 12 (No. 14), imperf	1,150.00
	Quantity: 56	

George Washington. February 22, 1890. Engraved.

2c lake (issued without gum)

IM 59	imperf pair NRI	100.00
	block of 4, imperf	225.00
	plate block of 12, imperf	—
	Quantity: *56+*	

2c carmine, May 12, 1890

IM 60	imperf pair NRI	125.00
	block of 4, imperf	275.00
	plate block of 12 (No. 18), imperf	*900.00*
	Quantity: 56	

Andrew Jackson. February 22, 1890. Engraved.

3c purple

IM 61	imperf pair NRI	150.00
	block of 4, imperf	350.00
	top plate block of 12 (No. 21), imperf	—
	Quantity: 56	

Pricing Note: Most examples of this series are heavily hinged, contain disturbed or partial original gum, and often contain faults. Prices are for stamps in such condition. Sound, lightly hinged stamps sell for 50% to 100% more. Never hinged copies are rare and worth 100% to 150% more.

Abraham Lincoln. June 2, 1890. Engraved.

4c dark brown

IM 62	imperf pair NRI	165.00
	block of 4, imperf	400.00
	Quantity: 56	

Ulysses S. Grant. June 2, 1890. Engraved.

5c chocolate brown

IM 63	imperf pair NRI	165.00
	block of 4, imperf	400.00
	top plate block of 12, imperf	—
	Quantity: 56	

James A. Garfield. February 22, 1890. Engraved.

6c brown red

IM 64	imperf pair NRI	175.00
	block of 4, imperf	420.00
	top plate block of 12 (No. 23), imperf	*1,200.00*
	Quantity: 56	

William T. Sherman. March 21, 1893. Engraved.

8c lilac

IM 65	imperf pair NRI	1,250.00
	block of 4, imperf	—
	Quantity: n/a	

Daniel Webster. February 22, 1890. Engraved.

10c green

IM 66	imperf pair NRI	225.00
	imperf block of 4	420.00
	Quantity: 56	

Henry Clay. February 22, 1890. Engraved.

15c indigo

IM 67	imperf pair NRI	500.00
	imperf block of 4	1,100.00
	plate block of 12 (No. 22), imperf	*3,750.00*
	Quantity: 56	

Thomas Jefferson. February 22, 1890. Engraved.

30c black

IM 68	imperf pair NRI	750.00
	imperf block of 4	1,650.00
	Quantity: 56	

Commodore O.H. Perry. February 22, 1890. Engraved.

90c orange

IM 69	imperf pair NRI	1,350.00
	imperf block of 4	2,500.00
	Quantity: 56	

Refer to note on pricing for this series preceding **IM 58**.

COLUMBIAN SERIES OF 1893

The B. K. Miller Collection at the New York Public Library Collection contains a complete set of imperforate horizontal pairs, 1c-$5. They were originally the property of John Wanamaker, Postmaster General 1889-93.

Columbus Landing. January 2, 1893. Engraved.

2c purple maroon

IM 70	imperf pair, ungummed PW	1,750.00
	imperf block of 4	*5,000.00*
	Quantity: 50-100	

These stamps are from a crumpled sheet, which was likely printer's waste. All known copies are ungummed and defective.

SERIES OF 1894

Similar to the Series of 1890 except triangles added to the upper corners. Printed on unwatermarked paper.

George Washington. October 5, 1894. Engraved.

2c pink, type I

IM 71	vrt pair, imperf hz	*2,250.00*
	Quantity: *rare*	

2c carmine, type I

IM 72	vrt pair, imperf hz	*1,750.00*
	Quantity: *rare*	
IM 73	hz pair, imperf between	*1,750.00*
	Quantity: *rare*	

2c carmine, type III

IM 74	hz pair, imperf vrt	1,500.00
	Quantity: *rare*	
IM 75	hz pair, imperf between	1,500.00
	Quantity: *rare*	

Andrew Jackson. September 24, 1894. Engraved.

3c purple

IM 76	imperf pair, ungummed **NRI**	200.00
	imperf block of 4, ungummed	420.00
	imperf plate block of 6, ungummed	—
	Quantity: 400	

Abraham Lincoln. September 11, 1894. Engraved.

4c dark brown

IM 77	imperf pair, ungummed **NRI**	200.00
	imperf block of 4, ungummed	420.00
	imperf plate block of 6 (No. 50), ungummed **LRS (4/98)**	1,760.00
	Quantity: 400	

Ulysses S. Grant. September 28, 1894. Engraved.

5c chocolate brown

IM 78	imperf pair, ungummed **NRI**	225.00
	imperf block of 4, ungummed	500.00
	imperf plate block of 6, ungummed	—
	Quantity: 300-400	
IM 79	vrt pair, imperf hz, with gum	*1,750.00*
	vrt strip of 3, imperf hz, with gum	*1,850.00*
	plate block of 6	—
	Quantity: uncertain, but reportedly less than one pane of 100	

James A. Garfield. July 18, 1894. Engraved.

6c dull brown

IM 80	vrt pair, imperf hz	*800.00*
	block of 4, imperf hz	—
	plate block of 6	—
	Quantity: 100	

Usually with disturbed gum or faults. Price is for copy with usual disturbed gum or faults. Sound copies sell for more.

Daniel Webster. September 17, 1894. Engraved.

10c dark green

IM 81	imperf pair, ungummed **NRI**	500.00
	imperf block of 4, ungummed	1,100.00
	plate block of 6	—
	Quantity: 400	

Lester Brookman mentions that the 50c denomination was reported as a single on cover. Brookman also describes a bottom margin pair with no perforations between the bottoms of the stamps and the selvage. He also mentions that the $1 denomination (type I, broken circle around the $1) exists imperforate, but does not mention its form, i.e., imperforate horizontally, vertically, or between.

Note: IM 76, IM 77, IM 78 and **IM 81** were issued without gum. Those with gum had it added later.

Although catalogue prices are based on the best information available at press time, readers should be aware that prices for error stamps fluctuate over time, and therefore, are advised to contact dealers active in the error stamp market for timely quotes when buying or selling.

SERIES OF 1895

Similar to the Series of 1894 except with double-line watermark USPS horizontally or vertically.

Like the Series of 1890, quantities of imperforate stamps of this series reached public hands, this time via Gilbert Jones, owner of the New York Times, who accepted them in exchange for services rendered to the Bureau of Engraving and Printing. They are gummed and identical to regular stamps of the series except for the lack of perforations. It is reported that the 1c, 2c, 3c, 4c and 8c denominations exist used philatelically on cover. Some regard this issue as proofs, however, we regard them as stamps that were not regularly issued.

Benjamin Franklin. January 17, 1898. Engraved. Double-line watermark.

1c dull blue

IM 82	imperf pair NRI	150.00
	block of 4, imperf	320.00
	plate block of 6, imperf	*2,000.00*
	used pair on cover, imperf	—
	Quantity: 900 stamps	
IM 83	hz pair, imperf vrt	—
	plate strip of 3, imperf vrt	—
	Quantity: 1-5 pairs	

George Washington. 1895. Engraved. Double-line watermark.

2c carmine, type III

IM 84	imperf pair NRI	175.00
	block of 4, imperf	400.00
	plate strip of 3, (No. 319), imperf	*675.00*
	plate block of 6 (No. 319), imperf	*2,250.00*
	Quantity: 500	

Pricing Note: Most examples of this series are heavily hinged, contain disturbed or partial original gum, and often contain faults. Prices are for stamps in such condition. Sound, lightly hinged stamps sell for 50% to 100% more. Never hinged copies are rare and worth 100% to 150% more.

Andrew Jackson. October 31, 1895. Engraved. Double-line watermark.

3c dark purple violet

IM 85	imperf pair NRI	200.00
	block of 4, imperf	420.00
	used pair on cover, imperf	—
	Quantity: 300	

Abraham Lincoln. June 5, 1895. Engraved. Double-line watermark.

4c black brown

IM 86	imperf pair NRI	200.00
	block of 4, imperf	420.00
	used pair on cover, imperf	—
	Quantity: 300	

Ulysses S. Grant. June 11, 1895. Engraved. Double-line watermark.

5c deep reddish brown

IM 87	imperf pair NRI	200.00
	block of 4, imperf	420.00
	Quantity: 300	

Where possible, illustrations of actual error stamps have been used. They are bordered in black. Illustrations of normal stamps have been used in cases where error stamp illustrations were not available, or where an error illustration would not adequately illustrate the error. Illustrations of normal stamps appear without black border.

James A. Garfield. August 31, 1895. Engraved. Double-line watermark.

6c claret brown

IM 88	imperf pair NRI	200.00
	block of 4, imperf	420.00
	plate block of 6, imperf	—
	Quantity: 300	

William T. Sherman. July 22, 1895. Engraved. Double-line watermark.

8c deep claret brown

IM 89	imperf pair NRI	300.00
	block of 4, imperf	625.00
	used pair on cover, imperf	—
	Quantity: 300	

Daniel Webster. June 7, 1895. Engraved. Double-line watermark.

10c pale dull green

IM 90	imperf pair NRI	225.00
	block of 4, imperf	475.00
	Quantity: 400	

Henry Clay. September 10, 1895. Engraved. Double-line watermark.

15c deep indigo

IM 91	imperf pair NRI	750.00
	block of 4, imperf	1,500.00
	Quantity: 100	

Thomas Jefferson. November 9, 1895. Engraved. Double-line watermark.

50c orange

IM 92	imperf pair NRI	750.00
	block of 4, imperf	1,500.00
	Quantity: 100	

Commodore O.H. Perry. August 12, 1895. Engraved. Double-line watermark.

$1 black, type I

IM 93	imperf pair NRI	1,250.00
	block of 4, imperf	2,600.00
	Quantity: 100	

James Madison. August 13, 1895. Engraved. Double-line watermark.

$2 blue

IM 94	imperf pair NRI	2,250.00
	block of 4, imperf	5,000.00
	Quantity: 100	

John Marshall. August 16, 1895. Engraved. Double-line watermark.

$5 dark green

IM 95	imperf pair NRI	2,500.00
	block of 4, imperf	5,250.00
	Quantity: 100	

Refer to the pricing note preceding **IM 82** regarding this series.

Troops Guarding Train. June 1898. Engraved.

8c violet brown

IM 96	vrt pair, imperf hz	22,500.00
	vrt strip of 4, imperf hz	—
	block of 4, top or bottom plate number, imperf hz	—
	Quantity: 25 pairs	

Price is for a sound copy.

IM 97   IM 98

George Washington. November 12, 1903. Engraved.

2c carmine

IM 97	vrt pair, imperf hz		5,000.00
	block of 4, imperf hz	**LRS (10/98)**	13,200.00
	Quantity: 20-25 pairs reported		
IM 98	vrt pair, imperf between		1,250.00
	Quantity: rare		

☛ Caution. Do not confuse **IM 97** and **IM 98** with similar stamps of 1906 which were regularly issued imperforate. Expert certificate recommended.

Pairs similar to **IM 98** exist rouletted between. Panes lacking perforations between the top two rows were rouletted by the postmaster in San Francisco and sold over the counter in the normal course of business.

Hinging. Prices for stamps preceding **IM 196** are for hinged copies. Never hinged copies sell for a premium ranging from 25% to 100% or more depending on the scarcity of an item, and the scarcity of never hinged copies of an item. These guidelines do not apply to prices for ultra-rare or unique items, which may not exist never hinged.

Thomas Jefferson. April 30, 1904. Engraved.

2c carmine

IM 99	vrt pair, imperf hz		9,000.00
	as above, line pair		—
	block of 4, imperf hz		18,000.00
	plate block of 4, imperf hz		—
	margin block of 4, arrow at lower left, imperf hz	**LRS (5/98)**	28,600.00
	Quantity: 19 pairs & 3 blocks as listed		

Well centered copies sell for a premium.

Benjamin Franklin. 1908. Booklet pane. Engraved. Double-line watermark.

1c green

IM 99A	hz pair, imperf between	**NRI**	1,000.00
	Quantity: n/a		

From a booklet pane experiment.

George Washington. February 12, 1912. Engraved. Single-line watermark. Perf 12.

1c green

IM 100	vrt pair, imperf hz	700.00
	vrt strip of three, imperf hz	—
	Quantity: rare	

☛ Caution. Do not confuse this stamp with that of identical design, which was regularly issued imperforate. Expert certificate recommended.

George Washington. 1914. Engraved. Single-line watermark. Perf 10.

1c green

IM 101	vrt pair, imperf hz LRS (4/00)	2,820.00
	used vrt pair, imperf hz	—
	Quantity: very rare	

IM 101A	vrt pair, imperf between LRS (5/00)	5,500.00
	Quantity: 2 reported	

IM 101A results from a foldover in which the upper right pair is imperf between and contains a straight edge at the top.

IM 102	booklet pane of 6, imperf, ungummed	1,750.00
	Quantity: 60 reported	

Price is for a sound, well centered pane.

George Washington. 1917. Engraved. No watermark. Perf 11.

1c green

IM 103	vrt pair, imperf hz	200.00
	block of 4, imperf hz	400.00
	Quantity: 1 pane of 100 reported	

IM 104	hz pair, imperf between	85.00
	Quantity: n/a	

IM 105	vrt pair, imperf between	400.00
	Quantity: scarce	

☛ Caution. It is possible to fabricate Nos. **IM 103**—**IM 108** by adding perforations to completely imperforate regularly issued stamps of identical design. Expert certificate strongly advised.

George Washington. 1917. Engraved. No watermark. Perf 11.

2c rose, type I

IM 106	vrt pair, imperf hz	150.00
	Quantity: n/a	

IM 107	hz pair, imperf vrt	250.00
	used hz pair, imperf vrt	*150.00*
	Quantity: 100 pairs reported	

IM 108	vrt pair, imperf between	500.00
	used vrt pair, imperf between	*250.00*
	Quantity: *very scarce*	

☛ Caution. Pairs are known with blind perfs that can be ironed out and eliminated to the naked eye, resulting in dangerous fakes. Pairs are also known with blind perfs occurring in the upper stamp due to a wandering perforating wheel. All pairs should be checked carefully. Copies lacking gum should be regarded with special caution. Expert certificate strongly advised.

George Washington. 1917. Engraved. No watermark. Perf. 11.

3c violet, type I

| IM 109 | vrt pair, imperf hz
Quantity: *25 pairs* | 400.00 |

3c dark violet, type II

| IM 110 | vrt pair, imperf hz
used vrt pair, imperf hz
Quantity: 40-50 pairs reported | *350.00*
150.00 |

George Washington. 1917. Engraved. No watermark. Perf 11.

5c blue

| IM 111 | hz pair, imperf between
hz pair, plate No. 8902 in top
  margin, imperf between
Quantity: *very rare* | 2,250.00

— |

Benjamin Franklin. 1917. Engraved. No watermark. Perf 11.

8c olive bistre

| IM 112 | vrt pair, imperf between
used vrt pair, imperf between
Quantity: 1 pair unused and
  2 pair used reported | —
— |

Benjamin Franklin. 1917. Engraved. No watermark. Perf 11.

20c light ultramarine

| IM 113 | vrt pair, imperf between
as above, used LRS (3/99)
Quantity: rare, used pair
  possibly unique | 1,500.00
1,437.50 |

☛ Caution. These stamps are often encountered with blind perfs that can be ironed out and eliminated to the naked eye, resulting in dangerous fakes. Copies lacking gum should be regarded with special caution. The discovery panes of this error contained mostly pairs with blind perforations and yielded only about 5 truly imperf pairs per pane. Blind-perf pairs are comparatively plentiful and can be deceptive.

Benjamin Franklin. 1917. Engraved. No watermark. Perf 11.

50c red violet

| IM 114 | vrt pair, imperf between
vrt pair, imperf between precanceled
  AKRON, OHIO   LRS (4/00)
Quantity: very rare | —

6,875.00 |

☛ Caution. Beware pairs with blind perfs.

George Washington. 1918. Offset lithography. No watermark. Perf 11.

1c gray green

| IM 115 | hz pair, imperf between
Quantity: n/a | 95.00 |

All known examples contain a straight edge on the right.

George Washington. 1919. Engraved. Rotary Press. No watermark. Design measures 19.5 to 20mm by 22 to 22.25mm. Perf 11x10.

1c green

IM 116	vrt pair, imperf hz	50.00
	used vrt pair, imperf hz	*75.00*
	block of 4, imperf hz	100.00
	top plate block of 6, imperf hz	750.00
	Quantity: 1,000+	

George Washington. 1919. Offset lithography. No watermark. Perf 12½.

1c gray green

IM 117	hz pair, imperf vrt	500.00
	block of 4, imperf vrt	—
	Quantity: n/a	

George Washington. 1919. Engraved. Rotary press. No watermark. Design measures 19.5 to 20mm by 22 to 22.25mm. Perf 11x10.

2c carmine rose, type III

IM 118	vrt pair, imperf hz	50.00
	used vrt pair, imperf hz	*125.00*
	block of 4, imperf hz	100.00
	plate block of 8, imperf hz	800.00
	Quantity: 1,000+	

IM 119	hz pair, imperf vrt	750.00
	Quantity: 25 pairs	

George Washington. 1920. Offset lithography. No watermark. Perf 11.

2c carmine, type V

IM 120	vrt pair, imperf hz	*850.00*
	Quantity: 2-3 pairs reported	
IM 121	hz pair, imperf vrt	*1,250.00*
	used hz pair, imperf vrt	—
	Quantity: n/a	

☛ Caution. Do not confuse **IM 120**—**IM 124** with the regularly issued imperforates of the same design.

2c carmine, type Va

IM 122	vrt pair, imperf between	*1,250.00*
	Quantity: rare	

2c carmine, type VI

IM 123	vrt pair, imperf hz	—
	Quantity: very rare	
IM 124	vrt pair, imperf between	*1,250.00*
	Quantity: very rare	

George Washington. 1921. Engraved. Rotary press. No watermark. Design 19 by 22.5mm. Perf 10.

1c green

IM 125	hz pair, imperf between	*1,000.00*
	Quantity: *rare*	

SERIES OF 1922/26

Stamps of 1922/26 series were printed by flat plate press and normally perforated 11. Designs measure 18.5 to 19mm by 22mm.

1922 Series, ½c–$5. Engraved. Flat plate press.

IM 127	½c Nathan Hale	
IM 128	1c Benjamin Franklin	
IM 129	1½c Warren G. Harding	
IM 130	2c George Washington	
IM 133	3c Abraham Lincoln	
IM 134	4c Martha Washington	
IM 137	5c Theodore Roosevelt	
IM 139	6c James A. Garfield	
IM 140	7c William McKinley	
IM 141	8c Ulysses S. Grant	
IM 142	9c Thomas Jefferson	
IM 143	10c James Monroe	
IM 145	11c Rutherford B. Hayes	
IM 147	12c Grover Cleveland	
IM 150	13c Benjamin Harrison	
IM 151	14c American Indian	
IM 152	15c Statue of Liberty	
IM 153	17c Woodrow Wilson	
IM 154	20c Golden Gate	
IM 156	25c Niagara Falls	
IM 158	30c Buffalo	
IM 159	50c Tomb of the Unknown Soldier	
IM 160	$1 Lincoln Memorial	
IM 161	$2 U.S. Capitol	
IM 162	$5 America	
	blocks of 4, imperf, ungummed **NRI**	—
	Quantity: *unique*	

The set of imperforate blocks of 4 as listed above, ½c through $5, was sold at auction in 1968 for $12,200. These stamps were not regularly issued, and as far as is known, the set of blocks is unique.

George Washington. January 15, 1923. Engraved. Flat plate press.

2c carmine

IM 131	hz pair, imperf vrt	200.00
	plate block of 6, imperf vrt	—
	Quantity: few hundred	

Exists misperfed horizontally.

IM 132	vrt pair, imperf hz	—
	Quantity: 3 pairs reported	

☛ Caution. It is possible to fabricate Nos. **IM 131-IM 132** regularly issued imperforate stamps of the same design. Beware fakes. Expert certificate advised.

Martha Washington. January 15, 1923. Engraved. Flat plate press.

4c brown

IM 135	hz pair, imperf between	—
	Quantity: reportedly unique	
IM 136	vrt pair, imperf hz	—
	Quantity: *unique*	

Theodore Roosevelt. October 27, 1922. Engraved. Flat plate press.

5c blue

IM 137A	imperf pair, gummed	1,500.00
	imperf plate block of 6, gummed	*7,500.00*
	Quantity: 1 pane of 100; 2 plate blocks	
IM 138	hz pair, imperf vrt	1,500.00
	Quantity: 10 pairs reported	

James Monroe. January 15, 1923. Engraved. Flat plate press.

10c yellow

IM 143	imperf pair, ungummed	1,750.00
	block of 4	—
	plate block of 6 LRS (6/96)	8,800.00
	Quantity: 2 panes	

Both panes contained large areas defaced by inspector's blue pencil marks. It is estimated that only 40 to 50 unmarked pairs exist. Blue pencil marked pairs sell for less. **IM 143** was issued without gum.

IM 144	vrt pair, imperf hz	1,250.00
	block of 4 LRS (12/99)	2,990.00
	Quantity: 50 pairs	

Most are poorly centered. Well centered pairs sell for a premium. Twenty-seven pairs contain splicing paper on the reverse or blue pencil marks on the front. All pairs originally contained penciled position numbers on the reverse. The numbers are missing on regummed pairs.

Rutherford Hayes. October 4, 1922. Engraved. Flat plate press.

11c light blue

IM 146	imperf vrt pair precanceled	
	SAN FRANCISCO, CALIFORNIA	—
	imperf vrt strip of 3 precanceled as above LRS (5/00)	17,600.00
	Quantity: 1 pair nearly severed by scissors cut and 1 strip of 3 reported	

Grover Cleveland. May 20, 1923. Engraved. Flat plate press.

12c brown violet

IM 148	imperf pair, gummed	—
	Quantity: rare	

IM 149	hz pair, imperf vrt	1,000.00
	block of 4, imperf vrt	—
	Quantity: *very scarce*	

Often without gum or with government splicing paper on reverse.

Golden Gate. May 1, 1923. Engraved. Flat plate press.

20c carmine rose

IM 155	hz pair, imperf vrt	2,000.00
	block of 4, imperf vrt	—
	Quantity: half pane of 100 reported	

Niagara Falls. November 11, 1922. Engraved. Flat plate press.

25c green

IM 157	vrt pair, imperf hz	1,000.00
	block with plate No. 14063 at right, imperf hz	—
	Quantity: rare	

The 1½c, 2c, 4c, 5c, 6c and 8c denominations of this series exist imperforate with various degrees of smearing or underinking. They are the result of impressions made during the cleaning of printing plates with solvent and are reported to have originally come on the market from a waste paper company. This catalogue does not recognize them as postage stamps. They are mentioned here for the record only.

Theodore Roosevelt. 1925. Engraved. Rotary press. Perf 10.

5c blue

IM 163   hz pair, imperf vrt precanceled
        PORTLAND, OREGON   LRS (5/00)   9,900.00
        Quantity: *very rare, possibly unique*

Benjamin Franklin. June 10, 1927. Engraved. Rotary press. Perf 11x10½.

1c green

IM 164   vrt pair, imperf between **LRS (6/98)**   2,640.00
        as above, used   —
        Quantity: very rare

IM 165   hz pair, imperf between   —
        Quantity: n/a

George Washington. December 10, 1926. Engraved. Perf 11x10½.

2c carmine

IM 166   hz pair, imperf between   2,250.00
        Quantity: very rare

IM 167   vrt pair, imperf between   —
        Quantity: very rare

William McKinley. March 24, 1927. Engraved. Rotary press. Perf 11x10½.

7c black

IM 168   vrt pair, imperf between   125.00
        as above, used   75.00
        block of 4, imperf between hz   250.00
        Quantity: n/a

☛ Caution. These stamps are known with blind perfs that can be ironed out and eliminated to the naked eye, resulting in dangerous fakes. Copies lacking gum should be regarded with special caution. Expert certificate advised.

IM 169   vrt pair, imperf between,
        precanceled **MOBILE, ALA.**   120.00
        Quantity: n/a

☛ Caution. Refer to note following **IM 168**.

Warren G. Harding. September 1, 1923. Engraved. Flat plate press. Design measures 19.25mm by 22.25mm.

2c black

IM 170 hz pair, imperf vrt   1,000.00
        Quantity: n/a

☛ Caution. It is possible to fabricate this error from regularly issued imperforate stamps of the same design. Expert certificate strongly advised. Most pairs are centered to bottom. Price is for a copy centered to bottom. Well centered pairs sell for more.

Battle of White Plains. October 18, 1926. Engraved.

2c carmine rose

IM 171 vrt pair, imperf between   —
        Quantity: very scarce

General Von Steuben. September 17, 1930. Engraved

2c carmine rose

IM 172 imperf pair   3,000.00
        block of 4, imperf   —
        plate block of 6, imperf   —
        Quantity: 1 pane of 100

Hinging. Prices for stamps preceding **IM 196** are for hinged copies. Never hinged copies sell for a premium ranging from 25% to 100% or more depending on the scarcity of an item, and the scarcity of never hinged copies of an item. These guidelines do not apply to prices for ultra-rare or unique items, which may not exist never hinged.

Although catalogue prices are based on the best information available at press time, readers should be aware that prices for error stamps fluctuate over time, and therefore, are advised to contact dealers active in the error stamp market for timely quotes when buying or selling.

Yorktown Sesquicentennial. October 19, 1931. Engraved.

2c carmine & black

IM 173 hz pair, imperf vrt   4,500.00
        block of 4, imperf vrt   9,500.00
        hz block of 6, imperf vrt   —
        hz center line block of 106, imperf vrt   —
        bottom plate block of 10, imperf vrt   —
        Quantity: 1 pane of 50

George Washington Bicentennial. June 16, 1932. Engraved.

3c violet

IM 174 vrt pair, imperf between   300.00
        as above, precanceled
            PHILADELPHIA, PENNSYLVANIA
            LRS (4/00)   880.00
        Quantity: n/a mint; 3 precanceled pairs

☛ Caution. Pairs are known with blind perforations that can be ironed out and eliminated to the naked eye, resulting in dangerous fakes. Copies lacking gum should be regarded with special caution.

William Penn. October 24, 1932. Engraved.

3c violet

IM 175 vrt pair, imperf hz   —
        Quantity: very rare

General Tadeusz Kosciuszko.   October 13, 1933. Engraved.

5c blue

IM 176	hz pair, imperf vrt	2,250.00
	block of 4, imperf vrt	5,000.00
	plate block of 8, imperf vrt	—
	Quantity: 1 pane of 100 stamps	

Often with heavy natural gum creases or bends.

Maryland Tercentenary. May 23, 1934. Engraved.

3c carmine rose

IM 177	hz pair, imperf between	LRS (89)	6,600.00
	Quantity: unique		

A single unique pair of **IM 177** exists in a block of 12 stamps, the error resulting from a foldover.

Wisconsin Tercentenary. July 7, 1934. Engraved.

3c violet

IM 178	vrt pair, imperf hz	350.00
	Quantity: n/a	

IM 179	hz pair, imperf vrt	450.00
	bottom plate strip of 10, imperf vrt	1,650.00
	Quantity: approx 80 pairs reported	

NATIONAL PARK SERIES OF 1934

The items listed below are errors of the fully gummed, perforated stamps of National Parks issue. They are similar in appearance to the Farley Special Printing which was issued fully imperforate and without gum.

Yosemite. July 16, 1934. Engraved.

1c green

IM 180	vrt pair, imperf hz, with gum	1,750.00
	Quantity: 16 pairs or strips of three	

☛ Caution. Fakes exist. All known genuine examples are signed "S.A." (Spencer Anderson) on the reverse in indelible pencil. Those rubber stamped "Sloane" are fakes.

☛ Caution. It is possible to fabricate **IM 178-IM 186** from completely imperforate stamps of identical designs from the Farley Special Printing of 1935, which were issued without gum. In 1940, the Bureau of Engraving & Printing offered to gum Farley Special Printing sheets submitted by collectors. Therefore, presence of government gum on part-perforate stamps is not necessarily an indication of genuineness. Expert certificate advised for part-perforate error stamps that have Farley Special Printing counterparts.

Hinging. Prices for stamps preceding **IM 196** are for hinged copies. Never hinged copies sell for a premium, which can range from 25% to 100% or more depending on the scarcity of an item, and the scarcity of never hinged copies of the item. These guidelines do not apply to prices for ultra-rare or unique items, which may not exist in never hinged condition.

Although catalogue prices are based on the best information available at press time, readers should be aware that prices for error stamps fluctuate over time, and therefore, are advised to contact dealers active in the error stamp market for timely quotes when buying or selling.

Grand Canyon. July 24, 1934. Engraved.

2c red

IM 181	vrt pair, imperf hz, with gum	600.00
	top plate block of 6, imperf hz, with gum	—
	Quantity: 2-3 panes	
IM 182	hz pair, imperf vrt, with gum	600.00
	bottom plate strip of 10, imperf vrt, with gum	2,500.00
	Quantity: 2-3 panes	

☛ Caution. Fakes exist. See second note following **IM 180**.

Mt. Rainier. August 3, 1934. Engraved.

3c violet

IM 183	vrt pair, imperf hz, with gum	450.00
	bottom plate block of 6, imperf hz, with gum	—
	Quantity: 1 pane	

☛ Caution. Fakes exist. See second note following **IM 180**.

Mesa Verde. September 25, 1934. Engraved.

4c brown

IM 184	vrt pair, imperf hz, with gum	650.00
	Quantity: 15 pairs	

Approximately 6-9 of the 15 known pairs have brown Post Office paper affixed to the reverse. Copies without brown paper sell for 50%-100% premium or more.

Yellowstone. July 30, 1934. Engraved.

5c blue

IM 185	hz pair, imperf vrt, with gum	700.00
	plate block of 6	—
	Quantity: 50 pairs	

☛ Caution. Fakes exist. See second note following **IM 180**.

Acadia. October 2, 1934. Engraved.

7c black

IM 186	hz pair, imperf vrt, with gum		600.00
	top plate strip of 10, imperf vrt, with gum	**LRS (4/98)**	4,675.00
	Quantity: 50 pairs		

☛ Caution. It is possible to fabricate **IM 178-IM 186** from imperforate stamps of the Farley Special Printing. Refer to note following **IM 180**.

PRESIDENTIAL SERIES OF 1938

Martha Washington. May 5, 1938. Engraved.

1½c brown

IM 188	hz pair, imperf between Quantity: n/a	150.00

IM 189	hz pair, imperf between, precanceled **SAINT LOUIS, MO.** Quantity: few thousand	20.00

Thomas Jefferson. June 16, 1938. Engraved.

3c violet

IM 190	imperf pair Quantity: very rare	*2,750.00*

☛ The 3c Jefferson was counterfeited to defraud the post office. The printer was raided and his stock seized; nevertheless, a small number of the counterfeits, fully gummed and imperforate, escaped. Counterfeits were lithographed and thus can be distinguished from engraved genuine stamps. Gum on counterfeits lacks the gum-breaking ridges found on genuine stamps and is much more yellow than gum on genuine stamps. **IM 190** should possess large outer margins.

IM 191	hz pair, imperf between booklet pane of 6, imperf between vrt booklet pane, imperf between vrt, vrt gutter between **LRS (2/99)** Quantity: 10 pairs; 1 pane with gutter	*1,100.00* — 2,415.00

☛ Refer to note following **IM 190**. The booklet pane with the vertical gutter contains 3 errors pairs plus 6 additional stamps or parts of stamps, one on either side of each error pair.

Woodrow Wilson. August 29, 1938. Engraved.

$1 purple & black

IM 192	vrt pair, imperf hz top plate block of 8, imperf hz arrow block of 6, imperf hz Quantity: 50 pairs reported, including the unique plate block	1,500.00 *8,500.00* —
IM 193	vrt pair, imperf between Quantity: very rare	*2,750.00*

Woodrow Wilson. August 31, 1954. Engraved.

$1 reddish purple & black

IM 194	vrt pair, imperf hz Quantity: 1-2 panes of 100 reported	1,000.00
IM 195	vrt pair, imperf between block of 4, imperf hz between Quantity: 10 pairs	*7,500.00* —

IM 194 and **IM 195** were printed by the dry process on somewhat thicker paper than that of **IM 192** and **IM 193**. The gum of the 1954 stamps is smooth and clear, and the purple color is decidedly more reddish than that of the 1938 issue.

Hinging. Prices for stamps before **IM 196** are for hinged copies. Never hinged copies sell for a premium, which can range from 25% to 100% or more depending on the scarcity of an item, and the scarcity of never hinged copies of the item. These guidelines do not apply to ultra-rare or unique items. Prices for stamps after **IM 196** are for never hinged copies; hinged copies sell for less.

NATIONAL DEFENSE SERIES OF 1940

Statue of Liberty. October 16, 1940. Engraved.

1c green

IM 196	vrt pair, imperf between Quantity: 100-200 pairs reported	500.00
IM 197	hz pair, imperf between Quantity: several thousand pairs	35.00
IM 198	hz pair, imperf between, precanceled GLENDALE, CALIF. Quantity: n/a	75.00

☞ Caution. Often with blind perfs or a few punched perf holes.

Anti-aircraft gun. October 16, 1940. Engraved.

2c rose carmine

IM 199	hz pair, imperf between Quantity: several thousand	40.00

☞ Caution. Often with blind perfs or few punched perf holes.

Buying or selling?
Consult the dealer directory at the back of the catalogue.

Torch. October 16, 1940. Engraved.

3c violet

IM 200	hz pair, imperf between Quantity: several thousand	25.00

☞ Caution. Often with blind perfs or a few punched perf holes.

Mt. Palomar. August 30, 1948. Engraved.

3c blue

IM 201	vrt pair, imperf between plate block of 4, imperf vrt between Quantity: *350+ pairs, 15+ plate blocks (each with 2 pairs) reported*	550.00 *750.00*

LIBERTY SERIES OF 1954

Statue of Liberty. June 24, 1954. Engraved.

3c deep violet

IM 202	imperf pair block of 6, imperf Quantity: 5-10 pairs reported	*2,500.00* —

IM 203	hz pair, imperf between booklet pane of 6, as above Quantity: 5-10 pairs	2,000.00 —

Abraham Lincoln. July 31, 1958. Booklet pane of 6. Engraved.

4c red violet

IM 204	booklet pane of 6, imperf hz Quantity: *very rare, possibly unique*	—
IM 205	hz pair, imperf between LRS (10/94) Quantity: *very rare, possibly unique*	3,575.00

IM 205 occurs as the result of a booklet pane foldover.

Theodore Roosevelt. March 1957. Engraved. BEP.

6c rose red

IM 205A	imperf block of 4 LRS (7/00) Quantity: 1 block of 4	23,000.00

IM 205A is of the dry printing version first released in March 1957.

Where possible, illustrations of actual error stamps have been used. They are bordered in black. Illustrations of normal stamps have been used in cases where error stamp illustrations were not available, or where an error illustration would not adequately illustrate the error. Illustrations of normal stamps appear without black border.

COIL STAMPS

George Washington. October 8, 1954. Coil. Engraved.

1c green

IM 206	imperf pair Quantity: 13 pairs reported	2,250.00

Thomas Jefferson. October 22, 1954. Coil. Engraved.

2c carmine rose

IM 207	imperf pair line pair, imperf spliced pair or strip, imperf Quantity: 100 pairs reported	600.00 *1,200.00* —

Transition multiples exist.

IM 208	imperf pair, precanceled **RIVERDALE, MD** line pair, imperf Quantity: 200 pairs reported	550.00 —

Statue of Liberty. July 20, 1954. Coil. Engraved.

3c deep violet

IM 209	imperf pair line pair, imperf used strip of 3, imperf Quantity: 30 pairs reported	1,500.00 — *850.00*

Abraham Lincoln. July 31, 1958. Coil. Engraved.

4c red violet

IM 210	imperf pair	90.00
	line pair, imperf	200.00
	spliced pair or strip, imperf	—
	used pair, imperf	*75.00*
	Quantity: 500+ pairs reported	

Exists miscut. Transition multiples exist and sell for a premium.

IM 211	imperf pair, precanceled	
	SEATTLE, WASH.	—
	Quantity: rare	

Paul Revere. February 25, 1965. Coil. Engraved.

25c green

IM 212	imperf pair	30.00
	line pair, imperf	75.00
	spliced pair or strip, imperf	—
	Quantity: 1,200 pairs reported	

Exists miscut. Most copies are poorly centered as illustrated. Price is for a poorly centered copy. Add 66% premium for well centered copy. Transition multiples exist and sell for a premium.

Jose de San Martin. February 25, 1959. Engraved.

4c blue

| IM 213 | hz pair, imperf between | 1,200.00 |
| | Quantity: 20 pairs reported | |

Often poorly centered. Price is for a poorly centered copy.

IM 214   IM 216

Ephraim McDowell. December 3, 1959. Engraved.

4c maroon

IM 214	vrt pair, imperf hz	300.00
	plate block of 4, imperf hz	—
	Quantity: 210 pairs reported	

| IM 215 | vrt pair, imperf between | 500.00 |
| | Quantity: 50+ pairs reported | |

Thomas G. Masaryk. March 7, 1960. Engraved.

4c blue

| IM 216 | vrt pair, imperf between | *3,250.00* |
| | Quantity: 10 pairs | |

Thomas G. Masaryk. March 7, 1960. Engraved.

8c yellow, blue & red

| IM 217 | hz pair, imperf between | — |
| | Quantity: 3 pairs reported | |

The term "transition multiple" refers to errors appearing in combination with normal or nearly-normal stamps. Generally, a pair, strip, or block containing one or more error stamps, one or more normal stamps, and, in the case of color-omitted errors, one or more stamps with color(s) partially omitted. Transition multiples sell for a premium.

SEATO. May 31, 1960. Engraved.

4c blue

IM 218   vrt pair, imperf between   150.00
         plate block of 4, imperf hz between   —
         Quantity: 100-200 pairs reported

Winslow Homer. December 15, 1962. Engraved.

4c multicolored

IM 219   hz pair, imperf between   6,750.00
         hz pair with plate No.,
           imperf between   —
         Quantity: 4 pairs reported

Although catalogue prices are based on the best information available at press time, readers should be aware that prices for error stamps fluctuate over time, and therefore, are advised to contact dealers active in the error stamp market for timely quotes when buying or selling.

George Washington. November 23, 1962. Engraved.

5c blue gray

IM 220   hz pair, imperf between LRS (7/00)   4,025.00
         hz pair (1 stamp, 1 label),
           imperf between   —
         booklet pane, imperf vrt between
           LRS (5/98)   5,750.00
         Quantity: very rare

IM 220 results from miscut booklet panes and also exists se-tenant with label containing slogan.

COIL STAMP

George Washington. November 23, 1962. Coil. Engraved.

5c blue gray

IM 221   imperf pair   450.00
         line pair, imperf   1,000.00
         spliced strip of 8 with 2 line pairs   —
         Quantity: *50+ pairs reported*

Transition multiples exist and sell for a premium. Exists tagged and untagged. Often with gum problems. Price is for copy with sound gum.

U. S. Flag. January 9, 1963. Engraved.

5c red & blue

IM 222   hz pair, imperf between   1,250.00
         Quantity: 3-4 pairs reported

☛ Caution. Pairs exist with blind perfs. Expert certificate advised.

Appomattox. April 9, 1965. Engraved.

5c blue & black

| IM 223 | hz pair, imperf vrt | — |

Quantity: *very rare*

☛ Caution. Pairs exist with nearly invisible blind perfs. Expert certificate advised.

COIL STAMPS

Thomas Jefferson. January 12, 1968. Coil. Engraved.

1c green

| IM 224 | imperf pair | 25.00 |
| | line pair, imperf | 55.00 |

Quantity: 1,000+ pairs

IM 225   IM 226

Francis Parkman. November 4, 1975. Coil. Engraved.

3c violet

| IM 225 | imperf pair | 27.50 |
| | line pair, imperf | 45.00 |

Quantity: 1,000+ pairs

IM 226	imperf pair, precanceled	
	Non-Profit ORG CAR-RT SORT	6.00
	line pair, imperf	20.00
	spliced pair or strip, imperf	—

Quantity: several thousand

Exists miscut. Transition multiples exist.

Abraham Lincoln. May 28, 1966. Coil. Engraved.

4c black

IM 227	imperf pair	850.00
	line pair, imperf	1,750.00
	spliced pair or strip, imperf	—

Quantity: 100 pairs reported

Transition multiples exist and sell for a premium.

| IM 227A | pair, imperf between | — |

Quantity: *very rare*

George Washington. September 8, 1966. Original design. Coil. Engraved.

5c blue

IM 228	imperf pair	150.00
	line pair, imperf	275.00
	spliced pair or strip, imperf	—
	used pair, imperf	—

Quantity: 200 pairs reported

Often with faults. Price is for a sound copy. Exists miscut. Transition multiples exist and sell for a premium.

IM 229	imperf pair, precanceled	
	MOUNT PLEASANT, IA	350.00
	line pair, imperf	*1,000.00*
	imperf pair or strip, gap in bars	*475.00*

Quantity: n/a

IM 229A	imperf pair, precanceled	
	CHICAGO, IL	1,500.00
	line pair, imperf	—

Quantity: *6 pairs and unique line pair reported*

Original Design   Revised Design

George Washington. Revised design; clean shaven. Coil. Engraved.

5c blue

IM 230	imperf pair	625.00
	line pair, imperf	—
	Quantity: *50-60 pairs reported*	

Franklin D. Roosevelt. December 28, 1967. Coil. Engraved. Horizontal format.

6c brown

IM 231	imperf pair	2,250.00
	line pair, imperf	—
	Quantity: 25-30 pairs reported	

Franklin D. Roosevelt. February 28, 1968. Coil. Engraved. Vertical format.

6c brown

IM 232	imperf pair	70.00
	line pair, imperf	125.00
	Quantity: approx 1,000 pairs	

Exists miscut. Transition multiples exist.

Dwight D. Eisenhower. August 6, 1970. Coil. Engraved.

6c grayish blue

IM 233	imperf pair	1,500.00
	line pair, imperf	—
	Quantity: 20-30 pairs reported	

Sometimes encountered with incomplete gum or without gum. Price is for pair with full gum, never hinged.

Dwight D. Eisenhower. May 10, 1971. Coil. Engraved.

8c dark claret

IM 234	imperf pair	40.00
	line pair, imperf	70.00
	spliced pair or strip, imperf	—
	used pair, imperf	—
	Quantity: 1,000+ pairs	

Exists miscut. Transition multiples exist and sell for a premium.

IM 235	pair, imperf between	6,500.00
	Quantity: 1 pair	

Oliver Wendell Holmes. June 14, 1978. Coil. Engraved. Exists with wet or dry finish gum.

15c carmine or bright carmine; type I, wet gum

IM 236	imperf pair	30.00
	line pair, imperf	75.00
	used pair, imperf	—
	Quantity: 600-800 pairs	

Exists miscut. Transition multiples exist and sell for a premium.

Type I   Type II

Type I. The tip of the tie touches or almost touches the coat. The downward sloping hatch lines in the tie are more pronounced. The upper bar of the cents symbol is aligned slightly to the left of the "E" of "POSTAGE."

Type II. The tip of the tie is well clear of the coat. The downward sloping hatch lines in the tie are almost eliminated. The third upward sloping line of the tie stops well short of the right side of the tie. The upper bar in the cents symbol is aligned almost directly under the "E" of "POSTAGE."

15c carmine or bright carmine; type I, dry gum

IM 236A	imperf pair	30.00
	line pair, imperf	65.00
	Quantity: several hundred pairs	

IM 237	pair, imperf between	175.00
	line pair, imperf between	—
	Quantity: 200-250 pairs reported	

15c carmine or bright carmine; type II, dry gum

IM 237A	imperf pair	75.00
	line pair, imperf	150.00
	Quantity: 150+ pairs	

Transition multiples exist and sell for a premium.

Where possible, illustrations of actual error stamps have been used. They are bordered in black. Illustrations of normal stamps have been used in cases where error stamp illustrations were not available, or where an error illustration would not adequately illustrate the error. Illustrations of normal stamps appear without black border.

Eugene O'Neill. January 12, 1973. Coil. Engraved.

$1 dark violet

IM 238	imperf pair	2,000.00
	line pair, imperf	*4,250.00*
	spliced pair or strip, imperf	—
	Quantity: 50 pairs, 3 line pairs reported	

Exists miscut. Transition multiples exist and sell for a premium.

Franklin D. Roosevelt. December 28, 1967. Booklet pane. Engraved.

6c brown

IM 238A	hz pair, imperf between	**LRS (5/98)**	1,650.00
	Quantity: very rare, possibly unique		

IM 238A results from a foldover.

Dwight D. Eisenhower. January 28, 1972. Booklet pane. Engraved.

8c dark claret

IM 239	block of 4 (incl label "Use Zip Code"), imperf hz between	850.00
	booklet pane of 7 + 1 label, imperf hz between	—
	Quantity: n/a	

The label "Use Zip Code" appears at the bottom left corner on normal booklet panes. It appears that **IM 239** occurs from sheets of perforated booklet panes that were separated along the perforations instead of being cut apart in the normal places. In addition, some examples are known as the result of a foldover. They generally sell for more.

Oliver Wendell Holmes. June 28, 1978. Booklet pane of 8. Engraved. Perf 10.

15c carmine

| IM 240 | booklet pane of 8, imperf vrt between **LRS (10/98)** Quantity: *2 panes reported* | 2,640.00 |

Davy Crockett. August 17, 1967. Engraved, lithographed. BEP.

5c black, yellow & green

| IM 241 | vrt pair, imperf between Quantity: 3-5 pairs reported | 5,000.00 |

U.S. Flag. January 24, 1968. Engraved. Design 19x22mm. Perf 11. BEP.

6c red, blue & green

IM 242	vrt pair, imperf hz	500.00
	as above, used	—
	Quantity: *very scarce*	

☛ Caution. Beware regumming. Most pairs lack gum, which was removed to eliminate faint perforation impressions. So long as impressions do not affect a stamp's paper, the stamp is considered imperforate. Check carefully for blind perfs. Price is for pair with original gum. Those without gum sell for less.

IM 243	vrt pair, imperf between	500.00
	as above, used	—
	Quantity: less than 50 pairs reported	

☛ Caution. Many offered as imperforates have traces of perforations. Check carefully.

U.S. Flag. August 7, 1970. Engraved. Design 18.25 by 21mm. Perf 11x10½. BEP.

6c red, blue & green

| IM 244 | hz pair, imperf between | 150.00 |
| | Quantity: 100-200 pairs | |

Often with clipped perfs, a normal result of trimming at the Bureau of Engraving & Printing.

Buying or selling?
Consult the dealer directory at the back of the catalogue.

U.S. Flag. May 10, 1971. Engraved. Perf 11x10½. BEP.

8c red, blue & green

IM 245	imperf vertical pair	40.00
	top or bottom plate block of 20, imperf	600.00
	Quantity: 500+ pairs reported	

Price is for copy with gum. Pairs without gum sell for less. Collected in vertical pairs or blocks to distinguish it from the coil imperforate of similar design.

IM 246	hz pair, imperf between	50.00
	Quantity: 600 pairs	

COIL STAMPS

U.S. Flag. May 30, 1969. Coil. Engraved. BEP.

6c red, blue & green

IM 247	imperf pair	500.00
	spliced pair or strip, imperf	—
	Quantity: 50-100 pairs reported	

Where possible, illustrations of actual error stamps have been used. They are bordered in black. Illustrations of normal stamps have been used in cases where error stamp illustrations were not available, or where an error illustration would not adequately illustrate the error. Illustrations of normal stamps appear without black border.

U.S. Flag. May 10, 1971. Coil. Engraved. BEP.

8c red, blue & green

IM 248	imperf pair	50.00
	spliced pair or strip, imperf	—
	Quantity: 750-1000 pairs reported	

Exists miscut, including 3 strips with complete plate number showing at bottom. Transition multiples exist and sell for a premium. Although it is generally accepted that line pairs, in the traditional sense, are not created on Huck press printed stamps, pairs with coloration between stamps resembling lines exist and are collected. They sell for about double the price of regular pairs.

Walt Disney. September 11, 1968. Photogravure. UCC.

6c multicolored

IM 249	imperf pair	650.00
	block of 4, imperf	—
	Quantity: 100 pairs	

IM 250	vrt pair, imperf hz	650.00
	plate block of 4, imperf hz	—
	Quantity: 50 pairs	

IM 251 hz pair, imperf between 5,000.00
Quantity: 5 pairs

☞ Caution. Expert certificate essential. This error can be fabricated from **IM 249**.

Waterfowl Conservation. October 24, 1968. Engraved, lithographed. BEP.

6c multicolored

IM 252 vrt pair, imperf between 475.00
Quantity: 100+ pairs

Christmas. November 1, 1968. Engraved, lithographed. BEP.

6c multicolored

IM 253 imperf pair, tagged 200.00
plate block of 10, imperf, tagged —
Quantity: 500 pairs

IM 254 imperf pair, untagged 250.00
Quantity: 250 pairs

IM 254 often occurs with mottled gum. Those with flawless gum sell for a premium.

Grandma Moses. May 1, 1969. Engraved, lithographed. BEP.

6c multicolored

IM 255 hz pair, imperf between 200.00
Quantity: 250 pairs reported, see note

☞ Caution. Many pairs have faint traces of blind perfs. Frequently, perf traces can be seen only on the gummed side. Pairs on cover have been reported, however, it is thought that they may have been thus used to disguise the presence of blind perfs and, therefore, when encountered, should be examined carefully. Of the quantity reported, it is not known how many pairs contain faint blind perfs.

Christmas. November 3, 1969. Engraved, lithographed. BEP.

6c multicolored

IM 256 imperf pair 1,000.00
Quantity: 25 pairs reported

Christmas. November 5, 1970. Se-tenant block of 4. Photogravure. GGI.

6c multicolored

a) Doll Carriage   b) Toy Horse

IM 257 used vrt margin pair (a & b) with
plate No. 31907, imperf —
used vrt margin pair (a & b) with
Mail Early slogan, imperf —
Quantity: each pair listed is unique

Each listed pair is postmarked Washington, DC, Nov. 5, 1970.

Tom Sawyer. October 13, 1972. Engraved, lithographed. BEP.

8c multicolored

IM 258	hz pair, imperf between	5,500.00
	plate block of 4, imperf vrt between	9,500.00
	Quantity: 7 pairs reported (one of which is damaged)	

George Gershwin. February 23, 1973. Photogravure. BEP.

8c multicolored

IM 259	vrt pair, imperf hz	200.00
	plate block of 12, imperf hz	—
	Quantity: 160-200 pairs	

Robinson Jeffers. August 13, 1973. Photogravure. BEP.

8c multicolored

IM 260	vrt pair, imperf hz	250.00
	Quantity: 80-100 pairs reported	

Willa Cather. September 20, 1973. Photogravure. BEP.

8c multicolored

IM 261	vrt pair, imperf hz	250.00
	Quantity: 80-100 pairs	

Buying or selling?
Consult the dealer directory at the back of the catalogue.

Lyndon B. Johnson. August 27, 1973. Photogravure. BEP.

8c multicolored

IM 262	hz pair, imperf vrt	325.00
	plate block of 12, imperf vrt	—
	Quantity: 128-160 pairs	

Rural America. October 5, 1973. Engraved, lithographed. BEP.

8c multicolored

IM 262A	used vrt pair, imperf hz LRS (11/95)	4,675.00
	Quantity: unique	

☛ Caution. Many pairs exist with blind perforations. Expert certificate essential. The listed pair is comprised of stamps 2 and 3 in a vertical strip of 5.

Where possible, illustrations of actual error stamps have been used. They are bordered in black. Illustrations of normal stamps have been used in cases where error stamp illustrations were not available, or where an error illustration would not adequately illustrate the error. Illustrations of normal stamps appear without black border.

Christmas. November 7, 1973. Photogravure. BEP.

8c multicolored

IM 263	vrt pair, imperf between Quantity: 50+ pairs	300.00

Pairs often contain a misplaced perforation in the design due to the nature of the error. Transition multiples exist and sell for a premium.

Crossed Flags. December 8, 1973. Engraved. BEP.

10c red & blue

IM 264	hz pair, imperf between top or bottom plate strip of 20 Quantity: several hundred pairs	50.00 —

Also exists with Salem, Ind. local precancel: price $100.

IM 264A	hz pair, imperf vrt hz strip of 4, imperf vrt Quantity: *8 pairs reported*	— 1,900.00

Most often encountered as a strip of 4 containing two error pairs.

IM 265	vrt pair, imperf block of 4, imperf Quantity: 35-60 pairs	950.00 1,900.00

Collected in vertical pairs or blocks to distinguish it from coil stamps of the same design

IM 265A	vrt pair, imperf between Quantity: *reportedly unique*	—

Jefferson Memorial. December 14, 1973. Engraved. BEP.

10c blue

IM 266	vrt pair, imperf hz Quantity: n/a	500.00

IM 266 is poorly centered. Price is for poorly centered copy.

IM 267	vrt pair, imperf between Quantity: n/a	800.00

IM 267 occurs from miscut booklet panes.

Hinging. Prices for stamps after **IM 196** are for never hinged copies. Hinged copies sell for less.

Although catalogue prices are based on the best information available at press time, readers should be aware that prices for error stamps fluctuate over time, and therefore, are advised to contact dealers active in the error stamp market for timely quotes when buying or selling.

COIL STAMPS

Liberty Bell. October 1, 1974. Coil. Engraved. BEP.

6.3c reddish orange

IM 268	imperf pair	150.00
	line pair, imperf	—
	Quantity: 200+ pairs reported	

Transition multiples exist.

IM 269	imperf pair, precanceled	
	WASHINGTON, DC	90.00
	line pair, imperf	200.00
	imperf pair or strip, gap in bars	—
	spliced pair or strip, imperf	—
	Quantity: 300-500 pairs reported	

Exists miscut. Transition multiples exist and sell for a premium.

IM 270	imperf pair, precanceled	
	COLUMBUS, OH	550.00
	line pair, imperf	—
	imperf pair or strip, gap in bars	—
	spliced pair or strip, imperf	—
	Quantity: rare	

IM 271	imperf pair, precanceled	
	GARDEN CITY, NY	850.00
	line pair, imperf	—
	Quantity: rare	

Flags. December 8, 1973. Coil. Engraved. BEP.

10c red & blue

IM 272	imperf pair	35.00
	line pair, imperf	50.00
	spliced pair or strip, imperf	—
	Quantity: 1,000+ pairs	

Refer to note after **IM 248**. Exists miscut. Transition multiples exist and sell for a premium.

Jefferson Memorial. December 14, 1973. Coil. Engraved. BEP.

10c blue

IM 273	imperf pair	35.00
	line pair, imperf	65.00
	spliced pair or strip, imperf	—
	used pair, imperf	*40.00*
	Quantity: 750+ pairs	

Exists miscut. Transition multiples exist and sell for a premium.

Skylab. May 14, 1974. Engraved, lithographed. BEP.

10c multicolored

IM 274	vrt pair, imperf between	—
	Quantity: n/a	

UPU. June 6, 1974. Se-tenant block of 8. Photogravure. BEP.

10c multicolored (block of 8)

a) Terboch e) Raphael
b) Chardin f) Hokusai
c) Gainsborough g) Peto
d) Goya h) Liotard

IM 275	block of 8, imperf vrt	*8,000.00*
	plate block of 16	—
	Quantity: 4 blocks of 8, including plate block	

Collective Bargaining. March 13, 1975. Photogravure. BEP.

10c multicolored

IM 276	imperf pair PW		350.00
	Quantity: 25 pairs reported		

☛ Printer's waste, refer to introduction.

Lexington & Concord. April 19, 1975. Photogravure. BEP.

10c multicolored

IM 277	vrt pair, imperf hz		425.00
	plate block of 12, imperf hz		—
	Quantity: 60-80 pairs		

Paul Laurence Dunbar. May 1, 1975. Photogravure. BEP.

10c multicolored

IM 278	imperf pair		1,250.00
	plate block of 10, imperf LRS (9/94)		7,425.00
	Quantity: 15 pairs		

Apollo-Soyuz. July 15, 1975. Se-tenant pair. Photogravure. BEP.

10c multicolored

a) Spacecraft & Globe
b) Spacecraft & Emblem

IM 279	vrt pair, imperf hz	2,100.00
	Quantity: 24-36 pairs	
IM 279A	imperf pair PW	—
	Quantity: *approximately 10 pairs*	

☛ **IM 279A** occurs from printer's waste, refer to introduction. All reported pairs are faulty and without gum.

Christmas. October 14, 1975. Photogravure. BEP.

10c multicolored

IM 280	imperf pair	100.00
	plate block of 12, imperf	*625.00*
	Quantity: several hundred pairs	

Where possible, illustrations of actual error stamps have been used. They are bordered in black. Illustrations of normal stamps have been used in cases where error stamp illustrations were not available, or where an error illustration would not adequately illustrate the error. Illustrations of normal stamps appear without black border.

Christmas. October 14, 1975. Photogravure. BEP.

10c multicolored

IM 281	imperf pair	100.00
	plate block of 12, imperf	—
	Quantity: several hundred pairs	

World Peace Through Law. September 29, 1975. Engraved. BEP.

10c multicolored

IM 281A	plate block, imperf vrt LRS (4/95)	13,750.00
	Quantity: unique plate block	

The plate block (plate No. 36535) consists of 2 pairs plus parts of 2 additional stamps at left, giving it the appearance of containing nearly six stamps.

AMERICANA SERIES OF 1975/1981

Flag & Independence Hall. November 15, 1975. Engraved. Huck Press. Perf 11x10½. BEP.

13c red, blue & brown

IM 282	hz pair, imperf between	50.00
	Quantity: approx 1,000 pairs	
IM 282A	hz pair, imperf vrt	—
	Quantity: *9 pairs reported*	

IM 283	vrt pair, imperf	500.00
	block of 4, imperf	—
	top plate strip of 20	—
	Quantity: 110-130 pairs	

Flag & Independence Hall. 1981. Engraved. Combination Press. Perf 11. BEP.

13c red, blue & brown

IM 284	vrt pair, imperf	125.00
	block of 4, imperf	250.00
	Quantity: 150-200 pairs reported	

IM 283 was printed on the Huck Press; plate numbers appear at the top or bottom of a pane. **IM 284** was printed on the Combination Press; plate numbers appear on the left or right of the sheet. In addition, **IM 283** has visible gum breaking ridges on the reverse, and tagging is usually in the form of a well defined block. **IM 284** has smooth gum without ridges, and tagging, while in block form, tends to be very irregular.

IM 283 and **IM 284** are collected in vertical pairs or blocks to distinguish them from coil imperforates of the same design.

Eagle & Shield. December 1, 1975. Photogravure. BEP.

13c multicolored

IM 285	imperf pair	45.00
	block of 4, imperf	100.00
	Quantity: approx 500 pairs	

Exists with color shift.

Buying or selling?
Consult the dealer directory at the back of the catalogue.

U.S. Flag. June 30, 1978. Engraved. BEP.

15c red, blue & gray

IM 286	vrt pair, imperf	17.50
	block of 4, imperf	35.00
	Quantity: 1,000+ pairs	

Collected in vertical pairs or blocks to distinguish from coil imperforate of the same design. Transition multiples exist and sell for a premium.

IM 286A vrt pair, imperf hz —
Quantity: *7 pairs reported*

IM 286B vrt pair, imperf between 500.00
Quantity: rare

IM 286B contains a natural straight edge at bottom. It is usually encountered in a strip of 3 or more.

Oil Lamp. September 11, 1979. Engraved, lithographed. BEP.

50c black, orange & tan

IM 287 vrt pair, imperf hz 1,750.00
Quantity: very rare

☛ Caution. Most pairs contain faint blind perfs and, therefore, do not qualify as errors. The blind perfs can be very deceptive. Extreme caution advised. Expert certificate necessary.

Where possible, illustrations of actual error stamps have been used. They are bordered in black. Illustrations of normal stamps have been used in cases where error stamp illustrations were not available, or where an error illustration would not adequately illustrate the error. Illustrations of normal stamps appear without black border.

BOOKLET PANE

Liberty Bell. October 31, 1975. Booklet pane. Engraved. BEP.

13c brown

IM 288 vrt pair, imperf between 300.00
booklet pane of 7 + 1 label —
Quantity: scarce

Some **IM 288** errors result from foldovers. Others are found in the form of complete booklet panes with perforations all around the outside edges. The complete panes, and vertical pairs taken from these panes, are almost certainly printer's waste. There is strong evidence to support this view. The slogan label appears at the lower left rather than the upper left, where it should normally be, suggesting that imperforate between panes were separated from uncut sheets along perforation lines instead of being cut apart in the normal places.

COIL STAMPS

Inkwell & Quill. March 6, 1981. Coil. Engraved. BEP.

1c blue (green paper)

IM 289	imperf pair	175.00
	line pair, imperf	250.00
	spliced pair or strip, imperf	—
	Quantity: 250+ pairs	

Transition multiples exist and sell for a premium.

Although catalogue prices are based on the best information available at press time, readers should be aware that prices for error stamps fluctuate over time, and therefore, are advised to contact dealers active in the error stamp market for timely quotes when buying or selling.

Guitar. October 25, 1979. Coil. Engraved. BEP.

3.1c dark red (yellow paper)

IM 290	imperf pair	1,350.00
	line pair, imperf	—
	Quantity: 30-50 pairs, 2 line pairs	

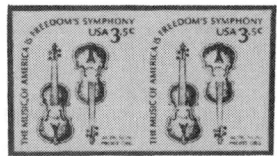

Violins. June 23, 1980. Coil. Engraved. BEP.

3.5c violet (yellow paper)

IM 291	imperf pair	200.00
	line pair, imperf	350.00
	Quantity: 250 pairs reported	

Prices are for well centered copies. Poorly centered copies sell for about half. Exists miscut. Transition multiples exist and sell for a premium.

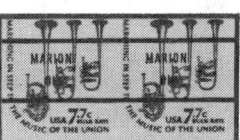

Saxhorns. November 20, 1976. Coil. Engraved. BEP.

7.7c brown (yellow paper)

IM 292	imperf pair, precanceled	
	MARION, OH	*1,950.00*
	Quantity: 7-10 pairs reported	

IM 293	imperf pair, precanceled	
	WASHINGTON, DC	1,650.00
	line pair, imperf	—
	imperf pair or strip, gap in bars	—
	Quantity: 40-50 pairs reported	

Drum. April 23, 1976. Coil. Engraved. BEP.

7.9c red (yellow paper)

IM 294	imperf pair	500.00
	line pair, imperf	—
	spliced pair or strip, imperf	—
	Quantity: 100+ pairs reported	

Transition multiples exist and sell for a premium.

Piano. July 13, 1978. Coil. Engraved. BEP.

8.4c blue (yellow paper)

IM 295	imperf pair, precanceled bars	17.50
	line pair, imperf	25.00
	imperf pair or strip, gap in bars	35.00
	Quantity: few thousand pairs	

Exists miscut. Some miscut pairs contain EE bars at top.

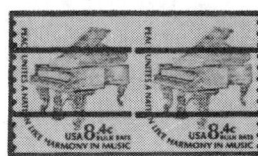

IM 296	pair, imperf between, precanceled bars	50.00
	line pair, imperf between	125.00
	pair, imperf between, gap in bars	65.00
	Quantity: several hundred pairs	

Buying or selling?
Consult the dealer directory at the back of the catalogue.

IM 297	imperf pair, precanceled	
	NEWARK, NJ	27.50
	line pair, as above	60.00
	imperf pair or strip, gap in bars	40.00
	Quantity: several hundred pairs	

Exists miscut.

IM 298	imperf pair, precanceled	
	BROWNSTOWN, IN	1,000.00
	imperf pair or strip, gap in bars	—
	spliced pair or strip, imperf	—
	Quantity: *rare, spliced strip unique*	

IM 299	imperf pair, precanceled	
	OKLAHOMA CITY, OK	1,500.00
	Quantity: *rare*	

Capitol Dome. March 5, 1976. Coil. Engraved. BEP.

9c green (gray paper)

IM 300	imperf pair	150.00
	line pair, imperf	350.00
	Quantity: few hundred pairs	

Exists miscut in various degrees. Price is for a well centered pair. Slightly miscut pairs sell for about half the well centered pair price. Drastically miscut pairs sell for about 66% of well centered pair price. Three line strips of six exist showing two full plate numbers at bottom.

IM 301	imperf pair, precanceled	
	PLEASANTVL, NY	800.00
	line pair, imperf	*2,000.00*
	Quantity: scarce, 2 line pairs reported	

Justice. November 4, 1977. Coil. Engraved. BEP.

10c violet (gray paper)

IM 302	imperf pair	60.00
	line pair, imperf	125.00
	spliced pair or strip, imperf	—
	Quantity: few hundred pairs	

Exists miscut. Exists with glossy gum and with dull gum. Transition multiples exist and sell for a premium.

Torch. April 8, 1981. Coil. Engraved. BEP.

12c red brown (gray paper)

IM 303	imperf pair	150.00
	line pair, imperf	275.00
	Quantity: 250 pairs	

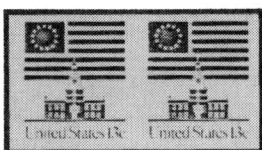

Flag & Independence Hall. November 15, 1975. Coil. Engraved. BEP.

13c red, blue & brown

IM 304	imperf pair	20.00
	line pair, imperf	50.00
	spliced pair or strip, imperf	—
	Quantity: several thousand pairs	

Refer to note after **IM 248**. Transition multiples exist and sell for a premium.

Hinging. Prices for stamps after **IM 196** are for never hinged copies. Hinged copies sell for less.

Liberty Bell. November 25, 1975. Coil. Engraved. BEP.

13c brown

IM 305	imperf pair	25.00
	line pair, imperf	55.00
	spliced pair or strip, imperf	—
	Quantity: few thousand pairs	

Exists miscut. Transition multiples exist and sell for a premium.

IM 306	pair, imperf between	—
	Quantity: scarce	

U.S. Flag. June 30, 1978. Coil. Engraved. BEP.

15c red, blue & gray

IM 307	imperf pair	20.00
	spliced pair or strip, imperf	—
	Quantity: several thousand pairs	

Exists miscut. Transition multiples exist and sell for a premium.

IM 308	pair, imperf between	150.00
	Quantity: 75-100 pairs	

Although catalogue prices are based on the best information available at press time, readers should be aware that prices for error stamps fluctuate over time, and therefore, are advised to contact dealers active in the error stamp market for timely quotes when buying or selling.

a)   b)   c)

The Spirit of '76. January 1, 1976. Se-tenant strip of 3. Photogravure. BEP.

13c multicolored

a) Drummer Boy
b) Adult Drummer
c) Fifer

IM 309	imperf strip of 3 (a-c)	1,150.00
	plate block of 12, imperf	—
	vertical pair (c), imperf	900.00
	imperf single (c), white border all around	350.00
	Quantity: 3 panes of 50 yielding 45 possible strips of 3 and 15 stamps as singles or pairs.	

BICENTENNIAL SOUVENIR SHEETS

A variety of perforation and color-omitted errors exist for this series. Some sheets contain multiple errors. Only those that exist imperforate are listed here, even though they may also contain color-omitted errors. Refer to the colors-omitted section for other varieties. Gaps in the numbering system exist for possible future listings.

Surrender at Yorktown. May 29, 1976. Souvenir sheet of 5. Lithographed. BEP.

13c multicolored

IM 310	imperf souvenir sheet, untagged, tied by postmark (5/29/76) to first day display card	2,250.00
	Quantity: 1-2 reported	

IM 310A	imperf souvenir sheet, tagged Quantity: possibly unique	—
IM 311	imperf souvenir sheet, untagged, USA 13c omitted on all stamps, with 5/29/76 PHILADELPHIA, PA precancel postmark Quantity: 1-2 reported	—
IM 312	imperf souvenir sheet, untagged, USA 13c omitted on 2nd, 3rd & 4th stamps, with 5/29/76 PHILADELPHIA, PA precancel postmark Quantity: 1-2 reported	2,500.00
IM 313	imperf souvenir sheet, USA 13c omitted on 1st & 5th stamps Quantity: *very rare*	450.00
IM 314	imperf souvenir sheet, USA 13c omitted on 1st & 5th stamps, with 5/29/76 PHILADELPHIA, PA first day cancellation Quantity: very rare, possibly unique	—

Declaration of Independence. May 29, 1976. Souvenir sheet of 5. Lithographed. BEP.

18c multicolored

IM 315	imperf souvenir sheet, tagged Quantity: very rare, possibly unique	—
IM 316	imperf souvenir sheet, USA 18c omitted on all stamps Quantity: very rare	2,750.00

Where possible, illustrations of actual error stamps have been used. They are bordered in black. Illustrations of normal stamps have been used in cases where error stamp illustrations were not available, or where an error illustration would not adequately illustrate the error. Illustrations of normal stamps appear without black border.

Washington Crossing the Delaware. May 29, 1976. Souvenir sheet of 5. Lithographed. BEP.

24c multicolored

IM 317	imperf souvenir sheet, untagged Quantity: very rare	2,500.00
IM 318	imperf souvenir sheet, untagged, USA 24c omitted from all stamps Quantity: *2-3 reported*	3,500.00
IM 319	imperf souvenir sheet, untagged USA 24c omitted on 4th & 5th stamps Quantity: very rare, possibly unique	—

Washington at Valley Forge. May 29, 1976. Souvenir sheet of 5. Lithographed. BEP.

31c multicolored

IM 322	imperf souvenir sheet, untagged, tied by 5/29/76 PHILADELPHIA, PA precancel postmark to first day display card Quantity: *very rare*	2,250.00
IM 323	imperf souvenir sheet, untagged, USA 31c omitted from all stamps Quantity: 6-8 reported	2,500.00

IM 324	imperf souvenir sheet, untagged, USA 31c omitted on 1st, 3rd & 5th stamps Quantity: *possibly unique*	—
IM 325	imperf souvenir sheet, untagged, USA 31c omitted on 2nd, 4th & 5th stamps Quantity: very rare	2,500.00

Olympics. July 16, 1976. Se-tenant block of 4. Photogravure. BEP.

13c multicolored

a) Diver   b) Skier
c) Runner   d) Skater

IM 329	imperf block of 4 (a-d)	625.00
	plate block of 12, imperf	—
	Zip block of 4, imperf	—
	imperf pair (a-b) or (c-d)	275.00
	Quantity: 200+ blocks of 4 reported	

Buying or selling?
Consult the dealer directory at the back of the catalogue.

Where possible, illustrations of actual error stamps have been used. They are bordered in black. Illustrations of normal stamps have been used in cases where error stamp illustrations were not available, or where an error illustration would not adequately illustrate the error. Illustrations of normal stamps appear without black border.

Clara Maass. August 18, 1976. Photogravure. BEP.

13c multicolored

IM 330	hz pair, imperf vrt Quantity: 60-80 pairs reported	450.00

Christmas. October 27, 1976. Photogravure. BEP.

13c multicolored

IM 331	imperf pair	90.00
	plate block of 12, imperf	—
	Quantity: few hundred pairs	

CHRISTMAS 1976

Stamps of the following design exist in two varieties, each printed by a different press. Type II is more gray and is washed out in overall appearance. The varieties also can be can be distinguished under UV light. Type I is completely tagged. Type II is tagged with rectangles that cover only the design area.

Christmas. October 27, 1976. Photogravure. BEP.

13c multicolored, type I

IM 332	imperf pair	100.00
	plate block of 12, imperf	—
	Quantity: few hundred pairs	

13c multicolored, type II

IM 333	imperf pair	110.00
	plate strip of 20, imperf	—
	Quantity: few hundred pairs	
IM 334	vrt pair, imperf between Quantity: *40-60 pairs*	—

Washington at Princeton. January 3, 1977. Photogravure. BEP.

13c multicolored

IM 335   hz pair, imperf vrt   575.00
Quantity: 20-40 pairs

Pueblo Art. April 13, 1977. Se-tenant block or strip of 4. Photogravure. BEP.

13c multicolored

a) Hopi Pottery   b) Acoma Pottery
c) Zia Pottery   d) San Ildefonso Pottery

IM 336   block of 4 (a-d), imperf vrt   2,250.00
strip of 4 (a-d), imperf vrt   2,000.00
Quantity: 16 blocks of 4, 4 strips of 4 reported

Panes of the Pueblo Pottery stamp are arranged so that the four designs are se-tenant (a-b-c-d) in a row. Additionally, rows alternate so that it is possible for the four designs to appear in a se-tenant block of four.

Although catalogue prices are based on the best information available at press time, readers should be aware that prices for error stamps fluctuate over time, and therefore, are advised to contact dealers active in the error stamp market for timely quotes when buying or selling.

Spirit of St. Louis. May 20, 1977. Photogravure. BEP.

13c multicolored

IM 337   imperf pair   1,000.00
Quantity: 85-100 pairs reported

Colorado. May 21, 1977. Photogravure. BEP.

13c multicolored

IM 338   hz pair, imperf vrt   850.00
Quantity: *35 pairs*

Butterflies. June 6, 1977. Se-tenant block of 4. Photogravure. BEP.

13c multicolored

a) Swallowtail   b) Checkerspot
c) Dogface   d) Orange-Tip

IM 339   block of 4 (a-d), plate numbers at left, imperf hz **LRS (91)**   12,100.00
block of 4 (a-d), perfs slightly in at lower right, imperf hz **LRS (5/98)** 12,100.00
Quantity: the 2 blocks as listed

Christmas. October 21, 1977. Photogravure. BEP.

13c multicolored

IM 340	imperf pair	70.00
	plate strip of 20, imperf	—
	Quantity: 1,000+ pairs	

Christmas. October 21, 1977. Photogravure. BEP.

13c multicolored

IM 341	imperf pair	300.00
	plate block of 10, imperf	—
	Quantity: few hundred	

Captain James Cook. January 20, 1978. Pane of 50 arranged so that each half pane contains 25 stamps of the same design. Five se-tenant pairs exist at the center of each pane. Engraved. BEP.

13c dark blue (a), green (b)

    a) Captain Cook   b) Ships at Anchor

IM 342	se-tenant pair (a-b), imperf between	4,250.00
	Quantity: fewer than 5 pairs reported	

Although **IM 342** appears to be imperf vertically, it is properly described as imperf between because of the presence of blind perfs at left and right.

☞ Caution. Pairs of the Captain Cook portrait design exist with blind perforations that give the appearance of being imperforate.

Hinging. Prices for stamps after **IM 196** are for never hinged copies. Hinged copies sell for less.

IM 343	vrt pair (b), imperf hz	—
	strip of 10 containing **IM 342** & **IM 343**	—
	Quantity: very rare	

☞ Caution. Pairs of the Captain Cook portrait design exist with blind perforations that give the appearance of being imperforate.

Indian Head Penny. January 11, 1978. Engraved. BEP.

13c brown & greenish (ocher paper)

IM 344	hz pair, imperf vrt	275.00
	Quantity: 300-375 pairs	

Eagle & A. May 22, 1978. Photogravure. BEP.

A (15c) orange

IM 345	imperf pair	90.00
	plate block of 4, imperf	—
	Quantity: few hundred pairs	

The sheet variety of this stamp was printed by photogravure; the coil stamp was engraved. Therefore, horizontal pairs of the sheet stamp are collectible because they cannot be confused with the coil stamp of same design.

IM 346	vrt pair, imperf hz	675.00
	plate block of 4, imperf hz	—
	Quantity: 15-20 pairs reported	

Most pairs exist with faint vertical perfs. Pairs with distinct perforations such as those in the illustration are much rarer.

COIL STAMP

Eagle & A. May 27, 1978. Coil. Engraved. BEP.

A (15c) orange

IM 347	imperf pair	90.00
	line pair, imperf	195.00
	spliced pair or strip	—
	Quantity: 150-200 pairs	

Well centered copies are scarcer and sell for a premium.

Where possible, illustrations of actual error stamps have been used. They are bordered in black. Illustrations of normal stamps have been used in cases where error stamp illustrations were not available, or where an error illustration would not adequately illustrate the error. Illustrations of normal stamps appear without black border.

BOOKLET PANE

Eagle & A. May 22, 1978. Booklet pane. Engraved. BEP.

A (15c) orange

IM 348	vrt pair, imperf between	1,750.00
	Quantity: 3-4 pairs reported	

CAPEX. June 10, 1978. Souvenir sheet of 8. Engraved, lithographed. BEP.

13c multicolored

a) Cardinal e) Moose
b) Mallard f) Chipmunk
c) Canada Goose g) Red Fox
d) Blue Jay h) Raccoon

IM 349	strip of 4 (a-d), imperf vrt	7,500.00
	Quantity: 2 strips of 4	

IM 350	strip of 4 (e-h), imperf vrt	—
	as above, in souvenir sheet	4,000.00
	Quantity: 6 strips of 4, including those within souvenir sheets	

Roses. July 11, 1978. Booklet pane of 8. Engraved. BEP.

15c green, orange & rose

IM 351	booklet pane, imperf	—
	imperf pair	500.00
	Quantity: 9 panes reported	

Trees. October 9, 1978. Se-tenant block of 4. Photogravure. BEP.

15c multicolored

a) Giant Sequoia b) White Pine
c) White Oak d) Gray Birch

IM 352	block of 4 (a-d), imperf hz	
	LRS (10/98)	17,600.00
	Quantity: unique	

Madonna. October 18, 1978. Photogravure. BEP.

15c multicolored

IM 353	imperf pair	90.00
	Quantity: 300-400 pairs	

Hobby Horse. October 18, 1978. Photogravure. BEP.

15c multicolored

IM 354	imperf pair	90.00
	plate block of 12, imperf	—
	Quantity: 400-500 pairs	
IM 355	vrt pair, imperf hz	2,000.00
	Quantity: 4-6 pairs or strips of 3	

IM 355 contains traces of blind vertical perfs that may give it the appearance of being completely imperforate.

Martin Luther King. January 13, 1979. Photogravure. BEP.

13c multicolored

IM 356	imperf pair	1,750.00
	Quantity: *10 pairs reported*	

☛ Caution. Many exist with blind perfs.

Buying or selling?
Consult the dealer directory at the back of the catalogue.

Folk Art. April 19, 1979. Se-tenant block of 4. Photogravure. BEP.

15c multicolored

a) Coffeepot b) Tea Caddy
c) Sugar Bowl d) Coffeepot

IM 357	block of 4 (a-d), imperf hz	4,000.00
	block of 6, imperf hz	4,250.00
	Quantity: 1 pane consisting of 4 blocks of 4 and 4 blocks of 6 reported	

Endangered Flora. June 7, 1979. Se-tenant block of 4. Photogravure. BEP.

15c multicolored

a) Persistent Trillium
b) Hawaiian Wild Broadbean
c) Contra Costa Wallflower
d) Antioch Dunes Evening Primrose

IM 358	block of 4 (a-d), imperf	500.00
	plate block of 12, imperf	—
	Quantity: 100+ blocks of 4; 50+ pairs	

Seeing for Me. June 15, 1979. Photogravure. BEP.

15c multicolored

IM 359	imperf pair	400.00
	Quantity: 100 pairs	

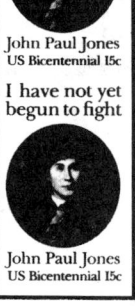      

IM 360   IM 361   IM 362

John Paul Jones. September 23, 1979. Photogravure. Two perforation varieties; Type I perf 11x12, Type II perf 11x11. JWF.

15c multicolored

IM 360	imperf pair PW	65.00
	Quantity: 500+ pairs	

☛ Printers waste, refer to introduction.

IM 361	vrt pair, type I, perf 12 vrt, imperf hz	175.00
	as above, Zip block of 4	—
	Quantity: 60-100 pairs	
IM 362	vrt pair, type II, perf 11 vrt, imperf hz	135.00
	as above, plate block of 10	—
	as above, Zip block of 4	—
	Quantity: 200-300 pairs	

The fully perforated version of this issue exists in a third variety, perf 12.

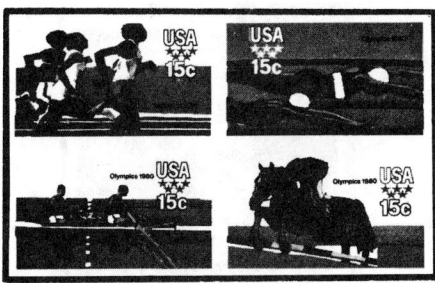

Summer Olympics. September 5, 1979. Se-tenant block of 4. Photogravure. BEP.

15c multicolored

a) Running b) Swimming
c) Rowing d) Horse Jumping

IM 363	block of 4 (a-d), imperf	1,500.00
	plate block of 12, imperf	*5,000.00*
	vrt pair (a & c), imperf	650.00
	vrt pair (b & d), imperf	650.00
	Quantity: 20 blocks of 4, 10 pairs	

Christmas Madonna. October 18, 1979. Photogravure. BEP.

15c multicolored

IM 364	imperf pair	90.00
	Quantity: 300-500 pairs	
IM 365	vrt pair, imperf between	2,250.00
	Quantity: *reportedly very rare*	
IM 366	vrt pair, imperf hz	700.00
	Quantity: at least 10-15 pairs	

Will Rogers. November 4, 1979. Photogravure. BEP.

15c multicolored

IM 367	imperf pair	200.00
	Quantity: several hundred pairs	

Benjamin Bannecker. February 15, 1980. Photogravure. ABN.

15c multicolored

IM 368	imperf pair **PW**	50.00
	Quantity: 500+ pairs	

☛ Printers waste, refer to introduction.

IM 369	hz pair, imperf vrt	750.00
	Quantity: *25 pairs reported*	

☛ Caution. Fakes exist made from printers waste. Expert certificate necessary.

COIL STAMP

Eagle & B. March 15, 1980. Coil. Engraved. BEP.

B (18c) violet

IM 370	imperf pair	95.00
	line pair, imperf	150.00
	spliced pair or strip, imperf	—
	used pair, imperf	—
	Quantity: 300-400 pairs	

Well centered pairs sell for a premium.

Although catalogue prices are based on the best information available at press time, readers should be aware that prices for error stamps fluctuate over time, and therefore, are advised to contact dealers active in the error stamp market for timely quotes when buying or selling.

Emily Bissell. May 31, 1980. Engraved. BEP.

15c red & black

IM 371   vrt pair, imperf hz   375.00
          Quantity: 40-60 pairs

Veterans Administration. July 21, 1980. Photogravure. ABN.

15c red & blue

IM 372   hz pair, imperf vrt   450.00
          Quantity: 50 pairs

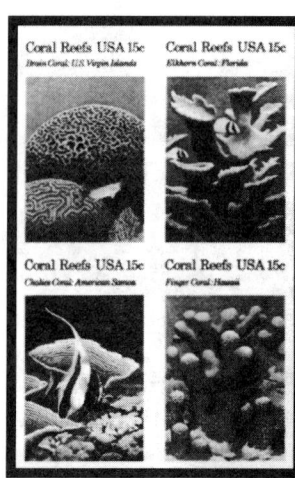

Coral Reefs. August 26, 1980. Se-tenant block of 4. Photogravure. BEP.

15c multicolored

a) Brain Coral   b) Elkhorn Coral
c) Chalice Coral   d) Finger Coral

IM 373   block of 4 (a-d), imperf   975.00
          any pair, imperf   400.00
          plate block of 12, imperf   —
          Quantity: 60-80 blocks of 4, 30-40 pairs

IM 374   block of 4 (a-d), imperf between vrt   3,750.00
          as above, any pair   —
          Quantity: 2 blocks of 4 and 2 pairs reported

IM 375   block of 4 (a-d), imperf vrt   2,975.00
          Quantity: 4 blocks reported

☞ Caution. Blind perfs may exist. Examine carefully.

Organized Labor. September 1, 1980. Photogravure. BEP.

15c multicolored

IM 376   imperf pair   375.00
          Zip block of 4, imperf   —
          Quantity: 100-150 pairs reported

Where possible, illustrations of actual error stamps have been used. They are bordered in black. Illustrations of normal stamps have been used in cases where error stamp illustrations were not available, or where an error illustration would not adequately illustrate the error. Illustrations of normal stamps appear without black border.

Learning Never Ends. September 12, 1980. Photogravure. ABN.

15c multicolored

IM 377	vrt pair, imperf vrt	225.00
	plate block of 8, imperf vrt	—
	Quantity: approx 100 pairs	

Madonna. October 31, 1980. Photogravure. BEP.

15c multicolored

IM 378	imperf pair	70.00
	plate block of 12, imperf	600.00
	Quantity: 1,000+ pairs	

Copies without gum sell for a substantial discount.

Drum. October 31, 1980. Photogravure. BEP.

15c multicolored

IM 379	imperf pair	70.00
	plate block of 20, imperf	*750.00*
	Quantity: 1,000+ pairs	

| IM 379A | vrt pair, imperf hz | — |
| | Quantity: 2-3 pairs reported | |

| IM 379B | hz pair, imperf between **LRS** (5/99) | 7,700.00 |
| | Quantity: 2 pairs, see note | |

The two listed pairs of **IM 379B** are contained in a block of 15 and occupy positions 4 & 5 and 9 & 10, and the **LRS** price is for the block.

GREAT AMERICANS SERIES OF 1980

Dorothea Dix. September 23, 1983. Engraved. BEP.

1c black

| IM 380 | imperf pair | 400.00 |
| | Quantity: *at least 100 pairs* | |

IM 380A   **IM 380B**

IM 380A vrt pair, imperf between   *3,000.00*
         Quantity: 3-5 pairs

Pairs of **IM 380A** contain a natural straight edge at bottom. Perfs at top should be clear of the design.

IM 380B vrt pair, imperf hz   —
         Quantity: *1-4 pairs reported*

Walter Lippmann. September 15, 1985. Engraved. BEP.

6c dark orange

IM 381	vrt pair, imperf between	*2,450.00*
	plate block of 4	—
	Quantity: 10 pairs	

Pairs of **IM 381** contain a natural straight edge at bottom.

Richard Russell. May 31, 1984. Engraved. BEP.

10c Prussian blue

IM 382	vrt pair, imperf between Quantity: 10-20 pairs	850.00

Pairs of **IM 382** contain a natural straight edge either at top or bottom.

IM 383	vrt pair, imperf hz Quantity: *10-17 pairs reported*	—

Do not confuse **IM 382** and **IM 383**. Vertical pairs of **IM 383** exist with perforations well into the stamp above the error pair. Such error pairs are considered to be imperforate horizontally, because the perforations in the third stamp do not occupy space between any stamps and are, therefore, completely extraneous to the error pair.

IM 383A	hz pair, imperf between Quantity: 10 pairs	2,000.00

IM 384	imperf pair, block tagged imperf strip of used on cover Quantity: *10 pairs reported*	1,200.00 —

☛ **IM 384** is block tagged. Imperf pairs without tagging exist and are printer's waste.

Sinclair Lewis. March 21, 1985. Engraved. BEP.

14c gray green

IM 385	hz pair, imperf between Quantity: several thousand pairs	8.00
IM 386	vrt pair, imperf hz Quantity: 200-250 pairs reported	125.00
IM 387	vrt pair, imperf between Quantity: 15-20 pairs reported	1,750.00

John J. Audubon. April 21, 1985. Engraved. BEP.

22c dark gray blue

IM 390	vrt pair, imperf hz Quantity: 10 pairs	2,500.00

Transition multiples exist.

IM 391	vrt pair, imperf between Quantity: *very rare, possibly unique*	—
IM 392	hz pair, imperf between Quantity: *10 pairs*	2,750.00

Transition multiples exist.

Grenville Clark. May 20, 1985. Engraved. BEP.

39c bright purple

IM 393	vrt pair, imperf hz strip of 3, imperf hz Quantity: *30-50 pairs reported*	575.00 —

Some copies exist with horizontal folds between stamps. Price is for copy without fold. Copies with fold sell for about one-third the price of those without folds.

IM 394	vrt pair, imperf between Quantity: 3-5 pairs reported	—

Buying or selling?
Consult the dealer directory at the back of the catalogue.

Alice Hamilton. July 11, 1995. Engraved. Dull gum. BCA.

55c gray green

IM 395	imperf pair	—
	Quantity: *10 pairs*	

Usually in a transition strip of 10.

Flag & Grain. April 24, 1981. Engraved. BEP.

18c red, blue & brown

IM 400	imperf pair	100.00
	Quantity: several hundred pairs	
IM 400A	vrt pair, imperf hz	850.00
	block of 4, imperf hz	—
	Quantity: *10-15 pairs reported*	

Although catalogue prices are based on the best information available at press time, readers should be aware that prices for error stamps fluctuate over time, and therefore, are advised to contact dealers active in the error stamp market for timely quotes when buying or selling.

Flag & Seashore. April 24, 1981. Coil. Engraved. BEP.

18c red, blue & brown

IM 401	imperf pair	18.00
	imperf strip with plate No. 2	*500.00*
	imperf strip with plate No. 3	—
	imperf strip with plate No. 4	—
	imperf strip with plate No. 5	175.00
	spliced pair or strip, imperf	—
	Quantity: 1,000+ pairs	

Exists miscut. Price for plate No. 2 is for a strip of 4 (the longest known strip); price for plate No. 5 for strip of 6. Plate No. 2 is most commonly encountered in pairs: price $125.00. Plate number pairs of No. 5 sell for about half the price of plate strips of 6.

At the time plate number coils were first introduced, the practice of saving plate numbers in strips had not yet been established. Therefore, many early plate number imperfs are relatively plentiful in pair form, but genuinely rare in longer strips.

IM 401A	hz pair, imperf between	—
	Quantity: *very rare*	

☛ Caution. Expert certificate necessary.

American Wildlife. March 15, 1981. Se-tenant booklet pane of 10. Engraved. BEP.

18c dark brown

a) Bighorn Sheep	b) Cougar
c) Seal	d) Bison
e) Bear	f) Polar Bear
g) Elk	h) Moose
i) Deer	j) Pronghorn Antelope

IM 402	booklet pane, imperf vrt between	*1,500.00*
	Quantity: 15 panes reported	

☛ Caution. Often with vertical row of perfs completely inside the design. Refer to the introduction for definitions of imperf errors.

Flag & Mountains se-tenant with numeral "6" in Circle of Stars. April 24, 1981. Booklet pane. Engraved. BEP.

6c red & blue, Numeral in Circle of Stars
18c red, blue & purple, Flag & Mountains

IM 403	booklet pane of 8 (6c & 18c), imperf vrt between	75.00
	pair (6c), imperf between	—
	pair (18c), imperf between	—
	Quantity: 1,000+ booklet panes	

COIL STAMP

Eagle & C. October 11, 1981. Coil. Photogravure. BEP.

C (20c) brown

IM 404	imperf pair	1,000.00
	line strip of 4, imperf	—
	Quantity: 60-70 pairs, 6+ line strips	

Gum along the edges of approximately half the pairs appears to have been slightly disturbed by moisture. Price is for a pair without moisture disturbance. Those with the disturbance sell for less.

Where possible, illustrations of actual error stamps have been used. They are bordered in black. Illustrations of normal stamps have been used in cases where error stamp illustrations were not available, or where an error illustration would not adequately illustrate the error. Illustrations of normal stamps appear without black border.

U.S. Flag. December 17, 1981. Engraved. BEP.

20c red, blue & black

IM 405	imperf vertical pair	35.00
	block of 4, imperf	75.00
	Quantity: 1,000+	

Collected in vertical pairs or blocks to distinguish it from the coil imperforate of the same design.

IM 406	vrt pair, imperf hz	475.00
	Quantity: very scarce	

Transition multiples exist and sell for a premium.

U.S. Flag. December 17, 1981. Coil. Engraved. BEP.

20c red, blue & black

IM 407	imperf pair	8.00
	used pair, imperf	—
	imperf strip with plate No. 1	—
	imperf strip with plate No. 2	350.00
	imperf strip with plate No. 3	450.00
	imperf strip with plate No. 4	400.00
	imperf strip with plate No. 5	300.00
	imperf strip with plate No. 6	1,250.00
	imperf strip with plate No. 8	150.00
	imperf strip with plate No. 9	175.00
	imperf strip with plate No. 10	150.00
	imperf strip with plate No. 11	—
	imperf strip with plate No. 12	850.00
	imperf strip with plate No. 13	950.00
	imperf strip with plate No. 14	1,250.00
	spliced pair or strip, imperf	—
	Quantity: several thousand pairs	

Exists miscut, some with EE bars at top or marginal markings at bottom. Transition multiples exist and sell for a premium. Exists untagged.

Prices are for plate strips of 6; plate strips of 5 sell for similar prices. Generally, plate strips of 3 sell for about 50% of the plate strip of six price, and plate pairs sell for about 33% of the strip of six price. There are exceptions depending on the issue and the plate number. Refer to second note following **IM 401**.

IM 408   pair, imperf between   1,000.00
            Quantity: 10-15 pairs

☛ Caution. Fakes exist. Expert certificate necessary.

BOOKLET PANE

Bighorn Sheep. January 8, 1982. Booklet pane of 10. Engraved. BEP.

20c gray blue

IM 409   booklet pane of 10, imperf vrt between   95.00
            complete booklet of 2 panes,
              imperf vrt between   185.00
            Quantity: *100-150 booklet panes*

Refer to note following **IM 402** and to introduction.

TRANSPORTATION SERIES OF 1982
COIL STAMPS

NOTE. Prices for imperf plate number coil (PNC) strips in this section are for strips of 6 unless otherwise noted. Generally, PNC strips of 5 sell for similar prices; PNC strips of 3 sell for about 50% of the strip of 6 price; and PNC pairs sell for about 33% of the strip of 6 price. There are exceptions, however, depending on issue and scarcity. Also, refer to the second note following **IM 401**.

Omnibus. August 19, 1983. Coil. Engraved. BEP.

1c violet

IM 410   imperf pair   625.00
            imperf strip with plate No. 5   —
            imperf strip with plate No. 6   —
            Quantity: 150-250 pairs

Omnibus. November 26, 1991. Coil. Engraved. BEP.

1c violet

IM 410A   imperf pair   2,400.00
             imperf strip with plate No. 1   —
             spliced pair or strip, imperf   —
             Quantity: 22-24 pairs

Transition multiples exist. Plate No. 1 is known on a transition strip in which the plate number appears on a perforated stamp.

Locomotive. May 20, 1982. Coil. Engraved. BEP.

2c black

IM 411   imperf pair   50.00
            used strip of 3, imperf   —
            imperf strip with plate No. 3   200.00
            imperf strip with plate No. 4   225.00
            imperf strip with plate No. 8   275.00
            imperf strip with plate No. 10   275.00
            Quantity: few thousand pairs

Transition multiples exist and sell for a premium. Prices are for plate strips of 6 with plate numbers & lines. Plate pairs sell for 33% less. Refer to second note following **IM 401**.

Stagecoach. August 19, 1982. Coil. Engraved. BEP.

4c reddish brown

IM 412   imperf pair, precanceled 2 bars
               & **NON-PROFIT Org.**   750.00
            imperf strip with plate No. 5   —
            imperf strip with plate No. 6   —
            imperf strip, gap in bars   —
            spliced pair or strip, imperf   —
            Quantity: *50-75 pairs*

Exists miscut. Transition multiples exist. The plate number appears at the top on plate number strips of plate No. 6. Plate number strips of **IM 412** exist only as strips of 3 or 4.

IM 412A	imperf pair, without precancel	850.00
	imperf strip with line & plate No. 1	—
	imperf strip with line & plate No. 2	—
	spliced pair or strip, imperf	—
	Quantity: 150 pairs reported	

Exists miscut.

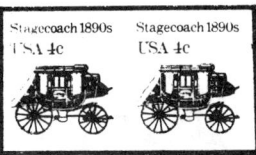

Stagecoach. August 15, 1986. Revised design. Coil. Engraved. BEP.

4c reddish brown

IM 412B	imperf pair	275.00
	imperf strip with plate No. 1	*1,500.00*
	Quantity: 250 pairs	

IM 412A contains a line on plate number pairs or strips. **IM 412B** contains a plate number only. Transition multiples exist.

Steam Carriage. August 31, 1990. Coil. Engraved. BEP.

4c dark purple

IM 412C	imperf pair	600.00
	imperf strip with plate No. 1	—
	spliced pair or strip, imperf	—
	imperf pair on first day cover	—
	Quantity: 100+ pairs; 5 first day covers	

Transition multiples exist and sell for a premium. Refer to note following **IM 434** regarding first day covers.

Motorcycle. October 10, 1983. Coil. Engraved. BEP.

5c gray green

IM 413	imperf pair	2,750.00
	imperf strip of 5 with plate No. 1	—
	imperf strip of 5 with plate No. 2	—
	spliced strip, imperf	—
	Quantity: 32 pairs; the 2 plate strips as listed above; unique spliced strip	

A transition multiple exists.

Circus Wagon. August 31, 1990. Coil. Engraved. BEP.

5c red

IM 413A	imperf pair	750.00
	imperf strip with plate No. 1	—
	spliced pair or strip, imperf	—
	Quantity: 72-88 pairs	

Transition multiples exist and sell for a premium. Wheels of the wagon are usually close to bottom or touch bottom. Price is for such a copy. Well centered copies exist and sell for more.

Circus Wagon. March 20, 1995. Coil. Photogravure. SVS.

5c carmine

IM 413B	imperf pair	—
	imperf strip with plate No. S2	—
	Quantity: *few hundred pairs*	

Some pairs possess counting numbers on the back.

Canoe. May 25, 1991. Coil. Engraved. BEP.

5c dark brownish violet & gray

IM 413C	imperf pair	250.00
	imperf strip with plate No. 1	—
	imperf strip with plate No. 2	—
	imperf pair on first day cover	—
	Quantity: 250+ pairs; 5 FDCs reported	

Exists miscut. Transition multiples exist. Refer to note following **IM 434** regarding first day covers.

Refer to the note preceding **IM 410** and the second note following **IM 401** for information about size and pricing of plate number coil strips.

Bicycle. May 17, 1982. Coil. Engraved. BEP.

5.9c blue

IM 414	imperf pair, precanceled 2 bars	150.00
	imperf strip with plate No. 3	—
	imperf strip with plate No. 4	—
	imperf pair or strip, gap in bars	—
	Quantity: 1,000+ pairs	

Exists miscut, some with EE bars at top. Transition multiples exist and sell for a premium.

Tricycle. May 6, 1985. Coil. Engraved. BEP.

6c red brown

IM 416	imperf pair, precanceled 2 bars & **NON-PROFIT Org.**	225.00
	imperf strip with plate No. 2	1,500.00
	Quantity: 250 pairs reported	

Wheel Chair. August 12, 1988. Coil. Engraved. BEP.

8.4c deep claret & red

IM 417	imperf pair	625.00
	imperf strip with plate No. 1	—
	imperf strip with plate No. 2	—
	Quantity: 100+ pairs reported	

Transition multiples exist and sell for a premium.

Mail Wagon. December 15, 1981. Coil. Engraved. BEP.

9.3c brownish purple

IM 418	imperf pair, precanceled 2 bars	115.00
	imperf strip with plate No. 1	*1,500.00*
	imperf strip with plate No. 2	*1,500.00*
	imperf strip with plate No. 3	—
	imperf strip with plate No. 4	—
	imperf pair or strip, gap in bars	—
	Quantity: 500 pairs	

Tractor Trailer. May 25, 1991. Coil. Engraved. BEP.

10c dark green & gray

IM 419	imperf pair	150.00
	imperf strip with plate No. 1	400.00
	Quantity: several hundred pairs	

Transition multiples exist and sell for a premium.

Canal Boat. April 11, 1987. Coil. Engraved. BEP.

10c blue

IM 419A	imperf pair	—
	imperf strip with Plate No. 1	—
	Quantity: 53 stamps	

Where possible, illustrations of actual error stamps have been used. They are bordered in black. Illustrations of normal stamps have been used in cases where error stamp illustrations were not available, or where an error illustration would not adequately illustrate the error. Illustrations of normal stamps appear without black border.

Although catalogue prices are based on the best information available at press time, readers should be aware that prices for error stamps fluctuate over time, and therefore, are advised to contact dealers active in the error stamp market for timely quotes when buying or selling.

Oil Wagon. April 18, 1985. Coil. Engraved. BEP.

10.1c slate blue

IM 420	imperf pair, precanceled 2 bars & **BULK RATE**	85.00
	imperf strip with plate No. 1	400.00
	spliced pair or strip, imperf	—
	imperf pair or strip, gap in bars	—
	Quantity: 500 pairs reported	

IM 420A	imperf pair, service inscribed **Bulk Rate Carrier Route Sort** in red	15.00
	imperf strip with plate No. 3	200.00
	spliced pair or strip, imperf	—
	Quantity: few thousand pairs	

Hansom Cab. March 26, 1982. Coil. Engraved. BEP.

10.9c purple

IM 421	imperf pair, precanceled 2 bars	135.00
	imperf strip with plate No. 1	—
	imperf strip with plate No. 2	—
	imperf pair or strip, gap in bars	—
	Quantity: 250+ pairs reported	

Pushcart. April 18, 1985. Coil. Engraved. BEP.

12.5c dark olive green

IM 423	imperf pair, precanc bars & **Bulk Rate**	50.00
	imperf strip with plate No. 1	250.00
	imperf pair or strip, gap in bars	—
	Quantity: 750-1,000 pairs	

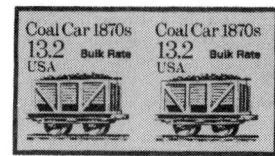

Coal Car. July 19, 1988. Coil. Engraved. BEP.

13.2c slate green & red

IM 424	imperf pair	95.00
	imperf strip with plate No. 1	275.00
	imperf strip with plate No. 2	—
	Quantity: several hundred pairs	

Transition multiples exist and sell for a premium.

Iceboat. March 23, 1985. Coil. Engraved. BEP.

14c light blue

IM 425	imperf pair	95.00
	imperf strip with plate No.1	450.00
	imperf strip with plate No.2	450.00
	Quantity: 350+ pairs reported	

Transition multiples exist and sell for a premium.

Tugboat. July 12, 1988. Coil. Engraved. BEP.

15c violet

IM 425A	imperf pair	750.00
	imperf strip with plate No. 2	—
	Quantity: 80-100 pairs	

Transition multiples exist and sell for a premium.

Buying or selling?
Consult the dealer directory at the back of the catalogue.

Popcorn Wagon. July 7, 1988. Coil. Engraved. BEP.

16.7 rose & black

IM 426	imperf pair	165.00
	imperf strip with plate No. 1	—
	Quantity: 150-200 pairs reported	

All known copies are miscut. Transition multiples exist and sell for a premium.

Electric Auto. June 25, 1981. Coil. Engraved. BEP.

17c blue

IM 427	imperf pair	165.00
	imperf strip with plate No. 1	1,000.00
	imperf strip with plate No. 2	1,000.00
	imperf strip with plate No. 3	1,000.00
	imperf strip with plate No. 4	1,000.00
	imperf strip with plate No. 5	—
	imperf strip with plate No. 7	—
	used pair, imperf	—
	spliced pair or strip, imperf	—
	Quantity: 350-400 pairs	

Exists miscut. Plate numbers often appear at top of strip due to miscut. Transition multiples exist and sell for a premium.

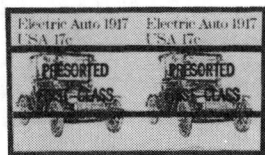

IM 428	imperf pair, precanceled 2 bars & **PRESORTED FIRST-CLASS**	575.00
	imperf strip with plate No. 3	—
	imperf strip with plate No. 4	—
	imperf pair or strip, gap in bars	—
	spliced pair or strip, imperf	—
	Quantity: 80-100 pairs reported	

Exists miscut. A unique strip exists containing three copies of **IM 428** spliced to three copies of **IM 407**.

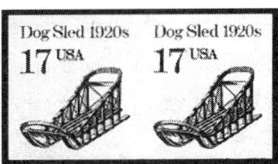

Dog Sled. August 20, 1986. Coil. Engraved. BEP.

17c blue

IM 429	imperf pair	450.00
	imperf strip with plate No. 2	—
	used strip of 3, imperf	—
	Quantity: 100-125 pairs reported	

Price for plate strip of 5 or 6 is the same. Exists miscut. Transition multiples exist and sell for a premium.

Racing Car. September 25, 1987. Coil. Engraved. BEP.

17.5c dark violet

IM 429A	imperf pair	2,500.00
	imperf strip with plate No. 1	—
	Quantity: *26 pairs; 3 plate strips of 6 reported*	

Transition multiples exist and sell for a premium.

Surrey. May 18, 1981. Coil. Engraved. BEP.

18c dark brown

IM 430	imperf pair	120.00
	imperf strip with plate No. 1	—
	imperf strip with plate No. 2	—
	imperf strip with plate No. 8	—
	imperf strip with plate No. 9	—
	imperf strip with plate No. 10	—
	imperf strip with plate No. 13	—
	spliced pair or strip, imperf	—
	Quantity: 400-500 pairs reported	

Exists miscut. Prices are for strips of 5 or 6 with plate number and line, except plate No. 13, which exists as a strip of 4. Also, refer to the second note following **IM 401**.

Hinging. Prices for stamps after **IM 196** are for never hinged copies. Hinged copies sell for less.

Fire Pumper. December 10, 1982. Coil. Engr. BEP.

20c red

IM 432	imperf pair	100.00
	imperf strip with plate No. 1	—
	imperf strip with plate No. 2	—
	imperf strip with plate No. 3	—
	imperf strip with plate No. 4	—
	imperf strip with plate No. 5	—
	imperf strip with plate No. 9	1,250.00
	imperf strip with plate No. 10	1,250.00
	imperf strip with plate No. 15	—
	imperf strip with plate No. 16	—
	Quantity: 600-800 pairs	

Exists miscut. Transition multiples exist and sell for a premium. Prices are for strips of 6 with plate number and line. Plate Nos. 1, 2, 4 and 5 are most commonly encountered in plate number pairs: price $200-$375. Plate strips of 3 or 4 generally sell for about 33%-50% of plate strips of 6.

Cable Car. October 28, 1988. Coil. Engraved. BEP.

20c blue violet

IM 433	imperf pair	45.00
	imperf strip with plate No. 2	275.00
	spliced pair or strip, imperf	—
	Quantity: 1,000+ pairs	

Transition multiples exist and sell for a premium.

Cog Railway. June 9, 1995. Coil. Engraved. BEP.

20c dark gray green

IM 433A	imperf pair	95.00
	imperf strip with plate No. 1	225.00
	Quantity: 400+ pairs	

Mail Car. August 16, 1988. Coil. Engraved. BEP.

21c olive green & red

IM 434	imperf pair	45.00
	imperf strip with plate No. 1	300.00
	imperf pair on first day cover	—
	Quantity: 1,000+ pairs, 36 FDCs reported	

Current Postal Service policy allows a grace period of 30 days (in some cases longer) after a stamp is issued during which covers may be submitted for first day cancellation. Because of this policy, controversy exists about the legitimacy of items that cannot conclusively be proved to have been postmarked on the actual first day of issue. Some regard imperfs on first day covers as contrived curiosities; others regard them as legitimately collectible. The publisher takes no position in this matter other than to report the existence of the covers.

Lunch Wagon. April 12, 1991. Coil. Engraved. BEP.

23c blue

IM 435	imperf pair	125.00
	imperf strip with plate No. 2	—
	imperf strip with plate No. 3	—
	spliced pair or strip, imperf	—
	Quantity: 400-500 pairs reported	

Exists miscut; some miscut pairs show EE bars at top. Transition multiples exist and sell for a premium. The gum on strips of plate No. 3 is mottled.

Breadwagon. November 22, 1986. Coil. Engr. BEP.

25c yellow brown

IM 436	imperf pair	10.00
	imperf strip with plate No. 1	—
	imperf strip with plate No. 2	225.00
	imperf strip with plate No. 3	225.00
	imperf strip with plate No. 4	225.00
	imperf strip with plate No. 5	—
	imperf pair, used	—
	spliced pair or strip, imperf	—
	Quantity: few thousand pairs	

Exists miscut, some with EE bars at top or marginal markings at bottom. Transition multiples exist and sell for a premium. Exists untagged.

IM 437	pair, imperf between	500.00
	strip of three pairs with plate No. 2	—
	Quantity: *10 pairs reported*	

Ferryboat. June 2, 1995. Coil. Engraved. BEP.

32c blue

IM 438	imperf pair	—
	imperf strip with plate No. 2	—
	imperf strip with plate No. 3	—
	imperf strip with plate No. 5	—
	Quantity: *70-80 pairs reported*	

Exists miscut, some with EE bars at top or marginal markings at bottom.

IM 438A	pair, imperf between	—
	Quantity: *new, n/a*	

Expert certificate necessary.

Seaplane. April 20, 1990. Coil. Engraved. BEP.

$1 red & gray blue

IM 439	imperf pair	3,000.00
	imperf strip with plate No. 1	—
	imperf pair, used	—
	Quantity: 54 mint stamps; 1 strip of 9 used & 1 strip of 4 used	

Of the 54 mint stamps, 22 are in a strip containing plate No. 1 and the balance, in pairs.

Refer to the note preceding **IM 410** and the second note following **IM 401** for information about size and pricing of plate number coil strips.

Where possible, illustrations of actual error stamps have been used. They are bordered in black. Illustrations of normal stamps have been used in cases where error stamp illustrations were not available, or where an error illustration would not adequately illustrate the error. Illustrations of normal stamps appear without black border.

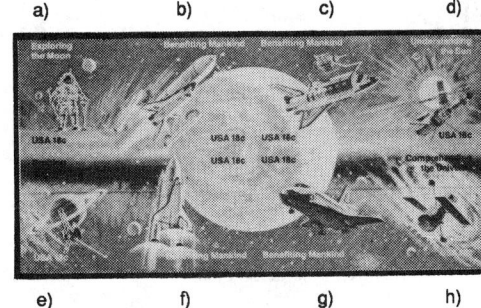

a) b) c) d)
e) f) g) h)

Space Achievement. Se-tenant block of 8. May 21, 1981. Photogravure. BEP.

18c multicolored

a) Exploring the Moon
b) Space Shuttle
c) Space Shuttle Launching Satellite
d) Understanding the Sun
e) Probing the Planets
f) Space Shuttle Blasting Off
g) Space Shuttle with Landing Gear Down
h) Comprehending the Universe

IM 440	block of 8 (a-h), imperf	9,000.00
	plate block of 8 (a-h), imperf	—
	Zip block of 8 (a-h), imperf	—
	Quantity: 4-6 blocks of 8 reported	

A block of 8 exists perforated horizontally at the top, and with vertical perforations extending about one-third the way down from the top. This creates four imperf stamps (e-h) along the bottom row and four imperf horizontally (a-e, b-f, c-g, and d-h) pairs.

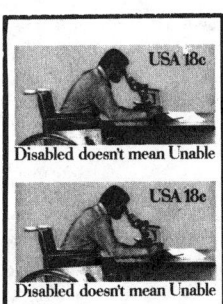

Year of the Disabled. June 29, 1981. Photogravure. BEP.

18c multicolored

IM 441	vrt pair, imperf hz	2,750.00
	plate block of 4, imperf	—
	Quantity: 10 pairs reported	

☛ Caution. Beware pairs with blind horizontal perfs. Error pairs contain blind vertical perforations, which are normal.

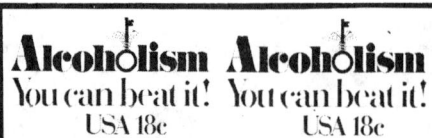

Beat Alcoholism. August 19, 1981. Engraved. BEP.

18c black & blue

IM 442	imperf pair	425.00
	Quantity: at least 50 pairs	

Price is for copy without disturbed gum. Copies with disturbed gum sell for less.

IM 442A	vrt pair, imperf hz	2,500.00
	Quantity: 3 pairs reported	

Frederic Remington. October 9, 1981. Engraved. BEP.

18c brown, dark green & gray

IM 443	vrt pair, imperf between	225.00
	Quantity: 200 pairs reported	

☛ Caution. Pairs or strips of 3 exist with blind perfs.

Madonna. October 28, 1981. Photogravure. BEP.

(20c) multicolored

IM 444	imperf pair	110.00
	Quantity: few hundred pairs	

IM 444A	vrt pair, imperf hz	1,550.00
	block of 4, imperf hz	—
	Quantity: 2-5 pairs reported	

Christmas Toys. October 28, 1981. Photogravure. BEP.

(20c) multicolored

IM 445	imperf pair	225.00
	Quantity: 200-300 pairs	

IM 446	vrt pair, imperf hz	2,500.00
	Quantity: *10-15 pairs*	

IM 446 results from blind perfs at left and right.

a)   b)   c)   d)

Cactus. December 11, 1981. Se-tenant block of 4. Engraved, lithographed. BEP.

20c multicolored

a) Barrel Cactus   b) Agave
c) Beavertail Cactus   d) Saguaro

IM 447	vrt pair (d only), imperf **LRS (2/96)**	6,600.00
	single (d), imperf	—
	Quantity: 2 pairs, 1 single	

The vertical imperf pair (d only) is contained in a block of 8.

Love. February 1, 1982. Photogravure. BEP.

20c multicolored

IM 448	imperf pair	250.00
	plate block of 4, imperf	—
	Quantity: 150-200 pairs	

Horizontal pairs usually sell for more than vertical pairs.

State Birds & Flowers. April 14, 1982. Se-tenant pane of 50. Photogravure. BEP.

20c multicolored.

IM 449	pane of 50, imperf **LRS (3/97)**		23,100.00
	imperf pair		—
	Quantity: 4 panes		

Of the four panes, two are completely imperf, one contains some blind perfs, and one was cut into pairs. The pane containing blind perfs realized $11,000 at auction in 1989.

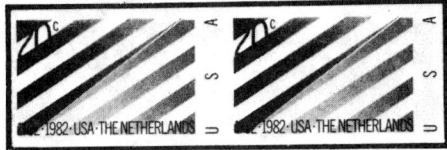

Netherlands/USA. April 20, 1983. Photogravure. BEP.

20c multicolored

IM 450	imperf pair	300.00
	Quantity: 94 pairs reported	

Consumer Education. April 27, 1982. Coil. Engraved. BEP.

20c light blue

IM 451	imperf pair	95.00
	imperf strip with plate No. 1	*1,650.00*
	imperf strip with plate No. 2	—
	imperf strip with plate No. 3	—
	imperf strip with plate No. 4	—
	Quantity: several hundred pairs	

Prices are for strips of 6 with plate number and line. Plate strips of 5 sell for similar prices. Plate pairs are much more common: price $275.00. Plate strips of 3 sell for about 33% the plate strip of 6 price. Exists miscut. Transition multiples exist and sell for a premium.

America's Libraries. July 13, 1982. Engraved. BEP.

20c red & black

IM 452	vrt pair, imperf hz	275.00
	Quantity: 100-120 pairs	

Touro Synagogue. August 22, 1982. Photogravure. BEP.

20c multicolored

IM 453	imperf pair	*2,750.00*
	Quantity: 25 pairs	

Ponce de Leon. October 2, 1982. Photogravure. BEP.

20c multicolored

IM 454	imperf pair	475.00
	plate block of 20, imperf	—
	Quantity: 125+ pairs reported	
IM 454A	vrt pair, imperf between	—
	Quantity: rare	

Puppy & Kitten. November 3, 1982. Photogravure. BEP.

13c multicolored

IM 455 imperf pair 650.00
Quantity: 75-100 pairs reported

Some pairs are faulty. Price is for a sound pair. Faulty pairs sell for considerably less.

Madonna. October 28, 1982. Photogravure. BEP.

20c multicolored

IM 456 imperf pair 150.00
plate block of 20, imperf —
Quantity: few hundred pairs

IM 457 hz, imperf vrt —
Quantity: 3-6 pairs reported

IM 457A vrt pair, imperf hz —
plate block of 4, imperf hz **LRS (6/98)** 4,025.00
Quantity: very rare

The plate block contains blind perforations on its sides and at bottom.

Where possible, illustrations of actual error stamps have been used. They are bordered in black. Illustrations of normal stamps have been used in cases where error stamp illustrations were not available, or where an error illustration would not adequately illustrate the error. Illustrations of normal stamps appear without black border.

Christmas Winter Scenes. October 28, 1982. Se-tenant block of 4. Photogravure. BEP.

20c multicolored

a) Snowman b) Sledding
c) Christmas tree d) Skating

IM 458 block of 4 (a-d), imperf 2,800.00
Quantity: 20 blocks of 4

IM 459 block of 4 (a-d), imperf hz —
Quantity: rare

Balloons. March 31, 1983. Se-tenant block of 4. Photogravure. BEP.

20c multicolored

a) Intrepid
b) Hot Air Ballooning
c) Hot Air Ballooning
d) Explorer II

IM 460 block of 4 (a-d), imperf 5,000.00
plate block of 4, imperf —
Zip block of 4, imperf —
copyright block of 4, imperf —
Quantity: 10 blocks of 4

In addition to the above, five blocks of 4 (a-d) exist with perforations on the three exterior sides of the right stamp (d) and blind perforations between the center two stamps (b-c) and the right stamp (d). Price $4,500.00.

Civilian Conservation Corps. April 5, 1983. Photogravure. BEP.

20c multicolored

IM 461	imperf pair	3,250.00
	plate block of 4, imperf	—
	Quantity: 7 pairs, including those in the plate block	
IM 461A	vrt pair, imperf hz	—
	Quantity: unique	

IM 461A results from blind perfs at its sides.

Volunteer Lend A Hand. April 30, 1983. Engraved. BEP.

20c black & red

IM 462	imperf pair	450.00
	Quantity: 25-50 pairs reported	

Some copies have an underinked appearance. Price is for underinked copy. Solidly colored copies sell for more.

Scott Joplin. June 9, 1983. Photogravure. BEP.

20c multicolored

IM 463	imperf pair	450.00
	Quantity: 50 pairs reported	

Santa Claus. October 28, 1983. Photogravure. BEP.

20c multicolored

IM 464	imperf pair	150.00
	plate bock of 6, imperf	450.00
	Quantity: 150+ pairs	

Love. January 31, 1984. Photogravure. BEP.

20c multicolored

IM 465	hz pair, imperf vrt	175.00
	Quantity: 150-175 pairs	

Hinging. Prices for stamps after **IM 196** are for never hinged copies. Hinged copies sell for less.

Although catalogue prices are based on the best information available at press time, readers should be aware that prices for error stamps fluctuate over time, and therefore, are advised to contact dealers active in the error stamp market for timely quotes when buying or selling.

Carter G. Woodson. January 31, 1984. Photogravure. ABN.

20c multicolored

IM 466 hz pair, imperf vrt 1,750.00
Quantity: 25 pairs reported

Summer Olympics. May 4, 1984. Photogravure. BEP.

a) Diving
c) Wrestling
b) Long Jump
d) Canoeing

20c multicolored

IM 466A block of 4, imperf vrt —
pair c & d, imperf vrt —
Quantity: 2 blocks of 4, 1 pair

The discovery pane contained the listed stamps in a strip of ten at left. The pane also contained a row of blind perfs between rows 7 and 8.

Douglas Fairbanks. May 23, 1984. Engraved, photogravure. BEP.

20c multicolored

IM 467 hz pair, imperf vrt —
Quantity: *reportedly unique*

Preserving Wetlands. July 2, 1984. Engraved. BEP.

20c blue

IM 468 hz pair, imperf vrt 375.00
hz strip of 3, imperf vrt 450.00
Zip block, imperf vrt —
Quantity: 95-120 pairs

The term "transition multiple" refers to errors appearing in combination with normal or nearly-normal stamps. Generally, a pair, strip, or block containing one or more error stamps, one or more normal stamps, and, in the case of color-omitted errors, one or more stamps with color(s) partially omitted. Transition multiples sell for a premium.

Smokey. August 13, 1984. Photogravure. BEP.

20c multicolored

IM 469	hz pair, imperf between	275.00
	plate block of 4, vrt imperf between	—
	Quantity: 100-125 pairs	
IM 469A	hz pair, imperf vrt	*1,600.00*
	Quantity: 20-25 pairs	
IM 470	vrt pair, imperf between	225.00
	Quantity: 160-200 pairs	

IM 471   block of 4, imperf hz & vrt (internally) between   *6,000.00*
Quantity: 6 blocks of 4 (including 1 faulty block)

Buying or selling?
Consult the dealer directory at the back of the catalogue.

Roberto Clemente. August 17, 1984. Photogravure. BEP.

20c multicolored

IM 472   hz pair, imperf vrt   2,000.00
hz strip of 3, vrt imperf   —
Quantity: 20 pairs, 3 strips of 3 reported

Family Unity. October 1, 1984. Photogravure. BEP.

20c multicolored

IM 473   hz pair, imperf vrt   525.00
Quantity: 50 pairs

IM 473A   hz pair, imperf between   —
Quantity: 1-2 pairs reported

IM 473B   vrt pair, imperf between   —
Quantity: n/a

IM 473B occurs with a natural straight edge at bottom.

Christmas. October 30, 1984. Photogravure. BEP.

20c multicolored

IM 473C   hz pair, imperf vrt   925.00
Quantity: 25 pairs

Most copies are poorly centered as in the illustration. Price is for a poorly centered copy.

Hispanic Americans. October 31, 1984. Photogravure. BEP.

20c multicolored

IM 474	vrt pair, imperf hz Quantity: 20 pairs reported	2,000.00

Eagle & D. February 1, 1985. Photogravure. BEP.

D (22c) green

IM 475	imperf vrt pair	40.00
	block of 4, imperf	80.00
	plate block of 4, imperf	125.00
	Zip block of 4, imperf	100.00
	copyright block of 4, imperf	100.00
	Quantity: 1,000+	
IM 476	vrt pair, imperf hz Quantity: 4 pairs reported	1,300.00

Hinging. Prices for stamps after **IM 196** are for never hinged copies. Hinged copies sell for less.

Eagle & D. February 1, 1985. Coil. Photogravure. BEP.

D (22c) green

IM 477	imperf pair	45.00
	imperf strip with plate No. 1	500.00
	imperf strip with plate No. 2	750.00
	spliced pair or strip, imperf	—
	Quantity: 1,000+	

Prices are for plate strips of 6. Plate strips of 5 sell for similar prices. Plate strips of 3 or 4 for sell for 33%-50% the price of plate strips of 6. Strips exist spliced with a variety of kinds and colors of cellophane, masking, and paper tapes, and the sell for a premium. Exists miscut. Exists untagged; quantity 200 pairs; price $125.00.

Eagle & D. February 1, 1985. Booklet pane of 10. Photogravure. BEP.

D (22c) green

IM 477A	booklet pane of 10, imperf hz between	—
	Quantity: *2 panes*	

Flag & Capitol. March 29, 1985. Coil. Engraved. BEP.

22c red, blue & black

IM 478	imperf pair	12.50
	imperf strip with plate No. 1	500.00
	imperf strip with plate No. 2	150.00
	imperf strip with plate No. 3	—
	imperf strip with plate No. 4	—
	imperf strip with plate No. 5	675.00
	imperf strip with plate No. 6	—
	imperf strip with plate No. 7	500.00
	imperf strip with plate No. 8	200.00
	imperf strip with plate No. 10	500.00
	imperf strip with plate No. 11	—
	imperf strip with plate No. 12	350.00
	imperf strip with plate No. 13	—
	imperf strip with plate No. 15	900.00
	imperf strip with plate No. 17	—
	imperf strip with plate No. 18	650.00
	imperf strip with plate No. 19	400.00
	imperf strip with plate No. 20	950.00
	imperf strip with plate No. 22	450.00
	spliced pair or strip, imperf	—
	Quantity: few thousand pairs	

Prices are for plate strips of 5 or 6. Strips of 3 or 4 sell for 33%-50% of the strip of 6 price. Exists miscut, some with EE bars at top or marginal markings at bottom. Transition multiples exist and sell for a premium.

Special Olympics. March 5, 1985. Photogravure. BEP.

22c multicolored

IM 479   vrt pair, imperf hz   500.00
          Quantity: 60-80 pairs reported

Love. April 17, 1985. Photogravure. BEP.

22c multicolored

IM 480   imperf pair   1,500.00
          Quantity: 15 pairs imperf, 5 pairs
          partially imperf, see note

Some pairs (often in transition strips) contain perfs at left, and on top and bottom of the left stamp. Often with paper crease. Price is for sound pair. Creased pairs sell for about 33% of sound pairs.

Sea Shells. April 4, 1985. Se-tenant booklet pane of 10. Engraved. BEP.

22c multicolored

        a) Frilled Dogwinkle
        b) Reticulated Helmet
        c) New England Neptune
        d) Calico Scallop
        e) Lightning Whelk

IM 481   booklet pane, imperf vrt between   600.00
          Quantity: 30-40 booklets reported

Panes removed from booklets usually contain tab faults. Price is for pane with tab faults.

Rural Electrification. May 11, 1985. Engraved, photogravure. BEP.

22c multicolored

IM 481A   vrt pair, imperf between   —
           Quantity: *reportedly unique*

Abigail Adams. June 14, 1985. Photogravure. BEP.

22c multicolored

IM 482   imperf pair   250.00
          Quantity: 150-200 pairs

Transition multiples exist and sell for a premium.

Poinsettia. October 31, 1985. Photogravure. BEP.

22c multicolored

IM 483   imperf pair   120.00
          block of 4, imperf   250.00
          plate block of 4, imperf   —
          Zip block of 4, imperf   —
          Quantity: 250-300 pairs

Where possible, illustrations of actual error stamps have been used. They are bordered in black. Illustrations of normal stamps have been used in cases where error stamp illustrations were not available, or where an error illustration would not adequately illustrate the error. Illustrations of normal stamps appear without black border.

Madonna. October 31, 1985. Photogravure. BEP.

22c multicolored

IM 484	imperf pair	80.00
	plate block of 4, imperf	200.00
	Zip block of 4, imperf	—
	Quantity: 300-400 pairs	

COIL STAMP

George Washington. November 6, 1985. Coil. Photogravure. BEP.

18c multicolored

IM 485	imperf pair, precanceled **PRESORTED FIRST-CLASS**	775.00
	imperf strip with plate No. 3333	—
	spliced pair or strip, imperf	—
	Quantity: 50-100 pairs reported	

Exists miscut. Transition multiples exist and sell for a premium.

IM 486	imperf pair, without precancel	950.00
	imperf strip with plate No. 1112	
	Quantity: 30-40 pairs reported	

Arkansas. January 3, 1986. Photogravure. ABN.

22c multicolored

IM 487	vrt pair, imperf hz	—
	Quantity: 25 pairs reported	

Texas. March 2, 1986. Photogravure. ABN.

22c multicolored

IM 488	hz pair, imperf vrt	1,100.00
	Quantity: 25 pairs	

Public Hospitals. April 11, 1986. Photogravure. BEP.

22c multicolored

IM 489	vrt pair, imperf hz	300.00
	Quantity: 50-75 pairs	

IM 489A	hz pair, imperf vrt	*1,250.00*
	Quantity: *20 pairs*	

Buying or selling?
Consult the dealer directory at the back of the catalogue.

Duke Ellington. April 29, 1986. Photogravure. ABN.

22c multicolored

IM 490	vrt pair, imperf hz	900.00
	plate block of 4, imperf hz	—
	used strip of 3, imperf hz	375.00
	Quantity: 40-60 pairs	

Presidents. May 22, 1986. Souvenir sheet of 9. Engraved, lithographed. BEP.

22c multicolored

IM 490A	imperf sheet of 9 LRS (2/93)	10,450.00
	Quantity: *very rare, possibly unique*	

Wood Carving. October 1, 1986. Se-tenant block of 4. Photogravure. ABN.

22c multicolored

a) Highlander Figure b) Ship Figurehead
c) Nautical Figure d) Cigar Store Indian

IM 491	block of 4 (a-d), imperf vrt	1,450.00
	pair (a-b or c-d), imperf vrt	300.00
	Quantity: 20 blocks of 4;	
	5 pairs each a-b & c-d	

Madonna. October 14, 1986. Photogravure. BEP.

22c multicolored

IM 491A	imperf pair	1,000.00
	Quantity: *20+ pairs reported*	

Where possible, illustrations of actual error stamps have been used. They are bordered in black. Illustrations of normal stamps have been used in cases where error stamp illustrations were not available, or where an error illustration would not adequately illustrate the error. Illustrations of normal stamps appear without black border.

Buying or selling?
Consult the dealer directory at the back of the catalogue.

William Faulkner. August 3, 1987. Engraved. BEP.

22c green

IM 491B imperf single, used PW —
Quantity: rare

☛ Caution. Genuine imperforate used singles of this issue are from printer's waste and are not tagged. Beware tagged used singles trimmed to resemble imperforates.

Flag & Fireworks. November 30, 1987. Booklet pane of 20. Photogravure. BEP.

22c multicolored

IM 491C vert pair, imperf btwn LRS (6/97) 1,980.00
Quantity: unique

IM 491C occurs as a result of a foldover.

COIL STAMP

Earth. March 22, 1988. Coil. Photogravure. BEP.

E (25c) multicolored

IM 492	imperf pair	70.00
	imperf strip with plate No. 1111	*475.00*
	imperf strip with plate No. 1211	—
	imperf strip with plate No. 1222	—
	imperf strip with plate No. 2222	—
	spliced pair or strip, imperf	—
	Quantity: 1,000+ pairs	

Prices are for plate strips of 6. Exists miscut. The plate number on plate strips of No. 1222 appear at the top due to a miscut. Transition multiples exist and sell for a premium.

Flag Over Yosemite. May 20, 1988. Coil. Block tagging. Engraved. BEP.

25c red, ultramarine & cobalt green

IM 493	imperf pair	25.00
	imperf strip with plate No. 2	600.00
	imperf strip with plate No. 3	425.00
	imperf strip with plate No. 4	—
	imperf strip with plate No. 5	700.00
	imperf strip with plate No. 7	500.00
	imperf strip with plate No. 8	750.00
	imperf strip with plate No. 9	750.00
	spliced pair or strip, imperf	—
	Quantity: several thousand pairs	

Exists miscut. Transition multiples exist and sell for a premium.

Flag Over Yosemite. February 14, 1989. Coil. Same design as IM 493. Phosphor tagging. Engraved. BEP.

IM 494	imperf pair	10.00
	imperf strip with plate No. 2	175.00
	imperf strip with plate No. 3	—
	imperf strip with plate No. 5	*750.00*
	imperf strip with plate No. 6	—
	imperf strip with plate No. 7	700.00
	imperf strip with plate No. 8	700.00
	imperf strip with plate No. 9	375.00
	imperf strip with plate No. 10	375.00
	imperf strip with plate No. 11	*600.00*
	imperf strip with plate No. 13	—
	imperf strip with plate No. 14	350.00
	imperf strip with plate No. 15	—
	imperf pair on first day cover	—
	spliced pair or strip, imperf	—
	Quantity: several thousand pairs	

Exists miscut, some with EE bands at top or marginal markings at bottom. Exists untagged. Transition multiples exist and sell for a premium. Prices are for plate strips of 6.
Block tagging on **IM 493** is rectangular in shape covering the design. Phosphor tagging on **IM 494** covers the entire stamp. Refer to note following **IM 434** regarding first day covers.

IM 494A	pair, imperf between	600.00
	strip of 6 with plate No. 9	—
	strip of 6 with plate No. 14	—
	Quantity: *20+ pairs reported*	

Expert certificate advised.

Honeybee. September 2, 1988. Coil. Engraved, lithographed. BEP.

25c multicolored

IM 495	imperf pair	50.00
	imperf strip with plate No. 1	250.00
	imperf strip with plate No. 2	250.00
	imperf pair on first day cover	—
	spliced pair or strip, imperf	—
	Quantity: several hundred pairs; 6 first day covers	

Exists miscut, some with EE bars at top. Some pairs contain lines that resemble Cottrell press lines. Prices are for plate strips of 6. Refer to the note following **IM 434** regarding first day covers.

☛ Caution. Pairs exist with blind perfs.

IM 496	pair, imperf between	—
	strip with plate No. 1, imperf between	—
	Quantity: *10 pairs, 1-2 plate number strips reported*	

Pheasant. April 29, 1988. Booklet pane of 10. Engraved, lithographed. ABN.

25c multicolored

IM 497	vrt pair, imperf between **PW**	—
	Quantity: several hundred pairs	

☛ Printer's waste. A few pairs exist as the result of a foldover. They are not printer's waste.

IM 498	vrt pair, imperf hz **PW**	75.00
	booklet pane, imperf hz	—
	Quantity: several hundred pairs	

☛ Printer's waste. Refer to introduction. Can be created by trimming perfs from top and bottom of **IM 497**.

IM 499	imperf pair **PW**	—
	Quantity: n/a	

☛ Printer's waste. Refer to introduction.

South Carolina. May 23, 1988. Photogravure. ABN.

25c multicolored

IM 499A	hz strip of 3, imperf vrt **LRS (9/92)**	10,450.00
	Quantity: unique strip of 3	

Love. July 4, 1988. Photogravure. BEP.

25c multicolored

IM 499B	imperf pair	3,250.00
	Quantity: *5 pairs or strips 3*	

Antarctic Explorers. August 25, 1988. Se-tenant block of 4. Photogravure. ABN.

25c multicolored

a) Nathaniel Palmer b) Charles Wilkes
c) Richard Byrd   d) Lincoln Ellsworth

IM 500	block of 4, imperf hz	3,000.00
	plate block of 4, imperf hz	—
	Quantity: 10 blocks of 4, 5 singles (a & c)	

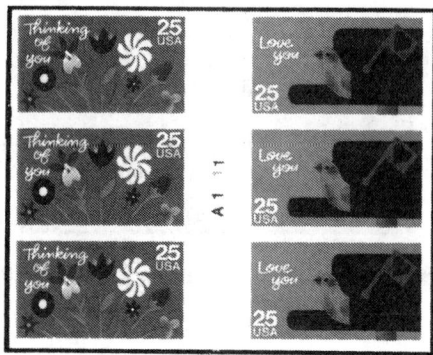

Special Occasions. October 22, 1988. Booklet pane of 6. Photogravure. ABN.

25c multicolored

    a) Flowers   b) Bird in mailbox

IM 501   booklet pane, imperf   —
            Quantity: unique

Montana. January 15, 1989. Engraved, litho. BEP.

25c multicolored

IM 501A   imperf pair   **PRF PW**   —
            Quantity: 100+ pairs

Ungummed, on heavy paper. Recent auction prices range from $40 to $175. At least one block of 4 exists with "First Day of Issue" postmark. It is almost certainly contrived.

Hemingway. July 17, 1989. Photogravure. ABN.

25c multicolored

IM 501B   vrt pair, imperf hz   —
            Quantity: 12 pairs reported

Of the 12 pairs, 6 are sound and 6 are faulty. Only 3 are well centered.

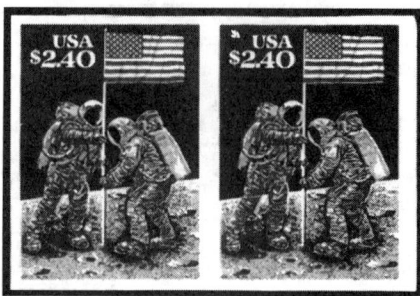

Astronauts on Moon. July 20, 1989. Engraved, lithographed. BEP.

$2.40 multicolored

IM 502   imperf pair   850.00
           plate block of 4, imperf   —
           Quantity: 200 pairs

Christmas. October 19, 1989. Photogravure. Perf 11. ABN.

25c multicolored

IM 503   vrt pair, imperf hz   750.00
           Quantity: 20+ pairs reported

Christmas. October 19, 1989. Booklet pane of 10. Photogravure. Perf 11½. BEP.

25c multicolored

IM 504   vrt pair, imperf hz   —
           booklet pane, imperf hz   —
           Quantity: 2 panes reported

IM 503 and **IM 504** can be distinguished in several ways. One of the easiest is to compare the color of the large package at the front and bottom of the sleigh. It is a light brown color on **IM 503** and dark maroon color on **IM 504**.

IM 504A   imperf pair   —
            block of 4, imperf   **LRS (12/98)**   1,265.00
            Quantity: rare

Hinging. Prices for stamps after **IM 196** are for never hinged copies. Hinged copies sell for less.

Eagle & Shield. November 10, 1989. Photogravure. Self-adhesive. Straight die cut. ABN.

25c multicolored

IM 505	pair, die cut omitted	300.00
	plate block of 4, die cut omitted	—
	Quantity: n/a	
IM 505A	pair, die cut omitted between	575.00
	Quantity: 27-36 pairs	

Love. January 18, 1990. Photogravure. USB.

25c multicolored

IM 506	imperf pair	750.00
	Quantity: 50 pairs	

American Indian Headdresses. July 6, 1990. Se-tenant booklet pane of 10. Engraved, lithographed. BEP.

25c multicolored

IM 506A	booklet pane of 10, imperf hz	—
	Quantity: very rare, possibly unique	

Although catalogue prices are based on the best information available at press time, readers should be aware that prices for error stamps fluctuate over time, and therefore, are advised to contact dealers active in the error stamp market for timely quotes when buying or selling.

Dwight D. Eisenhower. October 13, 1990. Photogravure. BEP.

25c multicolored

IM 507	imperf pair	2,250.00
	plate block of 4, imperf	—
	Quantity: 20 pairs	

Greetings. October 18, 1990. Photogravure. ABN.

25c multicolored

IM 507A	vrt pair, imperf hz	1,100.00
	Quantity: 19 sound pairs, 1 faulty pair	

Flower. January 22, 1991. Photogravure. Perf 13. USB.

F (29c) multicolored

IM 508	vrt pair, imperf	700.00
	Quantity: 20-30 pairs reported	

IM 508 is collected in vertical pairs or blocks in order to distinguish it from the imperforate coil stamp of the same design.

IM 509	hz pair, imperf vrt	1,250.00
	Quantity: 5 pairs reported	

Buying or selling?
Consult the dealer directory at the back of the catalogue.

Flower. January 22, 1991. Coil. Photogravure. BEP.

F (29c) multicolored

IM 510	imperf pair	35.00
	imperf strip with plate No. 1111	225.00
	imperf strip with plate No. 1222	—
	imperf strip with plate No. 2211	—
	imperf strip with plate No. 2222	225.00
	imperf pair on first day cover	—
	spliced pair or strip, imperf	—
	Quantity: 1,000+; 20 first day covers	

Prices are for plate strips of 5 or 6. Exists miscut. Transition multiples exist and sell for a premium. Refer to note following **IM 434** regarding first day covers.

Makeup Rate Stamp. January 22, 1991. Lithographed. ABN.

(4c) red & olive gold

IM 511	vrt pair, imperf hz	100.00
	plate block of 4, imperf hz	—
	Quantity: 400+ pairs	

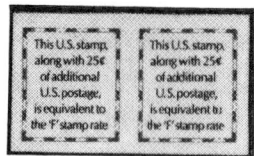

IM 511A	imperf pair	75.00
	plate block of 4, imperf	—
	Quantity: 300+ pairs	

IM 511A is likely printer's waste.

Switzerland. February 22, 1991. Photogravure. ABN.

50c multicolored

IM 511B	vrt pair, imperf hz	1,750.00
	Quantity: 20 pairs	

Flag & Mt. Rushmore. March 29, 1991. Coil. Engraved. BEP.

29c red, dark blue & dark purple

IM 512	imperf pair	20.00
	imperf strip with plate No. 1	450.00
	imperf strip with plate No. 2	—
	imperf strip with plate No. 3	375.00
	imperf strip with plate No. 4	350.00
	imperf strip with plate No. 6	350.00
	imperf strip with plate No. 7	250.00
	imperf strip with plate No. 9	—
	spliced pair or strip, imperf	—
	Quantity: 1,000+ pairs	

Exists miscut, some with EE bars at top. Prices are for plate strips of 6. Transition multiples exist and sell for a premium.

Hinging. Prices for stamps after **IM 196** are for never hinged copies. Hinged copies sell for less.

Flower. April 5, 1991. Booklet pane of 10. Photogravure. KCS.

29c multicolored

IM 514	hz pair, imperf vrt	250.00
	booklet pane, imperf vrt	1,850.00
	Quantity: *10-15 panes reported*	

IM 514 contains natural straight edges on right and left sides.

IM 515	hz pair, imperf between	—
	Quantity: *3-5 pairs reported*	

IM 515 results from a foldover.

IM 516	vrt pair, imperf hz	—
	booklet pane, imperf hz	—
	Quantity: *2-3 panes reported*	

Pairs of **IM 516** contain a natural straight edge on either the right or the left side.

Wood Duck. April 12, 1991. Booklet pane of 10. Photogravure. BEP.

29c multicolored & black numeral

IM 517	vrt pair, imperf hz	200.00
	booklet pane of 10, imperf hz	1,000.00
	Quantity: *20 panes reported*	

Wood Duck. April 12, 1991. Booklet pane of 10. Photogravure. KCS.

29c multicolored & red numeral

IM 518	vrt pair, imperf between	—
	Quantity: *2-3 reported*	

IM 518 results from a foldover.

IM 518A	imperf pair LRS (6/97)	3,960.00
	Quantity: *2 pairs reported*	

U.S. Flag & Olympic Rings. April 21, 1991. Booklet pane of 10. Photogravure. KCS.

29c multicolored

IM 519	vrt pair, imperf between	300.00
	booklet pane of 10, imperf between	—
	Quantity: *8-9+ panes reported*	

Vertical strips of 3 are known containing a pair imperf between plus an additional perforated stamp, raising the possibility that they originate from unsevered press sheets. At least one pane containing two full pairs as a result of a foldover is known.

Love. May 9, 1991. Photogravure. USB.

29c multicolored

IM 520	imperf pair	2,500.00
	Quantity: *25 pairs reported*	

Fishing Flies. May 31, 1991. Booklet pane of 5. Photogravure. ABN.

29c multicolored

a) Royal Wulff
b) Jock Scott
c) Apte Tarpon Fly
d) Lefty's Deceiver
e) Muddler Minnow

IM 520A	hz pair (c), imperf vrt PW	—
	Quantity: *5-6 pairs reported*	

☛ Printer's waste, refer to introduction. All pairs reported possess a vertical crease between stamps.

Buying or selling?
Consult the dealer directory at the back of the catalogue.

Cole Porter. June 8, 1991. Photogravure. ABN.

29c multicolored

IM 521	vrt pair, imperf hz	575.00
	Quantity: 50-60 pairs reported	

Hand & Torch. June 25, 1991. Booklet pane of 18. Photogravure. Self-adhesive. Straight die cut. AVR.

29c black, green & gold

IM 521A	pair, die cut omitted LRS (5/96)	3,740.00
	Quantity: 1 pane of 18	

Desert Storm. July 2, 1991. Photogravure. SVS.

29c multicolored

IM 522	vrt pair, imperf hz	1,500.00
	plate block of 4, imperf hz	—
	Quantity: 20-30 pairs reported	

Express Mail. June 16, 1991. Engraved, lithographed. ABN.

$9.95 black (engraved); black, yellow, red & cyan (lithographed)

IM 522A	imperf pair, black (engraved) omitted PW	—
	Quantity: at least 40 pairs	

☛ Printer's waste, refer to introduction.

Eagle & Olympic Rings. July 7, 1991. Engraved, lithographed. ABN.

$2.90 multicolored

IM 523	vrt pair, imperf hz	—
	Quantity: 4 pairs, 4 strips of 3	

Where possible, illustrations of actual error stamps have been used. They are bordered in black. Illustrations of normal stamps have been used in cases where error stamp illustrations were not available, or where an error illustration would not adequately illustrate the error. Illustrations of normal stamps appear without black border.

87

Boat. August 8, 1991. Coil. Photogravure. ABN.

19c multicolored

IM 524	imperf pair with gum PW	75.00
	imperf pair without gum PW	40.00
	imperf strip with plate No. A1112	—
	imperf strip with plate No. A7767	275.00
	Quantity: several hundred pairs	

Exists drastically miscut with printer's registration marks and color bars at bottom. Miscuts sell for a premium. Pairs and strips from plate number A1112 are without gum, reportedly spoiled by water.

☛ Printer's waste. Refer to the introduction.

Jan E. Matzeliger. September 15, 1991. Photogravure. ABN.

29c multicolored

IM 525	hz pair, imperf vrt	1,500.00
	Quantity: 50 pairs	

IM 526	vrt pair, imperf hz	1,500.00
	Quantity: 40-60 pairs	

IM 526A	imperf pair	*1,250.00*
	Quantity: 25-50 pairs	

Christmas. October 17, 1991. Photogravure. ABN.

29c multicolored

IM 527	hz pair, imperf vrt	275.00
	Quantity: 80-100 pairs	

Exists with rows of misplaced horizontal perforations.

IM 528	vrt pair, imperf hz	500.00
	Quantity: 50-80 pairs reported	

Santa in Chimney. October 17, 1991. Booklet pane of 4. Photogravure. BEP.

(29c) multicolored

IM 528A	booklet pane, imperf PW	—
	Quantity: n/a	

☛ **IM 528A-528D** are printer's waste. **IM 528A** contains 2 design types. The 2 stamps at left contain part of an extra brick on the left side of the top row of bricks. The two stamps at right do not.

Santa & Package. October 17, 1991. Booklet pane of 4. Photogravure. BEP.

(29c) multicolored

IM 528B	booklet pane, imperf PW	—
	Quantity: n/a	

Santa & Sack. October 17, 1991. Booklet pane of 4. Photogravure. BEP.

(29c) multicolored

IM 528C	booklet pane, imperf PW	—
	Quantity: n/a	

Santa & Sleigh. October 17, 1991. Booklet pane of 4. Photogravure. BEP.

(29c) multicolored

IM 528D	booklet pane, imperf PW	—
	Quantity: n/a	

Eagle & Shield, Bulk Rate-USA. December 13, 1991. Coil. Photogravure. ABN.

(10c) multicolored

IM 529	imperf pair	—
	imperf strip with plate No. A43335	—
	Quantity: *10-25 reported*	

Most **IM 529** are contained in plate number strips, most of which are transitional. Pairs are very rare. Three plate number strips of 6 or 7 have been reported, one of which is damaged. One of the plate number strips is a transition strip in which the plate number appears on a perforated stamp.

Eagle & Shield, USA-Bulk Rate. May 29, 1993. Coil. Untagged. Photogravure. BEP.

(10c) multicolored

IM 530	imperf pair	25.00
	imperf strip with plate No. 11111	125.00
	imperf strip with plate No. 22221	—
	imperf strip with plate No. 22222	175.00
	spliced pair or strip, imperf	—
	Quantity: several thousand pairs	

Exists miscut. Transition multiples exist and sell for a premium. Exists tagged.

Love. February 6, 1992. Photogravure. ABN.

29c multicolored

IM 532	hz pair, imperf vrt	750.00
	Quantity: 50 pairs	

Although catalogue prices are based on the best information available at press time, readers should be aware that prices for error stamps fluctuate over time, and therefore, are advised to contact dealers active in the error stamp market for timely quotes when buying or selling.

Flag & White House. April 23, 1992. Coil. Engraved. BEP.

29c red & gray blue

IM 533	imperf pair	17.50
	used pair, imperf	—
	imperf strip with plate No. 1	—
	imperf strip with plate No. 2	—
	imperf strip with plate No. 3	500.00
	imperf strip with plate No. 4	150.00
	imperf strip with plate No. 5	—
	imperf strip with plate No. 6	—
	imperf strip with plate No. 7	400.00
	imperf strip with plate No. 8	400.00
	imperf strip with plate No. 9	400.00
	imperf strip with plate No. 10	—
	imperf strip with plate No. 11	—
	imperf strip with plate No. 12	—
	imperf strip with plate No. 13	—
	spliced strip or pair, imperf	—
	Quantity: 1,000+ pairs	

☛ Caution. Beware blind perfs. Exists miscut. Imperforate strips from the edge of the printing web (plate No. 6) exist. They contain various printed elements: production bars, markings and/or plate numbers. At press time, 3 strips the length of a coil of 100 stamps were known, all from plate No. 6. Transition strips exist and sell for a premium.

IM 534	pair, imperf between	95.00
	Quantity: 250+ pairs reported	

☛ Exercise extreme caution. Rolls from which this error arises contain imperf pairs, imperf between pairs, and many ostensibly imperf between pairs with blind perfs. Check carefully to make sure that imperf between pairs are completely free of blind perfs between stamps. Exists with plate Nos. 3 or 4.

Flag & Pledge. September 8, 1992. Booklet pane of 10. Photogravure. BEP.

29c multicolored; black denomination

IM 534A	imperf pair	—
	Quantity: 10 pairs, including 4 with destruction marks	

COLUMBUS SOUVENIR SHEETS OF 1992

Voyages of Columbus. May 22, 1992. Souvenir sheet of 3. Engraved, lithographed. BEP.

5c chocolate, 30c orange brown & 50c slate blue

IM 534B souvenir sheet of 3, imperf PW   *450.00*
    Quantity: n/a

Voyages of Columbus. May 22, 1992. Souvenir sheet of 3. Engraved, lithographed. BEP.

1c deep blue, 4c ultramarine & $1 salmon

IM 534C souvenir sheet of 3, imperf PW   *450.00*
    Quantity: n/a

Imperforate Columbus souvenir sheets appeared on the market several years after original issue, and, by all indications, from a single source. Many contain faults—including wrinkles, edge faults, and offsets—not normally encountered on issued sheets, which were assembled and enclosed in printed envelopes. During manufacture, the Bureau of Engraving and Printing exercised extra vigilance precisely to avoid releasing faulty sheets and errors. Prior to discovery of the imperforate sheets, virtually no other Columbus souvenir sheet EFOs had surfaced. So, while one might expect to encounter a random error, the appearance of multiple copies of all six sheets over a short period of time leaves little doubt that they are printer's waste.

Voyages of Columbus. May 22, 1992. Souvenir sheet of 3. Engraved, lithographed. BEP.

10c brown black, 15c dark green & $2 purple

IM 534D souvenir sheet, imperf PW   *450.00*
    Quantity: n/a

Voyages of Columbus. May 22, 1992. Souvenir sheet of 3. Engraved, lithographed. BEP.

6c violet, 8c magenta & $3 olive green

IM 534E souvenir sheet of 3, imperf PW   *450.00*
    Quantity: n/a

Voyages of Columbus. May 22, 1992. Souvenir sheet of 3. Engraved, lithographed. BEP.

2c brown violet, 3c green & $4 crimson lake

IM 534F souvenir sheet of 3, imperf PW   *450.00*
    Quantity: n/a

Voyages of Columbus. May 22, 1992. Souvenir sheet of 1. Engraved, lithographed. BEP.

$5 black

IM 534G souvenir sheet, imperf PW   *450.00*
       Quantity: n/a

Hummingbirds. June 15, 1992. Booklet pane of 5. Photogravure. ABN.

29c multicolored

    a) Ruby-throated hummingbird
    b) Broad-bellied hummingbird
    c) Costa's hummingbird
    d) Rufous hummingbird
    e) Calliope hummingbird

IM 534H booklet pane of 5, imperf PW   —
       Quantity: n/a

☛ Printer's waste, refer to introduction.

Eagle & Shield. September 25, 1992. Pane of 17 plus label. Photogravure. Self-adhesive. Straight die cut. BCA.

29c multicolored, brown numeral

IM 535   pair, die cut omitted   175.00
        pane of 17, die cut omitted   1,500.00
        Quantity: 30-40 panes

IM 535 is often encountered with a fold or minor faults. Price is for a sound copy.

Wild Animals. October 1, 1992. Booklet pane of 5. Photogravure. SVS.

29c multicolored

    a) Giraffe
    b) Giant Panda
    c) Flamingo
    d) King Penguins
    e) White Bengal Tiger

IM 536   booklet pane, imperf   3,500.00
        Quantity: *6 panes reported*

Panes contain normal booklet bend between stamps b & c and gum disturbance from removal from booklet.

Chrome USA. October 9, 1992. Coil. Photogravure. BEP.

23c multicolored, deep blue background

IM 537   imperf pair   85.00
        imperf strip with plate No. 1111   250.00
        Quantity: 300-500 pairs

Christmas Toys. October 22, 1992. Se-tenant booklet pane of 4. Photogravure. ABN.

29c multicolored

a) Toy Horse b) Locomotive
c) Carriage d) Toy Ship

IM 538 booklet pane of 4, imperf hz
LRS (9/95) 6,875.00
Quantity: unique

IM 538A booklet pane of 4, imperf **PW** —
Quantity: n/a

Garden Flowers. May 15, 1993. Booklet pane of 5. Engraved, lithographed. BEP.

29c multicolored

a) Hyacinth
b) Daffodil
c) Tulip
d) Iris
e) Lilac

IM 539 booklet pane, imperf *2,500.00*
Quantity: 12-16 panes reported

Price is for pane with usual booklet bend between stamps b & c. A transition pane exists.

National Postal Museum. July 30, 1993. Engraved, lithographed. ABN.

29c multicolored

a) Ben Franklin b) Pony Express
c) Charles Lindbergh d) Stamps & Barcode

IM 540 block of 4, imperf 3,500.00
strip of 4, imperf —
plate block of 4, imperf —
Quantity: 8 blocks of 4; 2 strips reported

Country & Western Singers. September 25, 1993. Booklet pane of 4. Photogravure. ABN.

32c multicolored

a) Hank Williams
b) Carter Family
c) Patsy Cline
d) Bob Wills

IM 540A booklet pane, imperf —
Quantity: *8-10 reported*

Madonna. October 21, 1993. Booklet pane of 4. Engraved, lithographed. KCS.

29c multicolored

IM 541 imperf pair —
booklet pane of 4, imperf —
Quantity: *4 panes reported*

Young Readers' Classics. October 23, 1993.
Engraved, lithographed. ABN.

29c multicolored

    a) Huckleberry Finn   b) Little Women
    c) Rebecca   d) Little House

IM 542 block of 4, imperf   *3,000.00*
    strip of 4, imperf   *1,750.00*
    Quantity: *10-20 blocks of 4;*
    2-4 strips of 4

Pine Cone. November 5, 1993. Booklet pane of 18.
Engraved. Self-adhesive. Straight die cut. BCA.

29c multicolored

IM 543 pair, die cut omitted between   —
    used pair, die cut omitted between   *150.00*
    Quantity: *14-20 pairs reported*

Love. February 14, 1994. Booklet pane of 10.
Photogravure. ABN.

29c multicolored

IM 544 imperf pair   —
    booklet pane of 10, imperf   —
    Quantity: *n/a*

IM 544A hz pair, imperf between   *400.00*
    Quantity: *6-10 pairs reported*

Garden Flowers. April 28, 1994. Booklet pane of 5.
Engraved, lithographed. BEP.

29c multicolored

    a) Lily
    b) Zinnia
    c) Gladiola
    d) Marigold
    e) Rose

IM 545 booklet pane of 5, imperf   *2,000.00*
    Quantity: *16-20 panes reported*

Panes contain normal booklet bend between stamps b & c and tab faults from removal from booklet and are priced as such.

Locomotives. July 28, 1994. Booklet pane of 5.
Photogravure. SVS.

29c multicolored

    a) Hudson's General
    b) McQueen's Jupiter
    c) Eddy's No. 242
    d) Ely's No. 10
    e) Buchanan's No. 999

IM 545A pane of 5, imperf   —
    Quantity: *3 panes reported*

Panes contain normal booklet bend between stamps b and c.

Wonders of the Sea. October 3, 1994. Se-tenant block of 4. Lithographed. BCA.

29c multicolored

a) Motorboat & Buoy   b) Sailing Ship
c) Wheel on Sea Floor   d) Coral Outcropping

IM 546	block of 4, imperf	1,650.00
	plate block of 4, imperf	—
	Quantity: *48-60 blocks of 4*	

Legends of the West. October 18, 1994. Se-tenant pane of 20. Photogravure. SVS.

32c multicolored

IM 546A	pane of 20, partially imperf	—
	Quantity: *reportedly unique*	

Although catalogue prices are based on the best information available at press time, readers should be aware that prices for error stamps fluctuate over time, and therefore, are advised to contact dealers active in the error stamp market for timely quotes when buying or selling.

Madonna. October 20, 1994. Booklet pane of 10. Engraved, lithographed. BEP.

29c multicolored

IM 547	imperf pair	600.00
	booklet pane of 10, imperf	—
	Quantity: *8-10 panes reported*	

Transition panes exist.

Greetings. October 20, 1994. Lithographed. APU.

29c multicolored

IM 548	imperf pair	—
	Quantity: *at least 10 pairs*	

Christmas Stocking. October 20, 1994. Booklet pane of 20. Lithographed. APU.

29c multicolored

IM 549	vrt pair, imperf hz	—
	booklet pane, imperf hz	—
	Quantity: at least 8 panes	

Hinging. Prices for stamps after **IM 196** are for never hinged copies. Hinged copies sell for less.

Dove, G Make-Up Rate. December 13, 1994. Lithographed. ABN.

(3c) bright blue, red & tan

IM 550	imperf pair	175.00
	plate block of 4, imperf	—
	Quantity: *few hundred*	
IM 550A	imperf pair, bright blue omitted **PW**	—
	Quantity: *new, 100+ pairs*	

☛ Printer's waste, refer to introduction. May contain traces of blue, expert certificate recommended.

Flag & G. December 13, 1994. Photogravure. BEP.

G (20c) yellow background, black G

IM 550C	imperf pair	—
	Quantity: 35 stamps	

☛ Caution. The discovery pane of 100 contained 35 imperforate examples plus many others with blind perfs. Certificate advised.

Flag & G. December 13, 1994. Coil. Photogravure. BEP.

G (32c) multicolored; black G

IM 551	imperf pair	275.00
	imperf strip with plate No. 1111	—
	Quantity: *100-150 pairs reported*	
IM 552	pair, imperf between	—
	Quantity: n/a	

Flag & G. December 13, 1994. Booklet pane of 10. Photogravure. KCS.

G (32c) multicolored; red G

IM 553	hz pair, imperf between	—
	Quantity: *2-3 pairs reported*	

IM 553 results from a foldover; at least two of the pairs have a natural straight edge at the bottom. A booklet containing two panes, each with an error pair, sold at auction for $1,155.00 in July 1995.

IM 554	hz pair, imperf vrt	—
	Quantity: very rare	

One pair of **IM 554** is known attached to the top selvage of a booklet. It contains straight edges on both right and left sides, and if detached from the booklet selvage, would have the appearance of an imperf pair.

Flag & G. December 13, 1994. Booklet pane of 10. Photogravure. ABN.

G (32c) multicolored; blue G

IM 555	imperf pair	—
	booklet pane, imperf	—
	Quantity: *2 panes reported*	

Flag & Porch. May 19, 1995. Pane of 100. Photogravure. Water activated. Blue 1995 date. SVS.

32c multicolored

IM 556	imperf pair	75.00
	Quantity: 500+ pairs	

Often collected in vertical pairs to distinguish it from coil imperforates of similar design. Transition multiples exist.

Flag & Porch. May 19, 1995. Coil. Photogravure. Water activated. Red 1995 date. BEP.

32c multicolored

IM 557	imperf pair	35.00
	imperf strip with plate No. 11111	—
	imperf strip with plate No. 22222	—
	imperf strip with plate No. 33333	—
	imperf strip with plate No. 44444	350.00
	imperf strip with plate No. 45444	—
	imperf strip with plate No. 66646	—
	imperf strip with plate No. 66666	—
	imperf strip with plate No. 77767	350.00
	imperf strip with plate No. 78767	—
	imperf strip with plate No. 91161	—
	imperf strip with plate No. 99969	—
	spliced pair or strip, imperf	—
	imperf pair on first day cover	—
	Quantity: 1,000+ pairs	
	5 FDCs	

Exists miscut. Transition multiples exist and sell for a premium. Refer to the note following **IM 434** regarding first day covers.

Flag & Porch. May 21, 1996. Coil. Photogravure. Self-adhesive. Serpentine die cut. Red 1996. BEP.

32c multicolored

IM 558	pair, die cut omitted	40.00
	die cut omitted strip, plate No. 11111	—
	die cut omitted strip, plate No. 23222	—
	die cut omitted strip, plate No. 44444	—
	die cut omitted strip, plate No. 45444	—
	die cut omitted strip, plate No. 55555	—
	die cut omitted strip, plate No. 66666	—
	die cut omitted strip, plate No. 78777	—
	die cut omitted strip, plate No. 88888	175.00
	die cut omitted strip, plate No. 89898	—
	die cut omitted strip, plate No. 99999	—
	die cut omitted strip, plate No. 11111A	—
	die cut omitted strip, plate No. 13231A	—
	die cut omitted strip, plate No. 22222A	—
	die cut omitted strip, plate No. 44444A	—
	die cut omitted strip, plate No. 55555A	—
	die cut omitted strip, plate No. 66666A	—
	die cut omitted strip, plate No. 88888A	—
	spliced pair or strip, die cut omitted	—
	Quantity: 1,000+	

Exists miscut.

Flag & Porch. May 19, 1995. Booklet pane of 10. Photogravure. Water activated. Red 1995 date. BEP.

32c multicolored

IM 561	booklet pane of 10, imperf	—
	Quantity: *8-10 panes*	

Flag & Porch. April 18, 1995. Booklet pane of 20. Photogravure. Self-adhesive. Serpentine die cut. Small blue 1995 date. AVR.

32c multicolored

IM 562	pair, die cut omitted	—
	booklet pane of 20, die cut omitted between 2nd & 3rd row	—
	Quantity: very rare	

The backing paper of the self-adhesive error booklet pane contains the normal roulette for fold. It does not affect the status of the error.

Flag & Porch. May 21, 1996. Booklet pane of 10. Photogravure. Self-adhesive. Serpentine die cut. Red 1996 date. BEP.

32c multicolored

IM 564	booklet pane of 10, die cut omitted	250.00
	Quantity: 50+ panes reported	

The backing paper of **IM 564** contains the normal roulette for fold. It does not affect the status of the error.

Pink Rose. June 2, 1995. Booklet pane of 20. Photogravure. Self-adhesive. Serpentine die cut. SVS.

32c black, pink & olive green

IM 565	hz pair, die cut omitted btwn	—
	hz pair, 1 stamp & 1 label, die cut omitted between	—
	Quantity: 12 pairs, 2 pairs with label	

An intact booklet pane containing six error stamp pairs and one stamp-and-label error pair sold at auction for $1,650 in September 1996.

Yellow Rose. August 1, 1997. Coil. Photogravure. Self-adhesive. Serpentine die cut. Black 1997 date. BEP.

32c black, magenta, yellow & olive green

IM 565A	pair, die cut omitted	90.00
	die cut omitted strip, plate No. 1112	—
	die cut omitted strip, plate No. 1122	—
	die cut omitted strip, plate No. 2223	—
	die cut omitted strip, plate No. 4455	—
	die cut omitted strip, plate No. 5555	—
	die cut omitted strip, plate No. 5556	—
	die cut omitted strip, plate No. 5566	—
	die cut omitted strip, plate No. 5666	—
	die cut omitted strip, plate No. 6666	—
	die cut omitted strip, plate No. 7777	—
	Quantity: 450+ pairs	

Exists miscut. Plate number strips of 5556 exist miscut only. Transition multiples exist and sell for a premium.

IM 565B	pair, die cut & black omitted	—
	strip with plate No. 445, black omitted	—
	Quantity: *30 stamps*	

IM 565C	pair, die cut, black, yellow & olive green omitted	—
	strip with magenta plate No. 4	—
	strip with magenta plate No. 7	—
	Quantity: *22+ stamps*	

The initial discovery of **IM 565B** and **IM 565C** consisted of two rolls of 100 with die cutting omitted on all stamps and colors omitted on some. The first roll contained 5 normally colored stamps, 11 black omitted, 15 black, yellow and olive green omitted, and the balance of the roll with all colors omitted. The first roll contained only a single occurrence of plate number, the digit "7" in magenta, the black, yellow and olive green digits being omitted. The second roll contained 68 normally colored stamps, 1 black partially omitted, 19 black omitted, 1 black, yellow and olive green partially omitted, 6 black, yellow and olive green omitted, and 5 with all colors omitted. The second roll contained three strips with full plate No. 4455 and one strip with plate No. 445, the black digit being omitted. A third roll exists with die cuts, but miscut. It is listed in the Color Omitted section under **CO 199** and **CO 200**. A later find also yields a strip of **IM 565C** with a single digit "4."

Western Butte. March 10, 1995. Coil. Photogravure. SVS.

(5c) multicolored

IM 566	imperf pair	650.00
	imperf strip with plate No. S1111	—
	Quantity: *58-80 pairs reported*	

Some pairs have counting numbers on the back.

Mountain. March 16, 1996. Coil. Photogravure. SVS.

(5c) multicolored; blue-gray mountains

IM 568	imperf pair	450.00
	imperf strip with plate No. S111	—
	spliced pair or strip, imperf	—
	Quantity: 109 pairs,	
	10 plate No. strips	

Transition multiples exist. Some pairs have counting numbers on the back.

Cherub. May 12, 1995. Booklet pane of 10. Engraved, lithographed. Water activated. Design measures 19mm by 22½mm. BEP.

32c multicolored

IM 571	imperf pair	—
	pane of 10, imperf	—
	Quantity: *2 panes*	

The two panes each contain a black rejection mark.

Cherub. January 20, 1996. Booklet pane of 20. Engraved, lithographed. Self-adhesive. Serpentine die cut. BCA.

32c multicolored

IM 572	pair, die cut omitted	300.00
	pane of 20, die cut omitted	—
	Quantity: several panes	

Recreational Sports. May 20, 1995. Se-tenant strip of 5. Lithographed. BCA.

32c multicolored

a) Golf b) Volleyball c) Softball d) Bowling e) Tennis

IM 573	strip of 5, imperf	2,750.00
	Quantity: *8-12 strips of 5*	

The se-tenant designs vary in order of appearance from vertical strip to vertical strip within a pane.

Marilyn Monroe. June 1, 1995. Pane of 20. Photogravure. SVS.

32c multicolored

IM 574	imperf pair	625.00
	pane of 20, imperf	6,250.00
	Quantity: *15-20 imperforate panes;*	
	3 partially imperforate panes	

Due to the nature of the grinding process used to perforate this issue, perforations on partially perforated panes can appear in odd configurations such as a single row, multiple rows, or in a corner affecting only a few stamps. Because of the possible variety of partially perforated panes, no attempt has been made to list each one individually. A partially perforated pane sold for $3,737.50 in March 2000.

Challenger. June 22, 1995. Engraved, lithographed. APU.

$3 multicolored

IM 574A	hz pair, imperf between	—
	Quantity: *new, 3-4 pairs*	

Two panes initially reported. Each contained varying degrees of blind perfs. One pane yielded two error pairs, the second pane, one or two error pairs. Expert certificate essential.

Civil War. June 29, 1995. Se-tenant pane of 20. Photogravure. SVS.

32c multicolored

IM 575	pane of 20, imperf	2,000.00
	pane of 20, partially imperforate	—
	Quantity: *20-40 imperforate panes;*	
	4-5 partially imperforate panes	

Refer to the note following **IM 574**. Often encountered with light fingerprints on gum.

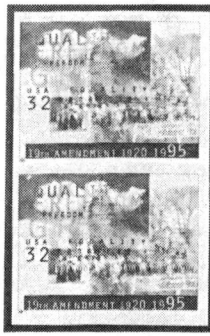

Women's Suffrage. August 26, 1995. Engraved, lithographed. APU.

32c multicolored

IM 576	imperf pair	1,500.00
	plate block of 4, imperf	—
	Quantity: *20 pairs reported*	

Often in transition strips.

Buying or selling?
Consult the dealer directory at the back of the catalogue.

Garden Flowers. September 19, 1995. Booklet pane of 5. Engraved, lithographed. BEP.

32c multicolored

a) Aster
b) Chrysanthemum
c) Dahlia
d) Hydrangea
e) Rudbeckia

IM 577   booklet pane of 5, imperf   —
Quantity: reportedly unique

The single known pane of this error contains a rejection mark at top.

Santa & Children. September 30, 1995. Se-tenant block of 4. Lithographed. APU.

32c multicolored

a) Santa & Chimney   b) Child & Jumping Jack
c) Child & Tree   d) Santa & Sled

IM 578   block of 4 (a-d), imperf   650.00
strip of 4 (a-d), imperf   —
Quantity: 75+ blocks of 4,
15 strips of 4

Comics. October 1, 1995. Se-tenant pane of 20. Photogravure. SVS.

32c multicolored

IM 579   pane of 20, imperf   —
pane of 20, partially imperf   —
Quantity: 1-2 imperforate pane,
3 partially imperforate panes

Refer to note following **IM 574**.

Midnight Angel. October 19, 1995. Booklet pane of 20. Lithographed. Self-adhesive. Serpentine die cut. BCA.

32c multicolored

IM 579A   pane of 20, die cut omitted from
third horizonal row & from the top
of the fourth horizontal row   —
Quantity: 15-20 reported

Also exists as a horizontal pair (one stamp and one reorder label) with die cut omitted between as the result of a foldover.

Although catalogue prices are based on the best information available at press time, readers should be aware that prices for error stamps fluctuate over time, and therefore, are advised to contact dealers active in the error stamp market for timely quotes when buying or selling.

Note. Quantities for listings appearing for the first time in this edition are marked "new." They are tentative and subject to change.

Garden Flowers. January 19, 1996. Booklet pane of 5. Engraved, lithographed. BEP.

32c multicolored

    a) Crocus
    b) Winter Aconite
    c) Pansy
    d) Snowdrop
    e) Anemone

IM 580 booklet pane of 5, imperf   —
    Quantity: *4 panes reported*

Year of the Rat. February 8, 1996. Pane of 20. Photogravure. SVS.

32c multicolored

IM 580A imperf pair   —
    plate block of 4, imperf   —
    Quantity: at least 2 panes

☛ Caution. Pairs exist with blind perfs.

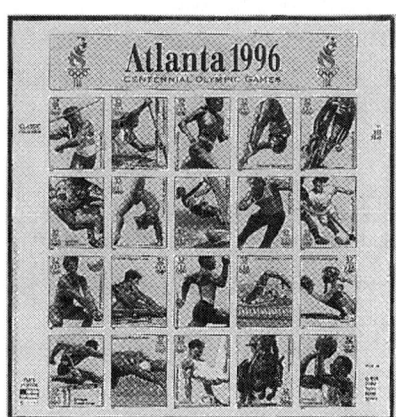

Olympics. May 2, 1996. Se-tenant pane of 20. Photogravure. SVS.

32c multicolored

IM 581 pane of 20, imperf   *1,500.00*
    pane of 20, partially imperf   —
    Quantity: 60+ panes

Refer to note following **IM 574**.

Georgia O'Keeffe. May 23, 1996. Pane of 15. Photogravure. SVS.

32c multicolored

IM 582 imperf pair   175.00
    pane of 15, imperf   —
    imperf pair on first day cover   —
    Quantity: 75-90 panes; 8 first day covers

Refer to note following **IM 574**. Refer to note following **IM 434** regarding first day covers.

James Dean. June 24, 1996. Pane of 20. Photogravure. SVS.

32c multicolored

IM 583 imperf pair   375.00
    pane of 20, imperf   —
    pane of 20, partially imperf   —
    Quantity: *30+ panes*

Refer to note following **IM 574**.

Buying or selling?
Consult the dealer directory at the back of the catalogue.

Christmas Scenes. October 8, 1996. Se-tenant in booklet pane of 20. Lithographed. Self-adhesive. Serpentine die cut. APU.

32c multicolored

a) Family at Fireside
b) Christmas Tree
c) Santa & Chimney
d) Shoppers

IM 584	strip of 4, die cut omitted	—
	block of 6, die cut omitted	—
	pane of 20, die cut omitted	3,000.00
	Quantity: 6-7 panes reported	

Designs are staggered, so the order of appearance in strips or blocks may vary. The illustration is cropped from the upper left corner of a pane. Strips of 4 contain each of the designs. However due to the layout, blocks of 6 are necessary to obtain all 4 designs in block form. Blocks may contain gutters. The backing paper of the self-adhesive error booklet pane contains the normal roulette for fold. It does not affect the status of the error.

Christmas Scenes. October 8, 1996. Se-tenant pane of 20. Lithographed. Water activated. Perforated. APU.

32c multicolored

a) Santa & Chimney
b) Shoppers
c) Family at Fireside
d) Christmas Tree

IM 585	strip of 4, c & d imperf	—
	plate block of 8	—
	Quantity: 1 strip, 1 block & 1 plate block	

Perforations appear between stamps a, b & c. In addition, perforations appear at top and bottom of stamps a, b & c. Stamp d lacks perforations on all sides.

Buying or selling?
Consult the dealer directory at the back of the catalogue.

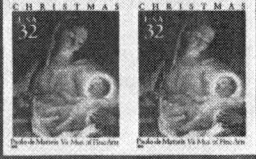

Madonna. November 1, 1996. Booklet pane of 20. Engraved, lithographed. Self-adhesive. Serpentine die cut. BEP.

32c multicolored

IM 586	pair, die cut omitted	75.00
	pane of 20, die cut omitted	—
	Quantity: 50-75 panes	

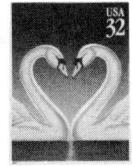

Swan. February 4, 1997. Booklet pane of 20. Lithographed. Self-adhesive. Serpentine die cut. BCA.

32c multicolored

IM 587	imperf pair	175.00
	pane of 20, imperf	—
	Quantity: 10-20 panes reported	

Statue of Liberty. February 1, 1997. Booklet pane of 20. Self-adhesive. Serpentine die cut. AVR.

32c multicolored

| IM 588 | pane of 20, die cut omitted | — |
| | Quantity: new, n/a | |

Note. Quantities for listings appearing for the first time in this edition are marked "new." They are tentative and subject to change.

Botanical Prints. March 3, 1997. Se-tenant booklet pane of 20. Photogravure. Self-adhesive. Serpentine die cut. SVS.

a) Citron b) Flowering Pineapple

32c multicolored

IM 589 vrt pair, die cut omitted btwn 475.00
Quantity: *28 pairs reported*

Error pairs in the initial discovery panes result from die cuts shifted downward one row from the top.

Dinosaurs. May 1, 1997. Pane of 15. Lithographed. APU.

32c multicolored

IM 590 pane of 15, bottom half imperf —
pane of 15, top half imperf **LRS (1/00)** 6,875.00
Quantity: *3 reported*

Celebrate the Century 1910s. February 3, 1998. Se-tenant pane of 15. Engraved, lithographed. APU.

32c multicolored

IM 592 pane of 15, five stamps imperf —
Quantity: unique

The error pane is the result of a perforation shift upward leaving 5 stamps without perforations. They are: Jim Thorpe, First Crossword Puzzle, Jack Dempsey, Construction Toys, and Child Labor Reform.

The term "transition multiple" refers to errors appearing in combination with normal or nearly-normal stamps. Generally, a pair, strip, or block containing one or more error stamps, one or more normal stamps, and, in the case of color-omitted errors, one or more stamps with color(s) partially omitted. Transition multiples sell for a premium.

Ring-necked Pheasant. July 31, 1998. Coil. Photogravure. Self-adhesive. Serpentine die cut. BEP.

20c multicolored

IM 594	pair, die cut omitted	—
	die cut omitted strip, plate No. 1111	—
	spliced pair or strip, die cut omitted	—
	Quantity: *70 pairs reported*	

Exists miscut. At press time, of the two known rolls, one was drastically miscut (yielding 50 pairs) and one was normal (yielding about 20 pairs).

Hat & H. November 9, 1998. Coil. Photogravure. Self-adhesive. Serpentine die cut. BEP.

(33c) multicolored

IM 596	pair, die cut omitted	—
	die cut omitted strip, plate No. 1111	—
	die cut omitted strip, plate No. 1131	—
	die cut omitted strip, plate No. 2222	—
	die cut omitted strip, plate No. 3333	—
	Quantity: 200+ pairs	

IM 597	pair, die cut & black omitted	—
	die cut omitted strip, plate No. 111	—
	Quantity: *new, 20 stamps*	

Red, blue and gray digits appear on the plate strip.

Flag Over City. February 25, 1999. Coil. Photogravure. Self-adhesive. Serpentine die cut. Red 1999 date. BEP.

33c multicolored

IM 600	pair, die cut omitted	—
	die cut omitted strip, plate No. 1111	—
	die cut omitted strip, plate No. 6666	—
	die cut omitted strip, plate No. 7777	—
	die cut omitted strip, plate No. 8888	—
	die cut omitted strip, plate No. 9999	—
	die cut omitted strip, plate No. 2222A	—
	Quantity: several hundred pairs	

Exists miscut.

Coyote & Roadrunner. April 6, 2000. Pane of 10. Photogravure. Self-adhesive. Serpentine die cut. BCA.

33c multicolored

IM 602	pane of 10, die cut omitted	—
	Quantity: new, n/a	

Where possible, illustrations of actual error stamps have been used. They are bordered in black. Illustrations of normal stamps have been used in cases where error stamp illustrations were not available, or where an error illustration would not adequately illustrate the error. Illustrations of normal stamps appear without black border.

Note. Quantities for listings appearing for the first time in this edition are marked "new." They are tentative and subject to change.

AIR MAIL STAMPS

Beacon on Sherman Hill. July 25, 1928. Engraved.

5c red & blue

IMA 1	vrt pair, imperf between vrt strip of 3, imperf between LRS (81)	7,100.00

Quantity: very rare, possibly unique

Winged Globe. February 10, 1930. Engraved. Flat plate press. BEP.

5c violet

IMA 2	hz pair, imperf between	5,000.00
	bottom strip of 5 with plate No., left pair imperf between	6,000.00

Quantity: very rare

Eagle & Shield. May 14, 1938. Engraved. BEP.

6c red & blue

IMA 3	vrt pair, imperf hz	325.00
	plate block of 4, imperf hz	1,250.00
	vrt line pair, imperf hz	450.00
	pair on cover postmarked 5/15/38	*300.00*

Quantity: 1,000 pairs

IMA 4	hz pair, imperf vrt	*12,500.00*
	hz strip of 5, left pair imperf vrt	*12,500.00*
	top plate block of 10, left 6 stamps imperf vrt LRS (9/94)	36,800.00

Quantity: 5 pairs

Transport Plane. June 25, 1941. Engraved. BEP.

6c carmine red

IMA 5	hz pair, imperf between	2,250.00
	plate strip of 10, containing two error pairs	—

Quantity: 20 pairs

Often sold in strips of 5 containing one error pair and three normal stamps. Government crayon marks are usually present on this error. Price is for pair or strip with crayon mark.

Where possible, illustrations of actual error stamps have been used. They are bordered in black. Illustrations of normal stamps have been used in cases where error stamp illustrations were not available, or where an error illustration would not adequately illustrate the error. Illustrations of normal stamps appear without black border.

Hinging. Prices for stamps after **IMA 6** are for never hinged copies. Hinged copies sell for less.

**Statue of Liberty at New York.   August 30, 1947.
Engraved. BEP.**

15c green

IMA 6	hz pair, imperf between	2,000.00
	as above, block of 4	—
	Quantity: 20 pairs	

All known pairs are poorly centered.

**Jet & Numeral.   August 19, 1960.   Booklet pane.
Engraved. BEP.**

7c carmine

IMA 6A	vrt pair, imperf between	—
	Quantity: 2 known	

IMA 6A occurs as a result of a foldover.

**Statue of Liberty.   June 28, 1961.   Engraved,
lithographed. BEP.**

15c orange & black

IMA 7	hz pair, imperf vrt **LRS (79)**	11,500.00
	strip of 5, 3 stamps & margin at left imperf vrt **LRS (5/00)**	7,150.00
	strip of 5, 3 stamps at left imperf vrt **LRS (81)**	15,400.00
	Quantity: 3 as listed above	

**Runway of Stars.   January 5, 1968.   Coil.   Engraved.
BEP.**

10c red

IMA 8	imperf pair	600.00
	line pair, imperf	950.00
	spliced pair, imperf	—
	Quantity: 100+ pairs	

Runway of Stars.   January 5, 1968.   Booklet pane of 8.   Engraved. BEP.

10c red

IM 8A	vrt pair, imperf between	—
	Quantity: possibly unique	

IM 8A occurs as the result of a foldover.

Jet Aircraft.   May 7, 1971.   Coil.   Engraved. BEP.

11c red

IMA 9	imperf pair	250.00
	line pair, imperf	425.00
	spliced pair, imperf	—
	Quantity: fewer than 200 pairs reported	

Exists miscut. Slightly miscut pairs usually sell for less than listed pairs; dramatically miscut pairs often sell for more than listed pairs. Transition multiples exist.

**Winged Envelope.   December 27, 1973.   Coil.
Engraved. BEP.**

13c red

IMA 10	imperf pair	75.00
	line pair, imperf	150.00
	Quantity: 500+ pairs	

Buying or selling?
Consult the dealer directory at the back of the catalogue.

Phillip Mazzei. October 13, 1980. Photogravure. BEP.

40c multicolored

IMA 11 imperf pair 3,500.00
Quantity: 15 pairs

IMA 11A hz pair, imperf vrt —
Quantity: very rare, possibly unique

Blanche Stuart Scott. December 30, 1980. Photogravure. BEP.

28c multicolored

IMA 11B imperf pair 10,000.00
Quantity: 4 pairs

Olympics. Se-tenant block of 4. June 17, 1983. Photogravure. BEP.

28c multicolored

a) Gymnastics   b) Hurdles
c) Basketball   d) Soccer

IMA 12 block of 4 (a-d), imperf vrt 7,500.00
as above, plate block of 4 —
Quantity: the 2 blocks as listed

Olympics. Se-tenant block of 4. April 8, 1983. Photogravure. BEP.

40c multicolored

a) Shot Put   b) Gymnastics
c) Swimming   d) Weight Lifting

IMA 13 block of 4 (a-d), imperf 1,350.00
plate block of 4, imperf —
copyright block of 4, imperf —
vrt pair (a & c) or (b & d), imperf 400.00
Quantity: 30-40 blocks of 4,
20-30 pairs reported

Although catalogue prices are based on the best information available at press time, readers should be aware that prices for error stamps fluctuate over time, and therefore, are advised to contact dealers active in the error stamp market for timely quotes when buying or selling.

Hinging. Prices for stamps after **IMA 6** are for never hinged copies. Hinged copies sell for less.

Alfred V. Verville. February 13, 1985. Photogravure. BEP.

33c multicolored

IMA 14	imperf pair	850.00
	plate block of 4, imperf	—
	Quantity: 50-100 pairs	

Junipero Serra. August 22, 1985. Photogravure. BEP.

44c multicolored

IMA 17	imperf pair	1,750.00
	Quantity: 19 pairs reported	

Most often encountered with disturbed gum or small faults. Price is for a sound copy. Those with faults sell for about 50% less.

Lawrence & Elmer Sperry. February 13, 1985. Photogravure. BEP.

39c multicolored

IMA 15	imperf pair	1,850.00
	plate block of 4, imperf	—
	Quantity: 25 pairs reported	

Reportedly, 14 of the 25 pairs are sound. Price is for a sound copy; those with faults sell for 50% or less depending on the degree of the fault.

Harriet Quimby. April 27, 1991. Photogravure. BEP.

50c multicolored

IMA 18	vrt pair, imperf hz	2,000.00
	plate block of 4, imperf hz	4,750.00
	Quantity: 25 pairs	

Many pairs contain a light rejection mark, which is nearly invisible. Price is for copy without rejection mark. Those with the rejection mark sell for less.

Transpacific Airmail 1935. February 15, 1985. Photogravure. BEP.

44c multicolored

IMA 16	imperf pair	850.00
	plate block of 4, imperf	—
	Quantity: 50 pairs reported	

Vertical pairs exist with perforations at bottom between stamp and selvage.

Although catalogue prices are based on the best information available at press time, readers should be aware that prices for error stamps fluctuate over time, and therefore, are advised to contact dealers active in the error stamp market for timely quotes when buying or selling.

SPECIAL DELIVERY

Messenger & Tablet. October 10, 1894. Engraved.

10c blue

IMSD 1 hz pair, imperf **LRS (11/93)**   4,675.00
vrt block of 6, without gum,
imperf **LRS (86)**   8,800.00
Quantity: very rare

Messenger & Tablet. October 16, 1895. Engraved.
Double line watermark.

10c blue

IMSD 2 imperf pair   4,500.00
sheet margin single, imperf   2,000.00
Quantity: very rare

Motorcycle Messenger. November 29, 1927.
Engraved. Rotary press.

10c violet

IMSD 3 hz pair, imperf between   300.00
plate block of 4, imperf vrt between   —
Quantity: 80-100 pairs

Many pairs are poorly centered. Price is for a poorly centered pair.
Well centered pairs sell for more.

Great Seal of the United States. February 10, 1936.
Engraved.

16c red & blue

IMSD 4 hz pair, imperf vrt   3,500.00
center line block of 4, imperf
vrt **LRS (6/97)**   8,625.00
Quantity: 10 pairs reported

POSTAGE DUE

SERIES OF 1879

Numeral. September 9, 1879. Engraved.

10c light brown

IMPD 1 imperf pair   2,250.00
Quantity: rare

SERIES OF 1891

Numeral. 1891. Engraved.

1c bright claret

IMPD 2 imperf pair **NRI**   400.00
Quantity: 46 stamps

Numeral. 1891. Engraved.

2c bright claret

IMPD 3 imperf pair **NRI**   400.00
Quantity: 46 stamps

Numeral. 1891. Engraved.

3c bright claret

IMPD 4 imperf pair **NRI**   *400.00*
Quantity: 46 stamps

Numeral. 1891. Engraved.

5c bright claret

IMPD 5 imperf pair **NRI**   *400.00*
Quantity: 46 stamps

Numeral. 1891. Engraved.

10c bright claret

IMPD 6 imperf pair **NRI**   *400.00*
Quantity: 46 stamps

Numeral. 1891. Engraved.

30c bright claret

IMPD 7 imperf pair **NRI**   *400.00*
Quantity: 46 stamps

Numeral. 1891. Engraved.

50c bright claret

IMPD 8 imperf pair **NRI**   *400.00*
Quantity: 46 stamps

See note for issues of the American Banknote Company, 1890/1893.

Numeral. August 14, 1894. Engraved.

1c deep claret

IMPD 9 imperf pair   250.00
             block of 4, imperf   —
Quantity: n/a

Usually encountered without gum. Price is for copy without gum.

IMPD 10 vrt pair, imperf hz   —
Quantity: n/a

OFFICIAL STAMPS

Post Office Department. Numeral. 1873. Engraved.

15c black

IMO 1 imperf pair   —
Quantity: rare

War Department. George Washington. 1879. Engraved.

3c rose red

IMO 2	imperf pair	900.00
	Quantity: rare	

COIL STAMPS

Official Mail. January 12, 1983. Coil. Engraved. BEP.

20c black, red & blue

IMO 3	imperf pair	2,000.00
	imperf strip with plate No. 1	—
	spliced strip, imperf	—
	Quantity: fewer than 25 pairs reported	

Official Mail. June 11, 1988. Coil. Engraved. BEP.

25c black, red & blue

IMO 5	imperf pair	1,850.00
	Quantity: 40-50 pairs, 1 used pair	

Official Mail. May 24, 1991. Pane of 100. Lithographed. BEP.

23c black, red & blue

IMO 6	imperf pair PW	125.00
	block of 4, imperf	—
	plate block of 4, imperf	—
	Quantity: few hundred pairs	

Printer's waste, refer to introduction.

MIGRATORY BIRD HUNTING STAMPS

Mallards. July 1934. Engraved. BEP.

$1 blue

IMWF 1	imperf pair PW	15,000.00
	vrt pair with plate No. 129199, imperf	—
	vrt strip of 3, imperf	20,000.00
	imperf single LRS (12/99)	4,950.00
	Quantity: 28 stamps	

Most copies of **IMWF 1** exist without gum and with faults. It is reported that 19 of the 28 stamps are off the market and will end up in the National Postal Museum.

IMWF 2	vrt pair, imperf hz PW	15,000.00
	vrt block of 8, imperf hz	—
	Quantity: very rare	

IMWF 2 is known to exist with gum on the front of the stamp. Some experts believe that it is likely that copies of **IMWF 1** have been created by trimming the perforations off and removing the gum from the front of **IMWF 2**.

COLOR OMITTED ERRORS

Red Cross. May 21, 1931. Engraved. BEP.

2c black & red

CO 1   red omitted   —
          Quantity: 2 reported

CO 1 results from a paper fold between the black design and the application of the red cross.

Ernst Reuter. December 29, 1959. Engraved. BEP.

8c ocher, carmine & ultramarine

CO 1A   ocher omitted   3,750.00
           Quantity: 3

CO 1B   ultramarine omitted   3,750.00
           Quantity: 3

CO 1C   ocher & ultramarine omitted   4,000.00
           Quantity: 2

CO 1A-CO 1C all result from a single pane that passed through the printing press with a sizable piece of extraneous paper adhering to the top of it. When overlaying flap of paper was removed, certain stamps were left with only a partial impression, including those listed above with colors omitted. **CO 1A** occurs in positions 10, 20 and 30; **CO 1B** occurs in positions 17, 36 and 46; and **CO 1C** occurs in positions 27 and 37. The intact pane sold for $11,550 in May 1996. The pane has since been broken up.

The term "transition multiple" refers to errors appearing in combination with normal or nearly-normal stamps. Generally, a pair, strip, or block containing one or more error stamps, one or more normal stamps, and, in the case of color-omitted errors, one or more stamps with color(s) partially omitted. Transition multiples sell for a premium.

Water Conservation. April 18, 1960. Engraved. BEP.

4c orange brown, green & ultramarine

CO 1D   orange brown omitted   **LRS (6/97)**   5,280.00
           Quantity: 4

American Music. October 15, 1964. Engraved. BEP.

5c black, red & blue (gray paper)

CO 2   blue omitted   950.00
          Quantity: 20-40 reported

Transition multiples exist and sell for a premium.

☛ Caution. Should contain no traces of blue. Copies with traces of blue do not qualify as major errors.

Florida Settlement. August 28, 1965. Engraved. BEP.

5c black, red & ocher

CO 3   ocher omitted   300.00
          Quantity: 300-400

☛ Caution. A shift in the ocher can give the stamp the appearance of having the color omitted. Examine carefully.

Ten vertical transition pairs exist, each with an error stamp at top and a normal stamp at bottom.

Marine Corps Reserve. August 29, 1966. Engraved, lithographed. BEP.

    5c black & ocher (engraved); red & blue (lithographed)

CO 4   black & ocher omitted LRS (5/95)   15,400.00
         Quantity: unique

Savings Bonds. October 26, 1966. Engraved, lithographed. BEP.

    5c black, red & dark blue (engraved); light blue (lithographed)

CO 5   black, red & dark blue (engraved) omitted   5,250.00
        Quantity: 6 reported

Transition multiples exist and sell for a premium.

CO 5A   dark blue (engraved) omitted —
         Quantity: *unique*

Davy Crockett. August 17, 1967. Engraved, lithographed. BEP.

    5c black & gray green (engraved); yellow & green (lithographed)

CO 6   gray green (engraved) omitted —
         Quantity: unique

CO 7   black & gray green (engraved) omitted —
         Quantity: unique

CO 8   yellow & green (litho) omitted —
         Quantity: unique

The Space Capsule stamp is known with the red flag omitted from the capsule. However, red litho dots are present elsewhere on the stamp, so it is not considered to be a 100% color-omitted error. Nevertheless, it is still a collectible variety, most often encountered as a block of nine with red omitted from the center stamp: price $185.00

Hemisfair '68. March 30, 1968. Engraved, lithographed. BEP.

    6c white (engraved); red & Prussian blue (lithographed)

CO 10   white omitted   1,250.00
         Quantity: 100

Hinging. Prices for stamps after **CO 1** are for never hinged copies. Hinged copies sell for less.

Walt Disney. September 11, 1968. Photogravure. UCC.

6c black, yellow, magenta, blue & ocher

CO 11	black omitted	2,000.00
	as above, plate block of 4	—
	Quantity: 35 reported	
CO 12	blue omitted	2,100.00
	as above, plate block of 4	—
	Quantity: 35 reported	
CO 13	ocher omitted	600.00
	as above, plate block of 4	—
	Quantity: 400-500	

Transition multiples exist for numbers **CO 11—CO 13**. They sell for a premium.

John Trumball. October 18, 1968. Engraved, lithographed. BEP.

6c black (engraved); magenta & ocher (litho)

CO 13A	black (engraved) omitted	—
	Quantity: 2	

The 2 error stamps resulted from a foldover on the lower right corner of a pane of 50. Two stamps above and 2 stamps to the left of the color omitted pair contain partial omission of engraved black in varying degrees. The pane sold for $20,900 in May 2000.

The term "transition multiple" refers to errors appearing in combination with normal or nearly-normal stamps. Generally, a pair, strip, or block containing one or more error stamps, or one or more normal stamps, and, in the case of color-omitted errors, one or more stamps with color(s) partially omitted. Transition multiples sell for a premium.

Waterfowl Conservation. October 24, 1968. Engraved, lithographed. BEP.

6c black (engraved); yellow, red, blue & blue green (lithographed)

CO 14	red & blue omitted	800.00
	as above, plate block of 4	—
	used, red & blue omitted	—
	Quantity: 100	

☛ Expert certificate recommended for used copies.

CO 15   CO 16

Christmas Angel. November 1, 1968. Engraved, lithographed. BEP.

6c black, red, blue & brown (engraved); yellow (lithographed)

CO 15	yellow omitted	55.00
	as above, plate block of 10	—
	Quantity: 1,000+	

☛ Caution. Beware copies with yellow partially omitted.

Grandma Moses. May 1, 1969. Engraved, lithographed. BEP.

6c black & Prussian blue (engraved); yellow, red, blue & blue green (lithographed)

CO 16	black & Prussian blue omitted	750.00
	as above, plate block of 4	—
	Quantity: 150	

Usually with mottled gum. Price is for copy with good gum. Deduct 33% for copy with mottled gum.

Professional Baseball. September 24, 1969. Engraved, lithographed. BEP.

    6c black (engraved); yellow, red & green (lithographed)

CO 17	black omitted Quantity: 300+	950.00

Price is for a well centered copy; poorly centered copies sell for less. Exists with tagging ghosts. Transition multiples exist and sell for a premium.

Christmas. November 3, 1969. Engraved, lithographed. BEP.

    6c dark green & dark brown (engraved); yellow, red, & light green (lithographed)

CO 18	yellow omitted Quantity: very rare	*2,500.00*
CO 19	light green omitted Quantity: 1,000+	25.00
CO 20	yellow, red & light green omitted as above, used Quantity: 50-60 unused, 6 copies used reported	850.00 —
CO 20A	yellow & red omitted Quantity: *very rare*	*2,850.00*

☛ Caution. Specks of red often present on **CO 20** and **CO 20A**. Expert certificate advised. Transition multiples exist for **CO 18** and **CO 20** and sell for a premium.

      CO 21   CO 22

Christmas Nativity Scene. November 5, 1970. Photogravure. GGI.

    6c black, magenta, blue & ocher

CO 21	black omitted Quantity: 50 reported	525.00

☛ Caution. Many copies similar to the error exist with partial black. However, in order to qualify as a major error no trace of black should be visible under 30-power magnification. Expert certificate advised. Transition multiples exist and sell for a premium.

Christmas Precancel. November 5, 1970. Photogravure.

    6c black, magenta, blue & ocher, precanceled with black bars

CO 22	blue omitted transition multiple, blue omitted Quantity: 15 reported	1,500.00 —

The term "transition multiple" refers to errors appearing in combination with normal or nearly-normal stamps. Generally, a pair, strip, or block containing one or more error stamps, one or more normal stamps, and, in the case of color-omitted errors, one or more stamps with color(s) partially omitted. Transition multiples sell for a premium.

Christmas Toys. November 5, 1970. Se-tenant block of 4. Photogravure. GGI.

6c black, magenta, blue & ocher

a) Doll carriage b) Toy Horse
c) Tricycle d) Locomotive

CO 23	block of 4, black omitted	—
	block of 4, black omitted on a & c	—
	any single, black omitted	2,300.00
	Quantity: 2 blocks, 5-6 of each single reported	

Some singles are unused on piece and, due to the rarity of the issue, sell for nearly the same price as mint copies.

Landing of Pilgrims. November 21, 1970. Engraved, lithographed. BEP.

6c black (engraved); yellow, red & blue (lithographed)

| CO 24 | yellow omitted | 875.00 |
| | Quantity: 200 | |

U.S. Flag. May 10, 1971. Engraved. BEP.

8c red, blue & slate green

| CO 24A | slate green omitted | 425.00 |
| | Quantity: 100 | |

Wool. January 19, 1971. Engraved, lithographed. BEP.

6c greenish blue, dark brown, olive green (engraved); yellow, cyan, orange, olive green (lithographed)

| CO 24B | greenish blue (engraved) omitted | — |
| | Quantity: 6-8 reported | |

CO 24B results from an upward shift of the engraved greenish blue portion of the design (the words "United States"). On some examples, the color is not completely shifted off the stamp and therefore, does not qualify as the error. Expert certificate advised. Transition multiples exist.

Wildlife Conservation. June 12, 1971. Se-tenant block of 4. Engraved, lithographed. BEP.

8c black, dark brown & dark green (engraved); red, blue, buff, olive green & bluish green (lithographed)

a) Trout b) Alligator
c) Polar Bear d) California Condor

CO 25	block of 4, olive & bluish green omitted from a & b	4,500.00
	as above, plate block of 4	—
	Quantity: 8 blocks including unique plate block	

CO 26	block of 4, red omitted from a, c & d	9,500.00
	used single (a), **LRS (11/96)**	1,320.00
	Quantity: very rare, possibly unique, used single unique	

Due to color schemes used in the four designs, some colors are normally not present in every stamp. For example, lithographic red was not used in the alligator design and, therefore, cannot be considered to have been omitted.

☛ Caution. The red head of the condor may appear to be omitted if shifted to the lower left. Expert certificate advised.

| CO 27 | CO 28 | CO 30 | CO 31 |

American Revolution Bicentennial. July 4, 1971. Engraved, lithographed.

    8c black & gray (engraved); red & blue (lithographed)

CO 27	black & gray omitted	675.00
	Quantity: 100-150	
CO 28	gray omitted	1,200.00
	Quantity: rare	

CO 28 often occurs in pairs or larger multiples with gray completely omitted from one stamp, and gray and black partially omitted from others. They sell for a premium.

Emily Dickinson. August 28, 1971. Engraved, lithographed. BEP.

    8c black & light olive green (engraved); dark olive green, red & flesh tone (lithographed); (greenish paper)

CO 30	black & light olive green omitted	750.00
	as above, plate block of 4	—
	Quantity: 150	
CO 31	pair, flesh tone omitted on one	*6,500.00*
	Quantity: 3-4	

Some examples of **CO 31** appear to have light olive green omitted, but traces are visible under magnification.

Space Achievement. August 2, 1971. Se-tenant pair. Engraved, lithographed. BEP.

    8c black (engraved); yellow, red, blue & gray (lithographed)

    a) Earth & Sun   b) Lunar Vehicle

CO 29	pair, red & blue omitted	1,400.00
	single (b), red & blue omitted	600.00
	plate block of 4, red & blue omitted	—
	Quantity: 40 pairs, 10 singles reported	

☞ Caution. The flag on the lunar lander is often shifted into the lander and not visible. Examine carefully.

Where possible, illustrations of actual error stamps have been used. They are bordered in black. Illustrations of normal stamps have been used in cases where error stamp illustrations were not available, or where an error illustration would not adequately illustrate the error. Illustrations of normal stamps appear without black border.

Buying or selling?
Consult the dealer directory at the back of the catalogue.

Normal Block

Historic Preservation. October 29, 1971. Se-tenant block of 4. Engraved, lithographed. BEP.

8c black brown (engraved); beige (lithographed); (buff paper)

a) Decauter Home b) The Charles W. Morgan
c) Cable Car d) San Xavier Mission

CO 32	block of 4, black brown omitted	2,250.00
	plate block of 4, black brown omitted	—
	Quantity: 16 blocks of 4 reported	

Five blocks are intact and undamaged. Price is for an undamaged, intact block.

CO 33	block of 4, beige omitted	—
	Quantity: 8 blocks of 4	

Two blocks of **CO 33** are damaged and one is reportedly broken.

Where possible, illustrations of actual error stamps have been used. They are bordered in black. Illustrations of normal stamps have been used in cases where error stamp illustrations were not available, or where an error illustration would not adequately illustrate the error. Illustrations of normal stamps appear without black border.

CO 34   CO 35

Christmas. November 10, 1971. Photogravure. BEP.

8c black, magenta, blue, ocher, light bistre & metallic gold

CO 34	gold omitted	475.00
	as above, plate block	—
	Quantity: 150-200	

Transition multiples exist and sell for a premium.

CARE. October 27, 1971. Photogravure. BEP.

8c black, blue, purple & violet

CO 35	black omitted	4,250.00
	Quantity: 10	

Transition multiples exist.

Family Planning. March 18, 1972. Engraved, lithographed. BEP.

8c black (engraved); dark brown, yellow, magenta & olive green (lithographed)

CO 35A	dark brown omitted LRS (5/92)	9,350.00
	Quantity: unique	

CO 35A results from a foldover and occupies the lower left corner position in a block of 15.

National Parks Centennial. April 5, 1972. Se-tenant block of 4. Engraved, lithographed. BEP.

    2c black & dark blue (engraved); black, yellow, red, blue & tan (lithographed)

    a) Wrecked Hull   b) Lighthouse
    c) Shorebirds   d) Shorebirds & Grass

CO 36   block of 4, black (litho) omitted   2,750.00
    Quantity: 25 blocks of 4 reported

Mt. McKinley. July 28, 1972. Engraved, lithographed. BEP.

    15c black, light blue, dark brown (engraved); yellow, magenta, gray, gray green, brown (lithographed)

CO 36A yellow omitted   —
    Quantity: reportedly unique

Wildlife Conservation. September 20, 1972. Se-tenant block of 4. Engraved, lithographed. BEP.

    8c black (engraved); yellow, red, blue, green & brown (lithographed)

    a) Fur Seal   b) Cardinal
    c) Brown Pelican   d) Bighorn Sheep

CO 37   block of 4, brown omitted   4,000.00
    as above, plate block of 4   —
    single (c or d), brown omitted   —
    Quantity: 8-16 blocks of 4 reported

CO 38   block of 4, blue & green omitted   4,750.00
    as above, plate block of 4   —
    Quantity: 8 blocks of 4 reported

CO 38A block of 4, red & brown omitted   4,250.00
    Quantity: 16 blocks of 4 reported

    CO 39   CO 40

Tom Sawyer. October 13, 1972. Engraved, lithographed. BEP.

    8c black & deep red (engraved); yellow, red, blue, & gray (lithographed)

CO 39   black & deep red (engraved) omitted   1,700.00
    as above, plate block of 4 (plate No. also omitted)   —
    Quantity: 150

CO 40   yellow & gray (litho) omitted   2,250.00
    as above, plate block of 4   —
    Quantity: 50, including unique plate block

Christmas Angels. November 9, 1972. Photogravure. BEP.

    8c black, yellow, magenta, blue, gray & pink

CO 41   black omitted   —
    multiple, black omitted on one   4,500.00
    Quantity: 10 pairs reported

CO 42   pink omitted   150.00
    pair, one with pink omitted   —
    plate block of 12, pink omitted   —
    Quantity: several hundred

Transition multiples exist and sell for a premium.

Pharmacy. November 10, 1972. Engraved, lithographed. BEP.

8c black (engraved); yellow, blue, purplish red & orange (lithographed)

CO 44	blue & orange omitted	750.00
	as above, plate block of 4	—
	Quantity: 150 reported	
CO 45	blue omitted	2,000.00
	Quantity: very rare	
CO 45A	orange omitted	*2,000.00*
	plate block of 4, 2 stamps with orange omitted **LRS (5/99)**	3,960.00
	Quantity: *very rare*	

☛ Caution. Expert certificate necessary for **CO 45A**. Transition pairs exist and sell for a premium.

Boston Tea Party. July 4, 1973. **Se-tenant block of 4.** Engraved, lithographed. BEP.

8c black (engraved); black, yellow, red & blue (lithographed)

a) Tea Cast Overboard b) Ship
c) Boat & Keel d) Pier

CO 47	block of 4, black (engraved) omitted	1,350.00
	hz pair (a & c) or (b & d) black (engraved) omitted	450.00
	Quantity: 32 blocks of 4 reported including one without gum; sets of horizontal pairs also exist	

Stamp Collecting. November 17, 1972. Engraved, lithographed. BEP.

8c brown & black (engraved); black & greenish blue (lithographed)

CO 46	black (litho) omitted	650.00
	as above, plate block of 4	—
	Quantity: 80-100	

The lithographed black part of the design consists of a pattern of dots printed on the greenish blue field. They are visible under magnification on the normal stamp.

CO 48	block or 4, black (litho) omitted	1,250.00
	as above, Zip block	—
	Quantity: 32 blocks 4	

Hinging. Prices for stamps after **CO 1** are for never hinged copies. Hinged copies sell for less.

Although catalogue prices are based on the best information available at press time, readers should be aware that prices for error stamps fluctuate over time, and therefore, are advised to contact dealers active in the error stamp market for timely quotes when buying or selling.

CO 49   CO 50

Copernicus. April 23, 1973. Engraved, lithographed. BEP.

8c black (engraved); yellow (lithographed)

CO 49	yellow omitted	950.00
	as above, plate block of 4	—
	as above, Zip block of 4	—
	Quantity: 100	

☛ Caution. Extremely dangerous fakes, including color changelings, exist. Genuine copies of this error each have an APS certificate. Expert certificate absolutely essential. Copies without certificates should be avoided.

CO 50	black omitted	1,000.00
	Quantity: 100	

Progress in Electronics. July 10, 1973. Engraved, lithographed. BEP.

8c black (engraved); orange, dark brown, tan, green & light violet (lithographed)

CO 51	tan & light violet omitted	1,250.00
	as above, plate block 4	—
	Quantity: 50	

CO 52	black omitted	450.00
	as above, plate block of 4	—
	Quantity: 300-400	

Progress in Electronics. July 10, 1973. Engraved, lithographed. BEP.

15c black (engraved); yellow, brown, gray & gray green (lithographed)

CO 53	black omitted	1,350.00
	Quantity: 50	

Rural America. October 5, 1973. Engraved, lithographed. BEP.

8c black, brown red & dark blue (engraved); yellow, green, orange brown & brown (lithographed)

CO 54	green & orange brown omitted	900.00
	Quantity: 100	

Rural America. August 16, 1974. Engraved, lithographed. BEP.

10c black & dark blue (engraved); yellow, red, gray blue & brown (lithographed)

CO 55	black & dark blue (engraved) omitted	750.00
	Quantity: 100	

Where possible, illustrations of actual error stamps have been used. They are bordered in black. Illustrations of normal stamps have been used in cases where error stamp illustrations were not available, or where an error illustration would not adequately illustrate the error. Illustrations of normal stamps appear without black border.

Crossed Flags. December 8, 1973. Engraved. BEP.

10c red & blue

CO 56	blue omitted	165.00
	pair, one normal & one with blue omitted	200.00
	single used on cover, blue omitted	—
	Quantity: 100-125 singles or pairs with one normal attached; 2-3 used	

Often with tagging ghosts.

Zip Code. January 24, 1974. Photogravure. BEP.

10c black, yellow, magenta & blue

CO 57	yellow omitted	50.00
	as above, plate block of 8	450.00
	Quantity: 1,000+	

☞ Caution. Extremely dangerous fakes, including color changelings, exist. Beware used copies. Expert certificate essential.

Horse Racing. May 4, 1974. Photogravure. BEP.

10c black, yellow, magenta, blue, red & ultramarine

CO 58	ultramarine omitted	850.00
	as above, Zip block of 4	—
	Quantity: 50-100	

CO 59	red omitted	—
	Quantity: 1-4 reported	

☞ Caution. To be considered a major error all traces of red must be absent under 30-power magnification. Many copies containing traces of red exist, therefore, expert certificate is advised.

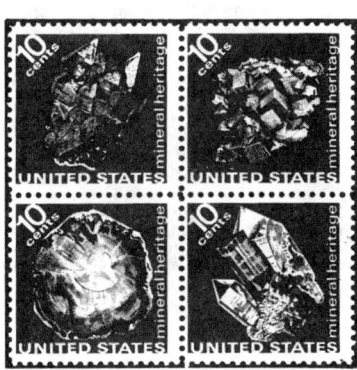

Mineral Heritage. June 13, 1974. Se-tenant block of 4. Engraved, lithographed. BEP.

10c black, red, violet (engraved); yellow, light blue, gray, brown & green (lithographed)

a) Amethyst b) Rhodochrosite
c) Tourmaline d) Petrified Wood

CO 60	block of 4, light blue omitted (a-d), yellow omitted (a & d)	2,000.00
	single a or d, yellow & lt blue omitted	—
	single b or c, light blue omitted	—
	Quantity: 24-28 blocks of 4	

Light blue (the lithographed background color) was printed on all four stamps. Lithographic yellow was printed only on stamps a and d, therefore its absence on stamps b and c is not the result of an error.

☞ Caution. Dangerous fakes exist.

CO 61	single b, black & red (engraved) omitted	—
	Quantity: 4	
CO 62	single c, black & violet (engraved) omitted	—
	Quantity: 4	

The error stamps **CO 61** and **CO 62** result from a single pane in which one se-tenant row, containing the two designs, lacked the engraved colors, black (inscription) and red or violet (mineral color) respectively.

Buying or selling?
Consult the dealer directory at the back of the catalogue.

Normal Stamp   Error Stamp

CO 65   CO 66

Kentucky Settlement. June 15, 1974. Engraved, lithographed. BEP.

10c black & dark green (engraved); black, light red, blue, light green & tan (lithographed)

CO 63	black & dark green (engraved), black, green & blue (litho) omitted Quantity: 29 reported including those in strips of 3 or 10	3,750.00

Exists in strips of 3 containing one normal, one with colors partially omitted and one with listed colors completely omitted. Also exists in strips of 10 (with various stages of colors omitted) which tend to sell for a substantial premium.

Energy Conservation. September 23, 1974. Engraved, lithographed. BEP.

10c black (engraved); yellow, blue, purple, orange (lithographed).

CO 65	blue & orange omitted Quantity: approx 100	850.00
CO 66	orange & green omitted plate block of 4 Quantity: 150-200	700.00

One pane of 50 has disturbed gum.

CO 64	black (litho) omitted as above, plate block of 4 used single, black omitted Quantity: 100-150 including 2 plate blocks	750.00 — —

Transition multiples exist and sell for a premium.

CO 64A	dark green (engraved) omitted Quantity: *very rare*	3,750.00
CO 64B	dark green (engraved) & black (litho) omitted Quantity: *very rare*	—

CO 67	green omitted Quantity: approx 100	875.00

Christmas. October 23, 1974. Photogravure. BEP.

10c black, yellow, magenta, blue, & very light buff

CO 68	buff omitted pane of 50, buff omitted Quantity: 75-100 panes of 50	10.00 300.00

☛ Caution. The buff color is a very light, transparent shade. Error stamps are extremely difficult to distinguish from normal stamps. Expert certificate strongly advised. Many prefer to collect this error in intact pane form because the omission of buff is more readily evident due to the absence of the buff plate number in the selvage.

Hinging. Prices for stamps after **CO 1** are for never hinged copies. Hinged copies sell for less.

Pioneer - Jupiter. February 28, 1975. Engraved, lithographed. BEP.

10c yellow & dark blue (engraved); dark yellow, red & blue (lithographed)

CO 69   dark blue omitted   825.00
        Quantity: 200 reported

CO 70   dark yellow & red omitted   1,250.00
        Zip block of 4   —
        Quantity: 50-100 reported

CO 70A dark yellow omitted LRS (7/97)   3,520.00
        Quantity: reportedly unique

CO 70A contains traces of red visible under magnification. To the naked eye, it is similar in appearance to CO 70.

Mariner 10. April 4, 1975. Engraved, lithographed. BEP.

10c black (engraved); red, blue & brown (lithographed)

CO 71   red omitted   425.00
        plate block of 4, red omitted   —
        Quantity: 300-400

☛ Caution. The red star may be shifted down and hidden in the spacecraft giving the appearance of being the error stamp. Examine carefully.

CO 72   blue & brown omitted   2,000.00
        Quantity: 50

Haym Salomon. March 25, 1975. Photogravure. BEP.

10c black, yellow, red, blue & gray; green inscription on reverse

CO 75   red omitted   225.00
        Quantity: 300+

☛ Caution. Expert certificate advised.

Refer to the **Reverse Inscription Omitted** section for this and other issues with reverse inscriptions omitted.

D. W. Griffith. May 27, 1975. Engraved, lithographed. BEP.

10c dark brown (engraved); yellow, magenta, & cyan (lithographed)

CO 77   dark brown omitted   625.00
        Quantity: 100-150

☛ Caution. Color variations and color shifts on this stamp are common and can be mistaken for the color-omitted error. Expert certificate advised.

Although catalogue prices are based on the best information available at press time, readers should be aware that prices for error stamps fluctuate over time, and therefore, are advised to contact dealers active in the error stamp market for timely quotes when buying or selling.

200 Years of Postal Service. September 3, 1975. Se-tenant block of 4. Photogravure. BEP.

10c black, yellow, red (2 plates), blue & ultramarine

    a) Locomotive   b) Stagecoach
    c) Satellite   d) Biplane

CO 78	block of 4, red (10c denomination) omitted	7,500.00
	as above, pair	—
	any single	—
	Quantity: 6-8 blocks of 4 reported, 2 pairs of each reported	

Two plates were used for red: one for the denomination, the other for design elements. Only the red denomination is omitted; red printed from the second plate appears elsewhere on the stamp.

Banking & Commerce. October 6, 1975. Se-tenant pair. Engraved, lithographed. BEP.

10c dark brown, green, greenish gray (engraved); yellow, blue & brown (lithographed)

    a) Banking   b) Commerce

CO 79	pair, blue & brown omitted	2,250.00
	single a or b, blue & brown omitted	500.00
	Quantity: 16-32 pairs; 8-16 singles	
CO 79A	pair, yellow, blue & brown omitted	2,750.00
	Quantity: 16 pairs, 8 singles (a)	

Buying or selling?
Consult the dealer directory at the back of the catalogue.

AMERICANA SERIES OF 1975/1981

    CO 80   CO 81

Eagle & Shield. December 1, 1975. Photogravure. BEP.

13c black, yellow, red, blue, brown & olive green

CO 80	yellow omitted	150.00
	pair, one with yellow omitted	200.00
	Quantity: 500	

☛ Caution. Dangerous fakes exist. Beware used stamps offered as CO 80. Expert certificate strongly advised.

Flag. June 30, 1978. Engraved. BEP.

15c red, blue & gray

CO 81	gray omitted	550.00
	pair, one with gray omitted	900.00
	Quantity: 100-200	

☛ Caution. Stamps with gray partially omitted exist.

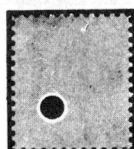

Lamp. September 11, 1979. Engraved, lithographed. BEP.

50c black (engraved); orange & tan (lithographed)

CO 82	black omitted	300.00
	transition pair or strip	375.00
	Quantity: 120-150 reported	

Transition multiples exist with some stamps showing partial omission of black. Transition multiples sell for a premium.

The term "transition multiple" refers to errors appearing in combination with normal or nearly-normal stamps. Generally, a pair, strip, or block containing one or more error stamps, one or more normal stamps, and, in the case of color-omitted errors, one or more stamps with color(s) partially omitted. Transition multiples sell for a premium.

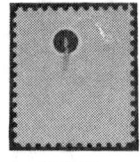 

CO 83　　　　　　CO 84

Candle Holder. July 2, 1979. Engraved, lithographed. BEP.

$1 dark brown (engraved); yellow, orange & tan (lithographed)

CO 83	dark brown omitted	250.00
	as above, plate block of 4	—
	transition strip, one with dark brown omitted	650.00
	Quantity: 1,000+	

Tagging ghosts exist.

CO 84	yellow, orange & tan omitted	300.00
	Quantity: 300-400	

Flag. June 30, 1978. Coil. Engraved. BEP.

15c red, blue & gray

CO 85	gray omitted	35.00
	pair, one with gray omitted	65.00
	Quantity: 1,000+	

Most show bleed of blue into area of gray.

BICENTENNIAL SOUVENIR SHEETS

A great variety of color-omitted and imperforate varieties exist, many with multiple errors. Those that are imperforate in addition to having colors omitted are listed in the imperforates section. Those normally perforated but lacking one or more colors are listed below.

Surrender at Yorktown. May 29, 1976. Souvenir sheet of 5. Lithographed. BEP.

13c multicolored

CO 86	yellow (USA 13c) omitted on 1st & 5th stamps	450.00
	as above, used, 5/29/76 Philadelphia, PA first day cancellation	—
	Quantity: rare	
CO 87	yellow (USA 13c) omitted on 5th stamp	550.00
	Quantity: very rare	
CO 88	brown (USA 13c) omitted on 2nd stamp, orange (USA 13c) omitted on 3rd & 4th stamps	500.00
	Quantity: very rare	
CO 89	orange (USA 13c) omitted on 3rd & 4th stamps	750.00
	Quantity: very rare	

For imperforate varieties of Bicentennial souvenir sheets with color(s) omitted refer to the imperforates section of the catalogue.

Hinging. Prices for stamps after CO 1 are for never hinged copies. Hinged copies sell for less.

Where possible, illustrations of actual error stamps have been used. They are bordered in black. Illustrations of normal stamps have been used in cases where error stamp illustrations were not available, or where an error illustration would not adequately illustrate the error. Illustrations of normal stamps appear without black border.

125

The Declaration of Independence. May 29, 1976.
Souvenir sheet of 5. Lithographed.

18c multicolored

CO 94	brown (USA 18c) omitted on 1st & 3rd stamps Quantity: rare	600.00
CO 95	orange (USA 18c) omitted on 2nd & 5th stamps, yellow (USA 18c) omitted on 4th stamp Quantity: rare	500.00
CO 96	orange (USA 18c) omitted on 2nd & 5th stamps Quantity: rare	500.00
CO 97	yellow (USA 18c) omitted on 4th stamp Quantity: rare	500.00
CO 98	black (screened dots for contrast in mural) omitted Quantity: very rare	*2,250.00*
CO 99	all process colors omitted, sheet blank except for USA 18c, tagging & perfs **LRS (5/99)** Quantity: very rare	3,300.00

The term "process colors" refers to those colors which were reduced to a pattern of dots and printed atop one another to achieve the effect of full color. The denominations and "USA" were added by a separate operation and printed in "solid color" rather than in a pattern of dots. The difference in printing can be seen on a normal sheet by examination under 10-power magnification.

CO 100	brown (USA 18c) omitted on 1st stamp Quantity: very rare	500.00
CO 101	yellow omitted (background color) Quantity: very rare, possibly unique	—
CO 102	orange (USA 18c) omitted on 2nd stamp, yellow (USA 18c) omitted on 4th stamp Quantity: very rare, possibly unique	—
CO 103	brown (USA 18c) omitted on 3rd stamp Quantity: very rare	—

Washington Crossing the Delaware. May 29, 1976.
Souvenir sheet of 5. Lithographed. BEP.

24c multicolored

CO 104	blue (USA 24c) omitted on 1st stamp, light blue (USA 24c) omitted on 2nd & 3rd stamps Quantity: very rare	500.00
CO 105	blue (USA 24c) omitted on 1st stamp, light blue (USA 24c) omitted on 2nd & 3rd stamps, with 5/29/76 Philadelphia, PA first day cancellation Quantity: very rare	500.00
CO 106	white (USA 24c) omitted on 4th & 5th stamps Quantity: very rare	450.00
CO 107	white (USA 24c) omitted on 4th & 5th stamps with 5/29/76 Philadelphia, PA first day cancellation, perforations inverted Quantity: very rare	450.00
CO 108	all process colors omitted, sheet blank except for 24c, tagging & perfs Quantity: reportedly unique	—

Refer to the note after **CO 99**.

Hinging. Prices for stamps after **CO 1** are for never hinged copies. Hinged copies sell for less.

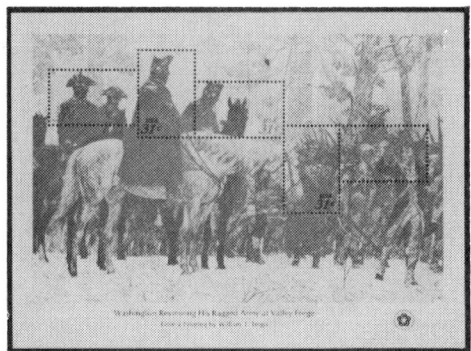

Washington at Valley Forge. May 29, 1976. Souvenir sheet of 5. Lithographed. BEP.

31c multicolored

CO 110   gray (USA 31c) omitted on 1st & 3rd stamps   450.00
Quantity: rare

CO 111   gray (USA 31c) omitted on 1st & 3rd stamps, white (USA 31c) omitted on 5th stamp   —
Quantity: very rare

CO 112   brown (USA 31c) omitted on 2nd & 4th stamps   *600.00*
Quantity: rare

CO 113   brown (USA 31c) omitted on 2nd & 4th stamps, white omitted on 5th stamp   500.00
Quantity: rare

CO 114   white (USA 31c) omitted on 5th stamp   450.00
Quantity: rare

CO 115   gray (USA 31c) omitted on 1st stamp, brown (USA 31c) omitted on 4th stamp, white (USA 31c) omitted on 5th stamp   —
Quantity: very rare

CO 116   brown (USA 31c) omitted on 4th stamp, white (USA 31c) omitted on 5th stamp   —
Quantity: very rare

CO 117   black (screened process dots in mural) omitted   2,000.00
Quantity: very rare

In process color printing a printed screen of black dots is often used to intensify contrast and add crispness to the finished illustration.

Benjamin Franklin. June 1, 1976. Engraved, lithographed. BEP.

13c dark blue (engraved); yellow, light blue & brown (lithographed)

CO 118   light blue omitted   250.00
        as above, plate block of 4   —
Quantity: 800-1000 reported

Carl Sandburg. January 6, 1978. Engraved. BEP.

13c black & dark brown

CO 119   dark brown omitted   —
Quantity: 10

Usually in transition strip or pair as illustrated.

CAPEX. June 10, 1978. Souvenir sheet of 8. Engraved, lithographed. BEP.

13c black & dark green (engraved); black, yellow, red, blue, brown & light green (lithographed)

a) Cardinal b) Mallard c) Canada Goose d) Blue Jay
e) Moose f) Chipmunk g) Red Fox h) Raccoon

CO 120   souvenir sheet of 8, all lithographed
        colors omitted   7,000.00
        as above, with plate No.   —
        Quantity: 6 souvenir sheets reported

CO 121   single (d or h), engraved black omitted   —
        Quantity: very rare

Christmas. October 18, 1979. Photogravure. BEP.

15c black, yellow, magenta, green, tan & purple

CO 123   yellow & green omitted, black
        misaligned   550.00
        Quantity: 150

CO 124   yellow, green & tan omitted,
        black misaligned   625.00
        Quantity: 250

Misalignment of black color occurs on all copies of **CO 123** and **CO 124**. Ten pairs exist containing one each of **CO 123** and **CO 124**: price $1,500.

The term "transition multiple" refers to errors appearing in combination with normal or nearly-normal stamps. Generally, a pair, strip, or block containing one or more error stamps, one or more normal stamps, and, in the case of color-omitted errors, one or more stamps with color(s) partially omitted. Transition multiples sell for a premium.

     CO 125   CO 126

General Bernardo Galvez. July 23, 1980. Engraved, lithographed. BEP.

15c dark brown, claret & light gray-blue (engraved); light yellow, red, blue & brown (lithographed)

CO 125   dark brown, claret & light gray-
        blue (engraved) omitted   750.00
        Quantity: 50

CO 126   light yellow, red, blue & brown
        (litho) omitted   1,300.00
        Quantity: 50

Christmas. October 31, 1980. Photogravure. BEP.

15c black, yellow, red, green & buff

CO 126A   buff omitted   25.00
         plate block of 20, buff omitted   450.00
         Quantity: several hundred

This error is very subtle and difficult to see. Certificate recommended.

Flag over Supreme Court. December 17, 1981. Engraved. BEP.

20c black, red & blue

CO 127   black omitted   300.00
        Quantity: n/a

Transition multiples exist and sell for a premium.

CO 128 blue omitted   75.00
Quantity: few hundred

☛ Caution. Stamps exist with colors partially omitted. Transition multiples exist and sell for a premium.

COIL STAMP

Flag over Supreme Court. Coil. December 17, 1981. Engraved. BEP.

20c black, red & blue

CO 129	black omitted	50.00
	pair, 1 normal, 1 black omitted	90.00
	Quantity: 1,000+	
CO 130	blue omitted	*1,500.00*
	Quantity: *very rare*	

Edna St. Vincent Millay. July 10, 1981. Engraved, lithographed. BEP.

18c black (engraved); black, yellow, magenta, blue, gray & buff (lithographed)

CO 132	black (engraved) omitted	325.00
	as above, plate block of 4	—
	as above, Zip block of 4	—
	used, black omitted	—
	Quantity: 500+	

Hinging. Prices for stamps after **CO 1** are for never hinged copies. Hinged copies sell for less.

Frederic Remington. October 9, 1981. Engraved, lithographed. BEP

18c dark brown (engraved); light brown & gray green (lithographed)

CO 133	dark brown (engraved) omitted	450.00
	as above, plate block of 4	—
	Quantity: 300-400	

Yorktown - Virginia Capes. October 16, 1981. Se-tenant pair. Engraved, lithographed. BEP.

18c black (engraved); red, light blue, dark blue, brown & tan (lithographed)

a) Yorktown   b) Virginia Capes

CO 134	pair, black (engraved) omitted	400.00
	as above, plate block of 4	—
	as above, Zip block of 4	—
	single a or b, black (engraved) omitted	150.00
	Quantity: 80 pairs, 10 of each single reported	

Cactus. December 11, 1981. Se-tenant block of 4. Engraved, lithographed. BEP.

20c dark brown, dark green & dark blue (engraved); yellow, magenta, brown, tan & cyan (lithographed)

a) Barrel Cactus   b) Agave
c) Beavertail Cactus   d) Saguaro

CO 134A	block of 4, dark brown (engraved) omitted	*8,000.00*
	Quantity: 10 blocks of 4	

Love. February 1, 1982. Photogravure. BEP.

    20c yellow, magenta, blue, violet & olive green

CO 135 blue omitted   225.00
    Quantity: 50-100 well centered
    150-200 poorly centered

Price is for well centered copy. Copies from some panes are centered high with the design running slightly off at the top; for those deduct 33%.

State Birds & Flowers. April 14, 1982. Se-tenant pane of 50. Photogravure. BEP.

    20c black, yellow, magenta & cyan

CO 135C black omitted   —
    Quantity: 2 stamps (1 each as described below)

Each of the two error stamps is contained in a horizontal transition pair. One pair contains the Rhode Island stamp (black completely omitted) and the South Carolina stamp (black partially omitted); the other pair contains the New Hampshire stamp (black completely omitted) and the New Jersey stamp (black partially omitted).

The Barrymores. June 8, 1982. Photogravure. BEP.

    20c black, yellow, magenta, cyan & ultramarine

CO 135D black omitted   —
    Quantity: unique.

The unique discovery copy occupies position 7 in a plate strip of 20.

International Peace Garden. June 30, 1982. Engraved, lithographed. BEP.

    20c black (engraved); yellow, red, green & gray (lithographed)

CO 136 black (engraved) omitted   250.00
    Quantity: 250-400 reported

Science & Industry. January 19, 1983. Engraved, lithographed. BEP.

    20c black (engraved); yellow, magenta & blue (lithographed)

CO 137 black (engraved) omitted   1,400.00
    plate block of 6 containing 2
    error stamps & 4 normal stamps   —
    Quantity: 40

Transition multiples exist and sell for a premium.

Medal of Honor. June 7, 1983. Engraved, lithographed. BEP.

    20c red (engraved); black, ocher, blue & green (lithographed)

CO 138 red omitted   275.00
    as above, plate block of 4   —
    Quantity: 320-400

Inventors. September 21, 1983. Se-tenant block of 4. Engraved, lithographed. BEP.

20c black (engraved); salmon (lithographed)

a) Charles Steinmetz   b) Edwin Armstrong
c) Nikola Tesla   d) Philo T. Farnsworth

CO 139 block of 4, black (engraved) omitted   375.00
as above, plate block of 4   —
as above, Zip block of 4   —
any single, black (engraved) omitted   95.00
Quantity: 200+ blocks of 4 reported

Streetcars. October 8, 1983. Se-tenant block of 4. Engraved, lithographed. BEP.

20c black (engraved); black, yellow, magenta, & blue (lithographed)

a) First Streetcar   b) Early Electric Streetcar
c) Bobtail Streetcar   d) St. Charles Streetcar

CO 140 block of 4, black (engraved) omitted   400.00
as above, plate block of 4   —
any single (a-d), black (engraved) omitted   75.00
Quantity: 120+ blocks of 4 reported

Although catalogue prices are based on the best information available at press time, readers should be aware that prices for error stamps fluctuate over time, and therefore, are advised to contact dealers active in the error stamp market for timely quotes when buying or selling.

AMERIPEX. May 25, 1985. Engraved, lithographed. BEP.

22c black, red & blue (engraved); gray & beige (lithographed)

CO 141 black, red & blue (engraved) omitted   175.00
Quantity: 700-800

CO 141A black & red (engraved) omitted   —
Quantity: *4-5 reported*

CO 141B red (engraved) omitted   2,250.00
Quantity: *2-3 reported*

a)   b)   c)   d)

Stamp Collecting. January 23, 1986. Booklet pane of 4. Engraved, lithographed. BEP.

22c black, bright green, purple, & dark blue (engraved); yellow, red, light blue & beige (lithographed)

a) American Philatelic Association
b) Youngster with Album
c) Magnifying Glass
d) Ameripex 86

CO 142 booklet pane of 4, black omitted   45.00
unexploded booklet of 2 panes, black omitted   90.00
used booklet pane on first day cover   150.00
Quantity: several thousand

Engraved black was printed only on stamps a & d; therefore, absence of black on stamps b & c is not the result of an error. Refer to note following **IM 434** *regarding first day covers.*

CO 142A booklet pane of 4, light blue (litho) omitted   2,350.00
Quantity: *4 booklets reported*

CO 142B booklet pane of 4, beige (litho) omitted   —
Quantity: *2-5 reported*

Texas. March 2, 1986. Photogravure. ABN.

22c black, red & dark gray blue

CO 142C red omitted   2,250.00
Quantity: *20 copies reported*

CO 142D dark gray blue omitted   —
Quantity: 2 stamps, which occur
in a plate block

The two error stamps, together with three color-partially-omitted stamps, were contained in the discovery pane of 50, which sold in May 1996 for $13,750.

Arctic Explorers. May 28, 1986. Se-tenant block of 4. Photogravure. ABN.

22c black, gray black, yellow, red, blue & gray

    a) Greely   b) Kane
    c) Peary, Henson   d) Stefansson

CO 143 block of 4, black omitted **LRS (6/97)** 11,550.00
block of 4, black omitted a & b;
c & d normal   —
Quantity: 4 blocks & 4 pairs reported

Buying or selling?
Consult the dealer directory at the back of the catalogue.

Sea Shells. April 4, 1985. Se-tenant booklet pane of 10. Engraved. BEP.

22c black, reddish brown & violet

    a) Frilled Dogwinkle
    b) Reticulated Helmet
    c) New England Neptune
    d) Calico Scallop
    e) Lightning Whelk

CO 144 booklet pane of 10, violet omitted   650.00
Quantity: 75-100+ reported

Presidents. May 22, 1986. Souvenir sheet of 9. Engraved, lithographed. BEP.

22c dark blue (engraved); black, red & beige (lithographed)

CO 145 sheet of 9, dark blue omitted   *3,500.00*
Quantity: 5-6 reported

CO 146 sheet of 9, black marginal
inscription omitted   2,000.00
Quantity: 6-10 reported

Presidents. May 22, 1986. Souvenir sheet of 9. Engraved, lithographed. BEP.

22c dark green (engraved); black, red & beige (lithographed)

CO 146A sheet of 9, black marginal
inscription omitted   3,000.00
Quantity: very rare

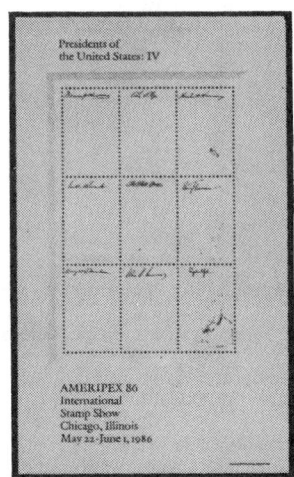

Presidents. May 22, 1986. Souvenir sheet of 9. Engraved, lithographed. BEP.

22c dark blue gray (engraved); black, red & beige (lithographed)

CO 147B sheet of 9, dark blue gray omitted
from left 6 stamps **LRS (1/94)**   2,240.00
Quantity: reportedly unique

Navajo Art. September 4, 1986. Se-tenant block of 4. Engraved, lithographed. BEP.

22c black (engraved); black, yellow, magenta & blue (lithographed)

a) Navajo Blanket   b) Navajo Blanket
c) Navajo Blanket   d) Navajo Blanket

CO 148 block of 4, black (engraved) omitted   375.00
any single (a-d), black omitted   —
Quantity: 150-200 blocks of 4

Presidents. May 22, 1986. Souvenir sheet of 9. Engraved, lithographed. BEP

22c dark brown (engraved); black, red & beige (lithographed)

CO 147 sheet of 9, black marginal
inscription omitted   2,750.00
Quantity: rare

CO 147A sheet of 9, dark brown (engraved)
omitted   —
Quantity: *very rare*

Pan American Games. January 29, 1987. Photogravure. BEP.

22c black, yellow, red, blue, & metallic silver

CO 149 metallic silver omitted 1,500.00
Quantity: 30 reported

All known examples are poorly centered. Transition multiples exist and sell for a premium.

Girl Scouts. March 12, 1987. Engraved, lithographed. BEP.

22c black & red (engraved); black, yellow, magenta, cyan & green (lithographed)

CO 150A black, yellow, magenta, cyan & green (litho) omitted 2,5000.00
as above, plate block —
Quantity: 46, including unique plate block

Many contain stray flecks of lithographed color in places where they would not normally occur, such flecks believed to have been deposited by the tagging roller. Price is for stamp with such flecks.

CO 150B black & red (engraved) omitted —
Quantity: 50 reported

The error is very subtle. The omission of color occurs in only a few merit badges. It can be easily overlooked. Expert certificate recommended.

Enrico Caruso. February 27, 1987. Photogravure. ABN.

22c black, yellow, magenta & gray

CO 150 black omitted 5,000.00
Quantity: 10

Transition multiples exist and sell for a premium.

Buying or selling?
Consult the dealer directory at the back of the catalogue.

Although catalogue prices are based on the best information available at press time, readers should be aware that prices for error stamps fluctuate over time, and therefore, are advised to contact dealers active in the error stamp market for timely quotes when buying or selling.

Wildlife. June 13, 1987. Se-tenant pane of 50. Photogravure. BEP.

22c black (2 plates), yellow, magenta & cyan

CO 151 any single, magenta omitted —
Quantity: unique pane of 50, see note

The discovery pane has been broken up and sold as individual stamps.

Friendship With Morocco. July 17, 1987. Engraved, lithographed. BEP.

22c dark rose & black

CO 152 black omitted 275.00
Quantity: 175-200 reported

Lacemaking. August 14, 1987. Se-tenant block of 4. Engraved, lithographed. BEP.

22c white (engraved); ultramarine (lithographed)

CO 153 block of 4, white omitted 800.00
single stamp, white omitted 165.00
Quantity: 80 blocks of 4; 80 singles reported

When separated from se-tenant blocks, single stamps of this error are indistinguishable from one another.

New Jersey. August 26, 1987. Photogravure. BEP.

22c black, yellow, red, cyan & tan

CO 154 black omitted 6,500.00
transition pair, black omitted
Quantity: 4 reported

Transition multiples exist.

Constitution Bicentennial. August 28, 1987. Booklet pane of 5. Photogravure. BEP.

22c black, yellow, red & greenish gray

a) The Bicentennial
b) We The People
c) Establish Justice
d) And Secure
e) Do Ordain

CO 154A any single, greenish gray omitted —
Quantity: 1-3 singles of each reported

☞ Caution. Expert certificate necessary. The greenish gray is the background color on the stamps. No intact booklet pane is known at this time. Pairs and strips of 3 exist. A set of the 5 a-e (a pair and a strip of 3) sold at auction for $4,400 in February 1993.

CPA. September 21, 1987. Engraved, lithographed. BEP.

22c black (engraved); black, red, green & tan (lithographed)

CO 155 black (engraved) omitted 700.00
Quantity: 300-400 reported

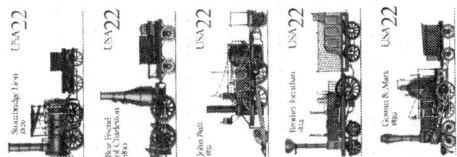

Locomotives. October 1, 1987. Se-tenant booklet pane of 5. Engraved, lithographed. BEP.

22c black (engraved); black, yellow, red, blue & dark green (lithographed)

 a) Stourbridge Lion
 b) Best Friend of Charleston
 c) John Bull
 d) Brother Jonathan
 e) Gowan & Marx

CO 155A booklet pane of 5, black omitted on e —
Quantity: very rare, possibly unique

CO 155B stamp (d), red omitted   LRS (1/92)   1,100.00
Quantity: 1 unused & 1 used reported

Honeybee. September 2, 1988. Coil. Engraved, lithographed. BEP.

25c black (engraved); black, yellow, magenta, blue, & beige (lithographed)

CO 156   black (engraved) omitted   65.00
as above, used   —
as above, used on cover   100.00
Quantity: several hundred unused; 20-50 used on cover

Cover listing is for contemporaneous use on commercial cover. Covers are known postmarked Midland, Texas during January 1990, and Midland, Texas during April 1990.

☛ Blocks and vertical pairs with engraved black omitted were purloined by employees at a paper recycling firm. They are printer's waste and are untagged. It is estimated that 150 may have been used on mail but no copies are known in collector's hands at this time.

CO 157   black (litho) omitted   475.00
Quantity: 100+ reported

☛ Caution. Many copies exist with a few black litho dots, which although invisible to the naked eye, are visible under magnification. In order to qualify as a color-omitted error, a stamp must contain no trace of lithographic black. Copies with traces of lithographed black sell for a small fraction of the price of true 100% black omitted copies.

CO 157A yellow (litho) omitted   1,000.00
Quantity: 50-60 reported

☛ Caution. Certificate necessary. Copies often exist with a few yellow litho dots, which although difficult to see with the naked eye, are visible under 30-power magnification. In order to be considered a yellow omitted error, a stamp must contain no trace of lithographic yellow.

Antarctic Explorers. September 14, 1988. Se-tenant block of 4. Photogravure. ABN.

25c black, gray black, yellow, magenta, cyan, brown & Prussian green

 a) Nathaniel Palmer   b) Lt. Charles Wilkes
 c) Richard E. Byrd   d) Lincoln Ellsworth

CO 158   black omitted   1,350.00
single stamp, black omitted   —
plate block of 4, black omitted   —
Quantity: 2 panes (20 blocks and 20 singles)

Madonna & Child. October 20, 1988. Engraved, lithographed. BEP.

25c black & red (engraved); yellow, red, blue, pale rose & metallic gold (lithographed)

CO 159   metallic gold omitted   25.00
plate block of 4, gold omitted   —
Quantity: few thousand

Although catalogue prices are based on the best information available at press time, readers should be aware that prices for error stamps fluctuate over time, and therefore, are advised to contact dealers active in the error stamp market for timely quotes when buying or selling.

Astronauts. July 20, 1989. Engraved, lithographed. BEP.

$2.40 black (engraved); black, yellow, red, blue & dark blue (lithographed)

| CO 161 | black (engraved) omitted plate block of 4 Quantity: 60-80 | 2,500.00 |

☛ Caution. No black engraved cross hatching should be visible on the white area of the space suits.

| CO 161A | black (litho) omitted plate block of 4 Quantity: *20-30 reported* | 3,250.00 |

Bill of Rights. September 25, 1989. Photogravure. BEP.

25c black (engraved); black, red & blue (lithographed)

| CO 162 | black (engraved) omitted Quantity: 200 | 300.00 |

Dinosaurs. October 1, 1989. Se-tenant block of 4. Engraved, lithographed. BEP.

25c black (engraved); black, yellow, magenta & cyan (lithographed)

a) Tyrannosaurus b) Pteranodon
c) Stegosaurus d) Brontosaurus

CO 163	block of 4, black (engraved) omitted	
	well centered block of 4	1,000.00
	poorly centered block of 4	800.00
	any single, a-d	175.00
	Quantity: 75-100 blocks of 4 reported	

Some copies of this error were discovered in postal vending machine packets in which the blocks had been folded along one row of perforations, and are, therefore, prone to separation. Price is for sound block with perforations that have not been folded. Folded blocks sell for less. Most blocks are poorly centered as in the illustration.

Christmas Madonna. October 19, 1989. Engraved, lithographed. BEP.

25c black & red (engraved); pink, yellow, magenta & pale gray blue (lithographed)

| CO 163A | red (engraved) omitted Quantity: 50 | 750.00 |

Christmas. October 19, 1989. Booklet pane of 10. Photogravure. ABN.

25c black, yellow, magenta, red & cyan

| CO 164 | booklet pane of 10, red omitted LRS (6/97) Quantity: *very rare* | 7,150.00 |

Hinging. Prices for stamps after CO 1 are for never hinged copies. Hinged copies sell for less.

20th UPU Congress. November 19, 1989. Se-tenant block of 4. Perf 11. Engraved, lithographed. BEP.

25c dark blue (engraved); black, yellow, magenta & cyan (lithographed)

a) Biplane b) Delivery Truck
c) Stagecoach d) Riverboat

CO 165   block of 4, dark blue (engraved) omitted
         well centered block of 4   900.00
         poorly centered block of 4   700.00
         any single (a-d), dark blue omitted   200.00
         plate block of 4, dark blue omitted   —
         Quantity: 60-80 blocks reported

Most copies of **IM 165** are poorly centered as in the illustration.

20th UPU Congress. November 27, 1989. Souvenir sheet of 4. Imperforate. Engraved, lithographed. BEP.

25c dark blue & gray (engraved); black, yellow, magenta & cyan (lithographed)

a) Stagecoach b) Riverboat
c) Biplane d) Delivery Truck

CO 165A   souvenir sheet, dark blue & gray
         (engraved) omitted   **LRS (12/99)**   6,875.00
         Quantity: 2 reported

Love. January 18, 1990. Booklet pane of 10. Photogravure. BEP.

25c black, red, blue & green

CO 166   booklet pane of 10, red omitted   1,850.00
         single stamp, red omitted   200.00
         Quantity: 20 panes of 10

Umbrella. February 3, 1990. Booklet pane of 10. Photogravure. BEP.

15c yellow, magenta, cyan, dark blue, green & buff

CO 167   booklet pane of 10, dark blue
         omitted   1,500.00
         single stamp, dark blue omitted   175.00
         Quantity: 75 panes reported

Wyoming. February 23, 1990. Engraved, lithographed. BEP.

25c black (engraved); black, yellow, magenta & cyan (lithographed)

CO 168   black (engraved) omitted   2,250.00
         as above, affixed to 4x5 card   *400.00*
         used, black (engraved) omitted   —
         Quantity: 30 mint copies, 10 of which
         are affixed to 4x5 cards; 1 used copy

Buying or selling?
Consult the dealer directory at the back of the catalogue.

Lighthouses. April 25, 1990. Booklet pane of 5. Engraved, lithographed. BEP.

25c white (engraved); black, yellow, magenta & cyan (lithographed)

CO 169	booklet pane of 5, white omitted	75.00
	unexploded booklet with 4 panes	275.00
	any single used	—
	any single, used on cover	—
	Quantity: 500+ booklets	

Price is for pane with usual tab disturbance, which is not considered a fault. Cover listing is for contemporaneous use on commercial cover.

☛ Caution. Copies exist with white ink lightly applied or with white shifted to the bottom of the design. White ink must be 100% omitted in order to qualify as a color-omitted error.

Fawn. March 11, 1991. Photogravure. BEP.

19c black, yellow, magenta, cyan & dark gray green

CO 170	magenta omitted	850.00
	Quantity: *100 reported*	

The non-omitted colors on **CO 170** are misregistered.

Sunfish. December 2, 1992. Engraved, lithographed. SVS.

45c black (engraved); black, yellow, magenta & cyan (lithographed)

CO 171	black (engraved) omitted	500.00
	used, black (engraved) omitted	—
	Quantity: 100-200 reported; 2 used copies	

Bobcat. June 1, 1990. Engraved, lithographed. BEP.

$2 black (engraved); black, yellow, magenta & cyan (lithographed)

CO 172	black (engraved) omitted	275.00
	plate block of 4, black omitted	1,200.00
	Quantity: 300-400 reported	

Many variations in the color of the green leaves occur on this issue. They are not color-omitted errors.

American Indian Headdresses. July 6, 1990. Se-tenant booklet pane of 10. Engraved, lithographed. BEP.

25c black (engraved); black, yellow, magenta, cyan & olive (lithographed)

a) Assiniboine
b) Cheyenne
c) Comanche
d) Flathead
e) Shoshone

CO 173	booklet pane of 10, black (engraved) omitted	3,500.00
	any single, black (engraved) omitted	350.00
	single (a) used on piece	—
	Quantity: *3 panes reported*	

Micronesia - Marshall Islands. September 28, 1990. Se-tenant pairs. Engraved, lithographed. BEP.

25c black (engraved); black, yellow, magenta, cyan & blue (lithographed)

a) Micronesia   b) Marshall Islands

CO 174	pair, black (engraved) omitted	3,500.00
	single (a), black (engraved) omitted	900.00
	Quantity: 20 pairs, 20 singles (a) reported	

☛ Caution. Often with minute flecks of black. Examine carefully under 30-power magnification.

Sea Mammals. October 3, 1990. Se-tenant block of 4. Engraved, lithographed. BEP.

25c black (engraved); black, yellow, magenta & cyan (lithographed)

    a) Killer Whale   b) Northern Sea Lion
    c) Sea Otter   d) Common Dolphin

CO 175 block of 4, black (engraved) omitted 750.00
    any single, black omitted 175.00
    any single, black omitted, used —
    Quantity: 100-120 blocks of 4

Fishing Flies. May 31 1991. Booklet pane of 5. Photogravure. ABN.

29c black, yellow, magenta, cyan & orange

    a) Royal Wulff
    b) Jock Scott
    c) Apte Tarpon Fly
    d) Lefty's Deceiver
    e) Muddler Minnow

CO 175A stamp a, black omitted —
    stamp b, black omitted —
    stamp c, black omitted —
    Quantity: each reportedly unique

Eagle. July 7, 1991. Engraved, lithographed. ABN.

$2.90 black (engraved); black, yellow red & cyan (lithographed)

CO 175B black (engraved) omitted —
    Quantity: *20 reported*

Of the 20 reported copies, 3 are sound, the balance with faults due to mishandling.

Express Mail. June 16, 1991. Engraved, lithographed. ABN.

$14 red (engraved); black, yellow, magenta & cyan (lithographed)

CO 175C red (engraved) omitted —
    Quantity: *very rare*

Editor's Note. The $10.75 Express Mail stamp of 1995 has been reported with cyan omitted, however we are not aware of any examples with cyan 100% omitted. Check under 30-power magnification.

Although catalogue prices are based on the best information available at press time, readers should be aware that prices for error stamps fluctuate over time, and therefore, are advised to contact dealers active in the error stamp market for timely quotes when buying or selling.

Note. Quantities for listings appearing for the first time in this edition are marked "new." They are tentative and subject to change.

World War II. September 31, 1991. Se-tenant block of 10. Engraved, lithographed. BEP.

29c black (engraved); black, yellow, magenta & cyan (lithographed)

a) Burma Road
b) Draft
c) Lend Lease
d) Atlantic Charter
e) Arsenal of Democracy
f) Reuben James
g) Civil Defense
h) Liberty Ship
i) Pearl Harbor
j) Declares War

CO 176 se-tenant block of 10, black
(engraved) omitted **LRS (6/94)***   12,650.00
Quantity: 1 pane containing 2 blocks of 10

* The **LRS** price of $12,650 is for the intact pane containing two blocks of 10.

Comedians. August 29, 1991. Booklet pane of 10. Engraved, lithographed. BEP.

29c red & violet (engraved); black, red & violet (lithographed)

a) Laurel & Hardy
b) Bergen & McCarthy
c) Jack Benny
d) Fanny Brice
e) Abbott & Costello

CO 177 booklet pane of 10, red & violet
(engraved) omitted   750.00
any single (a, c or e) red
(engraved) omitted   —
any single (b or d) violet (engraved)
omitted   —
first day cover with strip of 5 (a-e),
red & violet (engraved) omitted   —
Quantity: 100-150 booklet panes reported, 6 first day covers

Refer to note following **IM 434** regarding first day covers.

District of Columbia Bicentennial. September 7, 1991. Engraved, lithographed. BEP.

29c black (engraved); black, yellow, magenta & cyan (lithographed)

CO 178 black (engraved) omitted   125.00
plate block of 4, black omitted   525.00
Quantity: 1,000+

Christmas. October 17, 1991. Booklet pane of 10. Engraved, lithographed. BEP.

(29c) black & red (engraved); yellow, magenta, cyan & gold (lithographed)

CO 179 black & red (engraved) omitted   3,750.00
Quantity: 9 sound copies; 1 faulty copy

Alaska Highway. May 30, 1992. Engraved, lithographed. BEP.

29c black (engraved); black, yellow, magenta, cyan & dark brown (lithographed)

CO 180 black (engraved) omitted
well centered   850.00
poorly centered   475.00
used on cover, black omitted   *125.00*
Quantity: 220

Of the 220 copies, 100 copies are poorly centered as in the illustration and 120 copies are well centered. Cover price is for contemporaneous usage.

World War II. August 17, 1992. Se-tenant block of 10. Engraved, lithographed. BEP.

29c black (engraved); black, yellow, magenta & cyan (lithographed)

a) Tokyo Raid
b) Ration Stamps
c) Battle of Coral Sea
d) Corregidor
e) Aleutian Island
f) Secret Code
g) Yorktown Lost
h) Women in War
i) Guadalcanal
j) North Africa

CO 180A block of 10, red (litho) omitted **LRS (10/94)**   6,050.00
Quantity: 1 pane containing 2 blocks of 10

Minerals. September 17, 1992. Se-tenant block of 4. Engraved, lithographed. BEP.

29c black (engraved); black, yellow, magenta, cyan & silver (lithographed)

a) Azurite
b) Copper
c) Variscite
d) Wulfenite

CO 181 strip of 4, silver (litho) omitted   —
Quantity: 2 strips of 4 containing a-d

The strips of 4 of **CO 181** with color omitted are contained in blocks of 8 stamps that also contain 4 normal stamps.

☛ Copies with magenta (lithographed) omitted have been reported; however, we are not aware of any genuine examples. Beware fakes.

Eagle & Shield. September 25, 1992. Pane of 17 plus label. Photogravure. Self-adhesive. Straight die cut. BCA.

29c brown (engraved); black, yellow, magenta & cyan (lithographed)

CO 181B brown (engraved) omitted   400.00
Quantity: 75-150 reported

Juan Rodriguez Cabrillo. September 28, 1992. Engraved, lithographed. SVS.

29c black (engraved); black, yellow, magenta, cyan, dark red & tan (litho)

CO 181C black (engraved) omitted   4,250.00
Quantity: 8-10 reported

Sports Horses. May 1, 1993. Se-tenant block of 4. Engraved, lithographed. SVS.

29c black (engraved); black, yellow, magenta & cyan (lithographed)

a) Steeplechase
b) Thoroughbred Racing
c) Harness Racing
d) Polo

CO 182 block of 4, black (engraved) omitted   1,250.00
any single (a-d), black omitted   300.00
Quantity: 40-48 blocks of 4

Garden Flowers. May 15, 1993. Booklet pane of 5. Engraved, lithographed. BEP.

29c black (engraved); black, yellow, magenta & cyan (lithographed)

a) Hyacinth
b) Daffodil
c) Tulip
d) Iris
e) Lilac

CO 183   booklet pane, black (engraved) omitted   275.00
Quantity: 250+ panes reported

Individual panes usually contain a tab fault. Price is for pane with tab fault.

National Postal Museum. July 30, 1993. Engraved, lithographed. ABN.

29c black & dark red (engraved); black, yellow, magenta, cyan, tan & dark blue (lithographed)

a) Ben Franklin   b) Pony Express
c) Charles Lindbergh   d) Stamps & Barcode

CO 184   block of 4, black & dark red (engraved) omitted   —
hz strip of 4, black & dark red (engraved) omitted   —
pair, black and dark red (engraved) omitted   —
Quantity: *8-16 blocks of 4, 2 strips of 4*

Stars of the Silent Screen. April 27, 1994. Se-tenant block of 10. BEP.

29c red & pale violet (engraved); black, red & pale violet (lithographed)

a) Rudolph Valentino   f) Zasu Pitts
b) Clara Bow   g) Harold Lloyd
c) Charlie Chaplin   h) Keystone Cops
d) Lon Chaney   i) Theda Bara
e) John Gilbert   j) Buster Keaton

CO 185   block of 10, black (litho) omitted   —
Quantity: 2 blocks of 10

CO 186   block of 10, black (litho), red & pale violet (engraved) omitted   —
Quantity: 2 blocks of 10

Garden Flowers. April 28, 1994. Booklet pane of 5. Engraved, lithographed. BEP.

29c black (engraved); black, yellow, magenta & cyan (lithographed)

a) Lily
b) Zinnia
c) Gladiola
d) Marigold
e) Rose

CO 187   booklet pane, black (engraved) omitted   275.00
Quantity: 250-300 panes

Individual panes usually contain a tab fault. Price is for pane with tab fault.

Buying or selling?
Consult the dealer directory at the back of the catalogue.

Cranes. October 9, 1994. Se-tenant pair. Engraved, lithographed. BCA.

29c black & red (engraved); black, yellow, magenta & cyan (lithographed)

a) Black-necked Crane b) Whooping Crane

CO 188 pair, black & red (engraved) omitted 2,000.00
single (a or b), black & red omitted —
plate block of 4, black & red omitted
Quantity: *30-40 pairs*

Love. February 1, 1995. Pane of 20 plus label. Engraved, lithographed. Self-adhesive. Straight die cut. BCA.

(32c) red (engraved); black, yellow, magenta & cyan (lithographed)

CO 189 single stamp, red (engraved) omitted —
Quantity: 22-42 stamps

Three error panes are reported to exist. One contains three color-omitted stamps as a result of a color shift in which the red that should have been printed on the top three stamps was shifted one row lower. The other two panes contain 19-20 stamps each on which red is omitted. One of the reported panes contains the plate number B2222; the other contains plate number B3333.

Richard Nixon. April 26, 1995. Engraved, lithographed. BCA.

32c dark red (engraved); black, yellow, magenta & cyan (lithographed)

CO 190 dark red (engraved) omitted 1,400.00
Quantity: *70 reported*

Transition multiples exist and sell for a premium.

Recreational Sports. May 20, 1995. Se-tenant strip of 5. Lithographed. BCA.

32c black, yellow, magenta & cyan

a) Softball
b) Bowling
c) Tennis
d) Golf
e) Volleyball

CO 191 strip of 5, yellow, magenta & cyan omitted 2,500.00
Quantity: *8-16 strips reported*

CO 192 strip of 5, yellow omitted 2,500.00
Quantity: *12 strips reported*

Women's Suffrage. August 26, 1995. Engraved, lithographed. APU.

32c black (engraved); black, yellow, magenta & cyan (lithographed)

CO 193 black (engraved) omitted 425.00
plate block of 4 —
Quantity: *40-60 reported*

☞ Caution. This issue was prone to printing problems. Many varieties exist with colors partially omitted. Certificate recommended. Many copies of **CO 193** are poorly centered as illustrated. Price is for a poorly centered copy. Well centered copies sell for double.

Jazz Musicians. September 1, 1995. Se-tenant pane of 20 featuring 10 musicians. Lithographed. APU.

32c black, yellow, magenta, cyan, dark blue & red

CO 194 pane of 20, dark blue omitted   —
           Quantity: reportedly unique

The most noticeable omission on this error is the inscription "Jazz Musicians" at the top of the pane.

Madonna. October 19, 1995. Engraved, lithographed. BEP.

32c black (engraved); black, yellow, magenta & cyan (lithographed)

CO 195 black (engraved) omitted   225.00
           Quantity: 75-100 stamps

Computer vended postage (CVP) stamps exist with the denomination omitted. The denomination is added by the vending equipment at the point of sale and is not part of the initial *en masse* production process. Some denomination omissions were intentionally created by customer manipulation of the vended strip. Therefore, CVP stamps with omitted or misplaced denominations are not considered major errors. Their existence is mentioned here as a matter of record.

Jacqueline Cochran. March 9, 1996. Engraved, lithographed. BEP.

50c black (engraved); black, yellow, magenta & cyan (lithographed)

CO 196 black (engraved) omitted   70.00
           plate block of 4   —
           Quantity: several thousand

☛ Caution. Beware copies with black partially omitted.

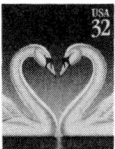

Swan. February 4, 1997. Booklet pane of 20. Lithographed. BCA.

32c black, yellow, magenta & cyan

CO 198 single, black omitted   —
           booklet pane, black omitted   600.00
           Quantity: n/a

Yellow Rose. August 1, 1997. Coil. Photogravure. Self-adhesive. Serpentine die cut. Black 1997 date. BEP.

32c black, magenta, yellow & olive green

CO 199 black omitted   —
           Quantity: *14 stamps*

CO 200 black, yellow & olive green omitted   —
           Quantity: *50-100 stamps*

The discovery roll of **CO 199** and **CO 200** is miscut. It contained 5 normal stamps, 14 black omitted, and 1 black, yellow and olive green omitted. Refer to **IM 565B** and **IM 565C** for combination die-cut omitted and color-omitted Yellow Rose errors. Since the discovery roll appeared, several additional partial rolls containing **CO 200** errors have surfaced. They exist for plate Nos. 2233, 3344 and 5555. Plate Nos. on these error strips appear as single magenta digits, "2," "3," and "5" respectively.

Celebrate the Century 1900s. February 3, 1998. Se-tenant pane of 15. Engraved, lithographed. APU.

32c red (engraved); black, yellow, magenta & cyan (lithographed)

CO 204 pane of 15, red engraved omitted
Quantity: *new, possibly unique*

Engraved red appears on only one stamp, the Gibson Girl. Engraved red was the only color used to print the Gibson Girl stamp. Its omission creates a blank stamp.

Holiday Wreaths. October 15, 1998. Se-tenant pane of 20. Lithographed. Self-adhesive. Serpentine die cut. BCA.

32c black, yellow, magenta, cyan, red & green

a) Evergreen Wreath   b) Chili Wreath
c) Colonial Wreath   d) Tropical Wreath

CO 205 block, red omitted   —
strip, red omitted   —
Quantity: *one pane reported*

The color red was used to print the denomination and salutation on stamps a and d; green was used on stamps b and c. Red appearing elsewhere on the stamps arises from magenta in the four-color process, not from the dedicated single-color red printing plate. The se-tenant designs vary in order of appearance from block to block within a pane. By virtue of the layout, each of the blocks of 4 contains plate numbers in its selvage.

Weather Vane. November 9, 1998. Lithographed. APU.

(1c) black, yellow, blue, red & dark blue

CO 206 black omitted   —
plate block, black omitted —
Quantity: *100-150 reported*

Note. Quantities for listings appearing for the first time in this edition are marked "new." They are tentative and subject to change.

Editor's Note. Dummy simulations bearing the design of the 32c Flag Over Porch coil stamp, but lacking the "USA 32," were included as leaders in a refrigerator-magnet stamp dispenser sold at some Wal-Mart stores in the spring of 1999. They are not color-omitted error stamps.

Hat & H. November 9, 1998. Coil. Photogravure. Self-adhesive. Serpentine die cut. BEP.

    (33c) black, red, blue & gray

CO 208 red omitted —
    strip, red omitted, plate No. 2222   —
    Quantity: 100 reported

On the discovery roll, the gray and blue portions of the design are shifted right as in the illustrated pair. **CO 208** can be collected as a single stamp or a pair. The listing is for a single stamp.

CO 209 black omitted —
    Quantity: *new, 35 reported*

Of the 35 copies, 17 have normal die cuts between stamps and 18 possess trace die cut impressions analogous to blind perfs.

Refer to **IM 597** for listings of black omitted and die cut omitted examples.

Flag Over City. February 25, 1999. Coil. Photogravure. Self-adhesive. Serpentine die cut. BEP.

    33c dark blue, light blue, red & yellow

CO 211 light blue & yellow omitted —
    strip, as above, plate No. 6666   —
    Quantity: new, 95

The dark blue and red portions of the design are misregistered in relation to one another, separated by about one eighth inch. In addition, the design is shifted to the right resulting in die cuts appearing to be misplaced. Only dark blue and red digits appear on plate number strips.

Note. Quantities for listings appearing for the first time in this edition are marked "new." They are tentative and subject to change.

AIR MAIL STAMPS

50th Anniversary of Airmail. May 15, 1968. Engraved, lithographed. BEP.

    10c black (engraved); red & blue (lithographed)

COA 1	red omitted	—
	as above, used pair on piece	
	LRS (82)	6,050.00
	Quantity: very rare	

☛ Caution. Dangerous fakes, including first day covers, exist. Expert certificate essential.

First Man on the Moon. September 9, 1969. Engraved, lithographed. BEP.

    10c black, red, & dark blue (engraved); yellow, red, light blue, blue & gray (lithographed)

COA 2	red (litho) omitted	550.00
	pair, one with red omitted	650.00
	Quantity: 250-300	

☛ Caution. Many copies exist with red shoulder patch omitted but with litho dots of red present in the visor and yellow area of the lunar lander. All traces of red must be absent in order for the stamp to qualify as a major error. Careful inspection under magnification is necessary. Also, note that the European standard for color-omitted errors differs from the accepted U.S. standard; the European standard requires only that the shoulder patch be omitted to qualify as an error. Price for copy with patch omitted, but other red litho dots present: $225.

Where possible, illustrations of actual error stamps have been used. They are bordered in black. Illustrations of normal stamps have been used in cases where error stamp illustrations were not available, or where an error illustration would not adequately illustrate the error. Illustrations of normal stamps appear without black border.

USA & Jet. May 21, 1971. Engraved, lithographed. BEP.

    21c black & dark blue (engraved); light blue & red (lithographed)

COA 2A	black omitted LRS (11/97)	12,100.00
	Quantity: 2	

This error occurs as the result of a foldover at the bottom right of a pane yielding 2 black omitted stamps. The price listed is for the intact pane.

National Parks Centennial. May 3, 1972. Engraved, lithographed. BEP.

    11c black (engraved); yellow, blue, orange & green (lithographed)

COA 3	blue & green omitted	950.00
	as above, plate block of 4	—
	Zip block of 4, blue & green omitted	—
	used single, blue & green omitted	—
	Quantity: 92 reported	

Progress in Electronics. July 10, 1973. Engraved, lithographed. BEP.

    11c black & deep red (engraved); black, red, brown, olive green & light violet (lithographed)

COA 4	red & olive green (litho) omitted	1,250.00
	Quantity: 100	

COA 4A	olive green (litho) omitted	—
	Quantity: *1 plate block of 4 reported*	

This error is visually similar to **COA 4** because the vermillion is nearly completely omitted, present only as small specks. The discovery examples are contained in a plate block of 4.

COA 5   COA 7

Wright Brothers. September 23, 1978. Vertical se-tenant pair. Engraved, lithographed. BEP.

    31c black & blue (engraved); black, yellow, magenta, blue & brown (lithographed)

        a) Wrights & Biplane
        b) Wrights, Biplane & Hanger

COA 5   pair, black & blue (engraved) omitted   725.00
         Quantity: 150 pairs reported

COA 6   pair, black (engraved) omitted   —
         Quantity: n/a

COA 7   pair, black, yellow, magenta,
         blue & brown (litho) omitted   2,250.00
         as above, plate block of 4   —
         Quantity: 15 pairs

Transition multiples exist and sell for a premium.

Octave Chanute. March 29, 1979. Vertical se-tenant pairs. Engraved, lithographed. BEP.

    21c black & blue (engraved); black, yellow, magenta, blue & brown (lithographed)

        a) Large Portrait
        b) Small Portrait

COA 8   pair, black & blue (engraved)
         omitted   4,500.00
         plate block of 4, colors omitted
         as above on right pair   —
         Quantity: 5 pairs reported

Transition multiples exist and sell for a premium.

20th UPU Congress. November 28, 1989. Se-tenant block 4. Perf 11. Engraved, lithographed. BEP.

    45c light blue (engraved); black, yellow, magenta & cyan (lithographed)

        a) Spacecraft   b) Hovercraft
        c) Lunar Rover   d) Space Shuttle

COA 10   block of 4, light blue
          (engraved) omitted   850.00
          block of 4 with hz gutter   —
          any single, a-d   200.00
          Quantity: 60-80 blocks of 4

The Sikorsky 36c airmail stamp is known with the red engraved inscriptions omitted in varying degrees. However, red specks (visible under magnification) are present on all stamps seen to date, so it is not considered to be a true 100% color-omitted error. Nevertheless, it is considered a collectible variety: price $75-$125, depending on the degree of red omitted.

Hinging. Prices for airmail color-omitted stamps are for never hinged copies. Hinged copies sell for less.

MIGRATORY BIRD HUNTING STAMPS

Canvasbacks. July 1, 1982. Engraved, lithographed. BEP.

$7.50 black (engraved); green, violet, pale yellow & orange

COWF 1 violet & orange omitted   7,500.00
Quantity: 5 reported

☛ Caution. Expert certificate necessary.

Fulvous Whistling Duck. July 1, 1986. Engraved, lithographed. BEP.

$7.50 black (engraved); yellow, pale blue, brown, gray green & light gray

COWF 2 black (engraved) omitted   3,750.00
Quantity: 62

King Eiders. June 30, 1991. Engraved, lithographed. BEP.

$15 black (engraved); black, yellow, magenta & cyan (lithographed)

COWF 4 black (engraved) omitted   7,500.00
Quantity: *6-10 reported*

Refer to the section **Reverse Inscriptions Omitted** for additional migratory bird hunting stamp errors.

Canvasbacks. June 30, 1993. Engraved, lithographed. BEP.

$15 black (engraved); black, yellow, magenta, cyan & tan (lithographed)

COWF 5 black (engraved) omitted   3,000.00
Quantity: 120-150

Transition copies exist with black partially omitted.

Buying or selling?
Consult the dealer directory at the back of the catalogue.

POSTAGE DUE STAMPS

Numeral of Value. June 19, 1959. Engraved, typographed. BEP.

COPD 1 single stamp, black omitted 275.00
plate block of 4, black omitted —
Quantity: several hundred

The red background for postage due stamps of this series were printed from common engraved plates. Denominations were added in black as demand required. When black is omitted, it is not possible to identify the denomination of an error, except in the case of pairs containing a normal stamp. Likewise, is it not possible to attribute black-omitted plate blocks to any specific denomination because denominations share plate numbers. Panes of postage due color-omitted errors usually contain a row of 10 pairs of one normal stamp and one error stamp. The balance of the pane consists of varying quantities of normal stamps and color-omitted stamps. Once the remaining color-omitted stamps have been detached from the pane, they are impossible to identify by denomination, and are listed above. Transition multiples also exist with black partially omitted from some stamps. They sell for a premium.

COPD 2 COPD 3

Numeral of Value. June 19, 1959. Engraved, typographed. BEP.

1c red (engraved); black (typographed)

COPD 2 pair, one with black omitted,
one normal 500.00
Quantity: 50+ pairs

Numeral of Value. June 19, 1959. Engraved, typographed. BEP.

3c red (engraved); black (typographed)

COPD 3 pair, one with black omitted,
one normal 700.00
Quantity: 40-60 pairs

Transition multiples exist for many denominations showing black partially omitted. They sell for a premium.

Numeral of Value. June 19, 1959. Engraved, typographed. BEP.

5c red (engraved); black (typographed)

COPD 4 pair, one with black omitted,
one normal 1,500.00
Quantity: 10 pairs reported

COPD 5 COPD 6

Numeral of Value. June 19, 1959. Engraved, typographed. BEP.

6c red (engraved); black (typographed)

COPD 5 pair, one with black omitted,
one normal 1,000.00
Quantity: 20 pairs

Numeral of Value. June 19, 1959. Engraved, typographed. BEP.

8c red (engraved); black (typographed)

COPD 6 pair, one with black omitted,
one normal 1,000.00
Quantity: 20 pairs

Hinging. Prices for postage due color-omitted stamps are for never hinged copies. Hinged copies sell for less.

STAMPED ENVELOPES

Prices are for unused entire envelopes unless otherwise noted.

Compass. October 13, 1975. Lithographed, embossed.

10c brown & blue (light brown paper)

COSE 1 brown omitted 125.00
Quantity: n/a

Quilt Design. February 2, 1976. Lithographed, embossed.

13c brown & blue green (light brown paper)

COSE 2 brown omitted 125.00
Quantity: n/a

Wheat Sheaf. March 15, 1976. Lithographed, embossed.

13c brown & green (light brown paper)

COSE 3 brown omitted 125.00
Quantity: n/a

Mortar. June 30, 1976. Lithographed, embossed.

13c brown & orange (light brown paper)

COSE 3A brown omitted —
Quantity: n/a

Tools. August 6, 1976. Lithographed, embossed.

13c brown & red (light brown paper)

COSE 4 brown omitted 125.00
Quantity: n/a

Golf. April 7, 1977. Photogravure, embossed.

13c black, blue & yellow green

COSE 5 black omitted *800.00*
Quantity: n/a

COSE 6 black & blue omitted *700.00*
Quantity: n/a

Although catalogue prices are based on the best information available at press time, readers should be aware that prices for error stamps fluctuate over time, and therefore, are advised to contact dealers active in the error stamp market for timely quotes when buying or selling.

Energy Conservation. October 20, 1977. Photogravure, embossed.

13c black, red & yellow

COSE 7	black omitted Quantity: n/a	*200.00*
COSE 8	black & red omitted Quantity: n/a	*350.00*
COSE 9	red & yellow omitted Quantity: n/a	275.00
COSE 10	yellow omitted Quantity: n/a	*200.00*

U.S.A. July 28, 1978. Photogravure, embossed.

16c blue; black "Revalued to 15c" surcharge

COSE 11	black surcharge omitted Quantity: n/a	200.00

Auto Racing. September 2, 1978. Photogravure, embossed.

15c black, red & blue

COSE 12	black omitted Quantity: n/a	125.00
COSE 13	black & blue omitted Quantity: n/a	—
COSE 14	red omitted Quantity: n/a	*125.00*
COSE 15	red & blue omitted Quantity: n/a	—

Exists albino.

Veterinary Medicine. July 24, 1979. Photogravure, embossed.

15c gray-black & brown

COSE 15A	gray-black omitted Quantity: n/a	*650.00*
COSE 15B	brown omitted **LRS (1/98)** Quantity: *5-7 reported*	990.00

Olympics 1980. December 10, 1979. Photogravure, embossed.

15c black, red & green

COSE 16	black omitted Quantity: n/a	*200.00*
COSE 17	black & green omitted Quantity: n/a	*200.00*
COSE 18	red & green omitted Quantity: n/a	*200.00*
COSE 19	red omitted Quantity: n/a	*450.00*

Exists albino.

Bicycle. May 16, 1980. Photogravure, embossed

15c blue & maroon

COSE 20	blue omitted Quantity: n/a	90.00

Honeybee.   October 10, 1980.   Photogravure, embossed.

15c brown, yellow, dark olive green

COSE 21 brown omitted   110.00
          Quantity: n/a

Blinded Veteran.   August 13, 1981.   Photogravure, embossed.

18c red & blue

COSE 24 red omitted   *250.00*
          Quantity: n/a

COSE 25 blue omitted   *350.00*
          Quantity: n/a

Great Seal of the United States.   June 15, 1982. Photogravure, embossed.

20c black, blue & red

COSE 26 blue omitted   *150.00*
          Quantity: n/a

COSE 26A blue & red omitted   —
          Quantity: n/a

Purple Heart.   August 6, 1982.   Lithographed, embossed.

20c black & purple

COSE 26B black omitted   —
          Quantity: *possibly unique*

Exists albino.

Paralyzed Veterans.   August 3, 1983.   Photogravure, embossed.

20c black, blue & red

COSE 27 black & red omitted   *150.00*
          Quantity: n/a

COSE 28 black & blue omitted   *150.00*
          Quantity: n/a

COSE 29 red omitted   *350.00*
          Quantity: n/a

COSE 30 blue omitted   *350.00*
          Quantity: n/a

COSE 30A black omitted   *175.00*
          Quantity: n/a

USA 25. March 26, 1988. Photogravure, embossed.

25c red & blue

COSE 31 red omitted   95.00
   Quantity: 160+

Often with printed corner card "Magnificent High School."

Frigate Constitution. April 12, 1988. Typographed, embossed.

8.4c black & blue

COSE 32 black omitted   —
   Quantity: *8 reported*

Love. September 22, 1989. Lithographed.

25c red, dark blue & pale cyan

COSE 33 dark blue omitted   —
   Quantity: *5 reported*

Space Station. December 3, 1989. Lithographed, hologram.

25c ultramarine & multicolored hologram

COSE 34 ultramarine omitted   575.00
   Quantity: *6-8 reported*

Star & USA. January 24, 1991. Lithographed, embossed.

29c red & ultramarine

COSE 34A ultramarine omitted LRS (5/98)   750.00
   Quantity: *6 reported*

COSE 34B red omitted   *325.00*
   Quantity: n/a

Love. May 9, 1991. Lithographed.

29c rose red & dull violet

COSE 35 rose red omitted   *350.00*
   Quantity: scarce

Star, USA & Bars. July 20, 1991. Lithographed.

29c dark blue & red

COSE 35A dark blue omitted   *575.00*
   Quantity: n/a

COSE 35B red omitted   —
   Quantity: n/a

Note. Quantities for listings appearing in this edition for the first time are marked "new." They are tentative and subject to change.

Football. September 17, 1994. Lithographed, embossed.

29c black & reddish brown

COSE 35C black omitted —
Quantity: *6 reported*

Liberty Bell. January 3, 1995. Lithographed, embossed.

32c gray green (bell) & blue

COSE 36 gray green omitted —
Quantity: *8-10 reported*

COSE 36A blue omitted 150.00
Quantity: *75 reported*

COSE 36A occurs on a No. 10 envelope with a printed Credit Union corner card. Exists tagged and untagged. The tagged variety is scarcer.

Old Glory. January 12, 1995. No. 10 business-size envelope. Lithographed.

G (32c) red & blue

COSE 37 red omitted *550.00*
Quantity: n/a

COSE 38 blue omitted —
Quantity: n/a

Paralympic Games. May 2, 1996. Lithographed.

32c black, blue, gold & red

COSE 39 blue & gold omitted —
Quantity: n/a

COSE 40 blue omitted —
Quantity: *2 initially reported*

COSE 41 black & red omitted —
Quantity: n/a

COSE 42 red omitted —
Quantity: n/a

Although catalogue prices are based on the best information available at press time, readers should be aware that prices for error stamps fluctuate over time, and therefore, are advised to contact dealers active in the error stamp market for timely quotes when buying or selling.

AEROGRAMMES

Prices are for complete aerogrammes unless otherwise noted.

Jet Aircraft. May 1959. Inscription on reverse in 2 lines. Typographed.

10c red & blue (blue paper)

COAG 1	red omitted Quantity: very rare, possibly unique	—
COAG 2	blue omitted Quantity: scarce	—

Jet Aircraft & Globe. June 16, 1961. Typographed.

11c orange red & dark blue (blue paper)

COAG 3	orange red omitted Quantity: n/a	550.00
COAG 4	dark blue omitted Quantity: n/a	750.00

John F. Kennedy. May 29, 1967. Typographed.

13c orange red & dark blue (blue paper)

COAG 5	orange red omitted Quantity: very rare	450.00
COAG 6	dark blue omitted Quantity: n/a	450.00

Buying or selling?
Consult the dealer directory at the back of the catalogue.

Human Rights Year. December 3, 1968. Photogravure.

13c black, gray, brown & orange (blue paper)

COAG 7	black omitted Quantity: rare	—
COAG 8	orange omitted Quantity: n/a	450.00
COAG 9	brown omitted Quantity: n/a	375.00

U.S.A. January 4, 1974. Photogravure.

18c red, white & blue (blue paper)

COAG 10	red omitted Quantity: n/a	—

U.S.A. December 29, 1980. Photogravure.

30c red, blue & brown (blue paper)

COAG 11	red omitted Quantity: 150	70.00

U.S.A. May 21, 1985. Photogravure.

36c black, blue, magenta & yellow (blue paper)

COAG 12	black omitted used entire, black omitted Quantity: 3 reported, 1 used entire	950.00 —

157

POSTAL CARDS

Prices are for unused entire cards unless otherwise noted.

☛ Caution. Many postal cards were available from the Postal Service in large uncut sheets. It is possible to cut individual cards from such sheets with the stamp design appearing in virtually any position. Occasionally intentionally miscut cards are offered to the unsuspecting as errors. They are not errors and have no philatelic value.

FIPEX. May 4, 1956. Lithographed.

2c red & violet black

| COPC 1 | violet black omitted
Quantity: n/a | 600.00 |

World Vacationland. August 30, 1963. Lithographed.

8c red & blue

| COPC 2 | blue omitted
Quantity: n/a | — |

U.S. Customs. February 22, 1964. Lithographed.

4c red & blue

COPC 3	blue omitted	500.00
	used entire, blue omitted	—
	Quantity: n/a	

| COPC 4 | red omitted
Quantity: n/a | — |

Social Security. September 26, 1964. Lithographed.

4c red & blue

| COPC 5 | blue omitted
Quantity: n/a | 750.00 |

| COPC 6 | red omitted
Quantity: n/a | — |

U.S. Coast Guard. August 4, 1965. Lithographed.

4c red & blue

| COPC 7 | blue omitted
Quantity: n/a | 450.00 |

Weather Services. September 1, 1970. Lithographed.

5c black, blue, red & yellow

| COPC 8 | black omitted
Quantity: n/a | 600.00 |

COPC 9	blue omitted	400.00
	used entire, blue omitted	—
	Quantity: rare	

COPC 9A	black & yellow omitted	—
	used entire, black & yellow omitted	850.00
	Quantity: n/a	

America's Hospitals. September 16, 1971. Lithographed.

6c black, blue, yellow & magenta

| COPC 10 | blue & yellow omitted
Quantity: n/a | 700.00 |

Figurehead. January 4, 1974. Lithographed.

12c black, yellow, magenta & blue

COPC 10A   black omitted   —
Quantity: *2 reported*

Eutaw Springs. September 8, 1981. Lithographed.

12c black, yellow, magenta & blue

COPC 10B   yellow & magenta omitted   —
Quantity: *2 reported*

Rochambeau. July 11, 1980. Lithographed.

10c black, yellow, magenta & cyan

COPC 10C   magenta & cyan omitted   —
Quantity: *possibly unique*

Philadelphia Academy of Music. June 18, 1982. Lithographed.

13c dark brown, red & cream (buff paper)

COPC 11   dark brown & cream omitted   950.00
Quantity: *4 reported*

Olympics. August 5, 1983. Lithographed.

13c black, blue, yellow & magenta

COPC 12   black, yellow & magenta omitted   —
Quantity: *1 reported*

COPC 13   yellow & magenta omitted   —
Quantity: n/a

Rancho San Pedro. September 16, 1984. Lithographed.

13c black, blue, yellow, & magenta

COPC 14   black & blue omitted   675.00
Quantity: *5 reported*

Buffalo. March 23, 1988. Lithographed.

15c black, yellow, magenta & cyan

COPC 15   black omitted   —
Quantity: n/a

Exists printed front and back.

COPC 16   black, yellow & cyan omitted   —
Quantity: n/a

COPC 17   black & magenta omitted   —
Quantity: n/a

Yorkshire Packet. June 29, 1988. Lithographed.

28c black, yellow, magenta & cyan

COPC 19 black, yellow & cyan omitted   —
Quantity: n/a

Settling of Ohio. July 15, 1988. Lithographed.

15c black, yellow, magenta & cyan

COPC 22 black, yellow & cyan omitted   —
Quantity: n/a

COPC 23 black & magenta omitted   —
Quantity: n/a

Hearst Castle. September 20, 1988. Lithographed.

15c black, yellow, magenta & cyan

COPC 25 black, yellow & cyan omitted   —
Quantity: n/a

COPC 26 black & magenta omitted   —
Quantity: n/a

AIR MAIL POSTAL CARDS

Virgin Islands. March 31, 1967. Lithographed.

6c black, blue, yellow & magenta

COAPC 1 magenta & yellow omitted   —
Quantity: n/a

World Jamboree. August 4, 1967. Lithographed.

6c black, blue, yellow & magenta

COAPC 2 black & blue omitted   —
Quantity: n/a

COAPC 3 blue omitted   —
Quantity: n/a

COAPC 4 magenta & yellow   —
Quantity: n/a

Angel Weathervane. December 17, 1975. Lithographed.

21c black, yellow, red & blue

COAPC 5 blue & red omitted   —
Quantity: n/a

INVERT ERRORS

In this section, centers are described as inverted, without regard to the order in which the plates were printed. The visual relationship of design elements to one another is the most convenient way to describe an error: the inverted Jenny, the inverted candle flame, etc.

NOTE. Prices for classic errors vary widely according to condition and may be substantially higher or lower than prices listed.

Columbus Landing. 1869. Engraved.

15c brown & blue

IV 1	center inverted	150,000.00
	used, center inverted	7,500.00
	Quantity: 3 unused (1 with original gum, 2 without gum); 88-100 used	

Used copies almost always contain faults. Used price is for copy with faults; sound copies sell for 100% or more of the price of a faulty copy, such as the nicely centered used copy that sold at auction for $30,800 in 1998. An unused copy with original gum sold for $247,500 in 1993.

IV 2	used, center double printed, one inverted **LRS (86)**	20,900.00
	Quantity: 3 used examples	

One copy is quite faulty and extensively repaired.

Declaration of Independence. April 7, 1869. Engraved.

24c green & violet

IV 3	center inverted	100,000.00
	used, center inverted	10,000.00
	used block of 4, center inverted **LRS (9/93)**	569,250.00
	on cover	—
	Quantity: 4 unused; 85-90 used	

Used copies usually contain faults. Used price is for copy with faults; sound copies sell for 100% or more of the price of a faulty copy. The finest known unused copy sold for $258,500 in September 1993. Refer to notes following **IV 1** and **IM 25**. The copy on cover is unique.

One hundred sets of plate proofs on card of the 1869 Series (15c, 24c, 30c & 90c) exist with centers inverted. The 90c value exists as an invert in proof form only. Market value per set of 4 single proofs is $10,000-$12,000. Plate blocks exist: 24c, two plate blocks of 8; 30c, one plate block 4 and one plate block of 8; 90c, two plate blocks of 8.

Eagle and Shield. May 15, 1869. Engraved.

30c red & blue

IV 5	center inverted	100,000.00
	used, center inverted	40,000.00
	Quantity: 7 unused; 36-40 used	

Almost all used copies contain faults; only 3 sound copies are known. Used price is for copy with faults: sound copies sell for 100% premium or more. One of the finest known unused copies sold at auction for $170,500 hammer price in 1991 and one of the finest used copies sold for $104,500 in 1998.

Steamship. May 1, 1901. Engraved.

1c black & green

IV 6	center inverted	10,000.00
	block of four **LRS (10/98)**	33,000.00
	used, center inverted	6,000.00
	used on cover	—
	Quantity: 250+	

Unused copies typically are poorly centered, have disturbed gum and small faults. Price is for a reasonably centered, hinged, sound copy with undisturbed gum. Copies with disturbed gum and faults sell for 50% or less of listed price; choice sound copies sell for more than listed price. Used price is for a sound copy.

Train. May 1, 1901. Engraved.

2c black & red

IV 7	center inverted	35,000.00
	intact block of 4 **LRS (89)**	203,500.00
	repaired block of 4 **LRS (10/98)**	148,500.00
	used, center inverted	12,500.00
	Quantity: 75-85 unused; 5-7 used; 2 blocks of 4 listed above	

Refer to price and condition note following **IV 6**. A select mint copy of **IV 6** sold at auction for $60,000 hammer price in 1999.

Antique Automobile. May 1, 1901. Engraved.

4c black & brown

IV 8	center inverted **NRI**	10,000.00
	block of 4 **LRS** (10/98)	104,500.00
	single, with **SPECIMEN** overprint	5,000.00
	Quantity: 100 without overprint, 186 with **SPECIMEN** overprint	

Distributed by the Third Assistant Postmaster General, many were marked with the word "Specimen." Additional copies were traded by the National Museum for stamps needed for their collection. Most copies with "Specimen" overprint are centered toward the bottom.

Usually encountered with small faults or disturbed gum (from being stuck down to a Post Office archive book prior to dispersal). Price is for copy with usual small faults. Fault free copies, either unused or used, sell for 100% to 150% premium. One of the finest known copies of **IV 8** sold for $27,500 in May 2000.

Dag Hammarskjold. October 23, 1962. Engraved.

4c black, brown & yellow

IV 9	yellow background inverted, used on first day cover postmarked October 23, 1962	3,000.00
	used on cover postmarked Cuyahoga Falls, November 14, 1962	—
	pane of 50, signed per note below	—
	Quantity: 25-40 covers estimated	

☛ The discovery pane of 50 was signed in its margin by ten well-known philatelists, among them George W. Linn, Leo August and Ernest A. Kehr. So far as is known, it remains intact. After the discovery of the Hammarskjold error, the government reissued the stamp intentionally inverting the yellow. **IV 9** is identical to the re-issued stamp (issued November 16, 1962). Aside from the autographed discovery pane, the only positive way to identify the true error is by cover dated before November 16, 1962. First day covers exist postmarked either New York, NY or Brooklyn, NY. Of the first day covers, 22 are reported to be postmarked New York, NY. Covers also exist machine postmarked Cuyahoga Falls, Ohio, November 14, 1962, and notarized in the lower left corner by George W. Swartz, Notary Public.

☛ Caution. Counterfeit first day covers exist. An expert certificate is absolutely necessary for **IV 9** because of its similarity to the re-issue.

Washington Crossing the Delaware. May 29, 1976. Souvenir sheet of 5. Lithographed. BEP.

24c multicolored

IV 10	white (USA 24c) from 4th & 5th stamps inverted	—
	Quantity: very rare	

Note. The 24c and 31c souvenir sheets of the Bicentennial issue exist with perforations inverted in relation to the design.

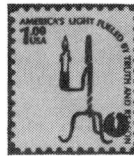

Candle Holder. July 2, 1979. Engraved, lithographed. BEP.

$1 dark brown (engraved); yellow, orange & tan (lithographed)

IV 11	candle flame inverted	14,500.00
	as above, white vertical stripe	—
	block of 4, candle flame inverted	—
	Quantity: one pane of 100 located of which 95 were purchased, including 8 white stripe varieties; the other 5 are presumed to have been lost in use.	

Copies of the 32c Nixon stamp with the lithographed portion of its design (Nixon's bust and the denomination) inverted in relation to the engraved (Richard Nixon) legend found their way onto the market in 1996, having been stolen by an employee of one of the printing plants. The employee has since been arrested, tried and convicted of theft of government property. The Postal Service ordered all copies seized; however, one or two copies are not accounted for.

AIR MAIL

Biplane. May 13, 1918. Engraved. BEP.

24c red & blue

IVA 1	center inverted	*125,000.00*
	block of 4, centers inverted	—
	center line block, centers inverted	—
	margin block of 4 with blue plate No., centers inverted	—
	Quantity: 100	

Prices for this stamp vary substantially according to condition. Each copy must be valued according to its merits. The listed price is only an average. Select copies have sold in the $125,000-$150,000 range during the past couple of years. An especially nice, lightly hinged, very fine copy sold at auction for $192,500 in October 1998; another sold for $176,00 in May 1999. Less desirable copies have sold for as little as $65,000.

Buying or selling?
Consult the dealer directory at the back of the catalogue.

POSTAL CARD INVERTS

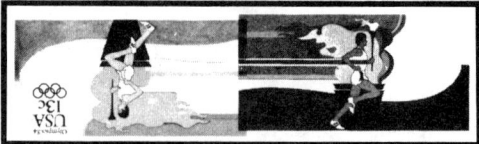

Olympics 1984. April 30, 1984. Lithographed.

13c black, blue, yellow & magenta

IVPC 2 yellow & black inverted & to the
left of basic design —
Quantity: 5 reported

Although catalogue prices are based on the best information available at press time, readers should be aware that prices for error stamps fluctuate over time, and therefore, are advised to contact dealers active in the error stamp market for timely quotes when buying or selling.

REVERSE INSCRIPTION ERRORS

REVERSE INSCRIPTION OMITTED

YOUTHFUL HEROINE
On the dark night of April 26, 1777, 16-year-old Sybil Ludington rode her horse "Star" alone through the Connecticut countryside rallying her father's militia to repel a raid by the British on Danbury.

Reverse Inscription

Sybil Ludington. March 25, 1975. Photogravure. BEP.

8c multicolored, green reverse inscription

RO 1   green reverse inscription omitted   200.00
       Quantity: 100-150

☞ Caution. Green reverse inscription is printed in partially water soluble ink. Used copies without expert certificates should be regarded with suspicion.

GALLANT SOLDIER
The conspicuously courageous actions of black foot soldier Salem Poor at the Battle of Bunker Hill on June 17, 1775, earned him citations for his bravery and leadership ability.

Reverse Inscription

Salem Poor. March 25, 1975. Photogravure. BEP.

10c multicolored, green reverse inscription

RO 2   green reverse inscription omitted   200.00
       Quantity: 300+ reported

☞ Caution. Refer to note following RO 1.

FINANCIAL HERO
Businessman and broker Haym Salomon was responsible for raising most of the money needed to finance the American Revolution and later to save the new nation from collapse.

Reverse Inscription

Haym Salomon. March 25, 1975. Photogravure. BEP.

10c multicolored; green reverse inscription

RO 3   green reverse inscription omitted   200.00
       as above, used single   —
       Quantity: 400+ reported

☞ Caution. Refer to note following RO 1.

Olympics. May 2, 1996. Se-tenant pane of 20. Photogravure. SVS.

32c multicolored; black reverse inscription

RO 4   pane of 20, black reverse inscription
       omitted on the leftmost vertical row
       of stamps (positions 1, 6, 11 & 16)   —
       Quantity: unique

RO 4 is due to a shift in printing of the reverse inscriptions so that the description for "Decathlon" (the top leftmost stamp) is shifted right one stamp and appears on the reverse of the "Men's Canoeing" stamp (the second stamp from the left on the top row). Each of the 16 non-inscription-omitted stamps contains a shifted inscription.

MIGRATORY BIRD HUNTING STAMPS

TAKE PRIDE IN AMERICA
BUY DUCK STAMPS
SAVE WETLANDS
•
SEND IN ALL BIRD BANDS
•
SIGN YOUR DUCK STAMPS
IT IS UNLAWFUL TO HUNT WATERFOWL OR USE THIS STAMP AS A NATIONAL WILDLIFE ENTRANCE PASS UNLESS YOU SIGN YOUR NAME IN INK ON THE FACE OF THIS STAMP

Black Bellied Whistling Duck. June 30, 1990. Engraved, lithographed. BEP.

$12.50 multicolored

ROWF 1   reverse inscription omitted   275.00
         Quantity: 150

☞ Caution. The reverse inscription is printed on top of the gum. Beware regummed copies offered as inscription omitted copies. Expert certificate strongly advised. Beware other waterfowl hunting stamps offered as reverse inscription omitted errors. It is possible to emulate this type of error by washing gum off (along with the inscription) then regumming a stamp.

REVERSE INSCRIPTION INVERTED

Reverse inscriptions are normally oriented with the top of an inscription at the top of a stamp. Inverted inscriptions appear to be upside down when turning a stamp in the same fashion as turning the page of a book.

Blue Geese. July 1, 1955. Engraved. BEP.

    $2 blue

RIWF1 reverse inscription inverted   —
       Quantity: *new, 1 mint, 1 used*

American Eiders. July 1, 1957. Engraved. BEP.

    $2 yellow green

RIWF 2 reverse inscription inverted   —
       Quantity: 7-8

Labrador Retriever & Mallard. July 1, 1959. Engraved, lithographed. BEP.

    $3 multicolored

RIWF 3 reverse inscription inverted   —
       Quantity: one reported

IMPERFORATE PLATE NUMBER COIL STRIPS - QUANTITIES KNOWN

The table lists the catalogue number, description of the stamp, plate number, length of the strip, and number of strips known or reported at press time. Additional plate numbers or quantities of strips may exist and not be known to publisher. Items listed in italics are either new or tentative; additional strips may surface.

TRANSPORTATION SERIES COILS

IM 410 1c Omnibus
Plate No. 5	strip of 5 or 6	10 strips
Plate No. 6	strip of 5 or 6	3 strips
Plate No. 6	strip of 10	1 strip

IM 410A 1c Omnibus (revised design)
Plate No. 1	strip of 6	*1-2 strips*

IM 411 2c Locomotive
Plate No. 3	strip of 6	50-100 strips
Plate No. 3	strip of 18	1 strip
Plate No. 4	strip of 6	50-100 strips
Plate No. 4	strip of 18	1 strip
Plate No. 8	strip of 6	100+ strips
Plate No. 10	strip of 6	100+ strips

IM 412 4c Stagecoach (precancelled)
Plate No. 5	strip of 3	4 strips
Plate No. 5	strip of 4	1 strip
Plate No. 6	strip of 3	4 strips

IM 412A 4c Stagecoach
Plate No. 1	strip of 6	8 strips
Plate No. 1	strip of 18	1 strip
Plate No. 2	strip of 6	8 strips
Plate No. 2	strip of 18	1 strip

IM 412B 4c Stagecoach (revised design)
Plate No. 1	strip of 6	12 strips
Plate No. 1	strip of 18	1 strip

IM 412C 04c Steam Carriage
Plate No. 1	strip of 6	4 strips
Plate No. 1	strip of 7	1 strip
Plate No. 1	strip of 9	1 strip

IM 413 5c Motorcycle
Plate No. 1	strip of 5	1 strip
Plate No. 2	strip of 5	1 strip

IM 413A 5c Circus Wagon
Plate No. 1	strip of 6	1 strip
Plate No. 1	strip of 18	1 strip

IM 413B 05c Circus Wagon
Plate No. S2	strip of 6	n/a
Plate No. S2	strip of 18	1 strip

IM 413C 5c Canoe
Plate No. 1	strip of 6	6 strips
Plate No. 1	strip of 18	1 strip
Plate No. 2	strip of 6	8 strips
Plate No. 2	strip of 18	1 strip

IM 414 5.9c Bicycle
Plate No. 3	strip of 6	62-63 strips
Plate No. 4	strip of 6	62-63 strips

IM 416 6c Tricycle
Plate No. 2	strip of 6	9 strips

IM 417 8.4c Wheelchair
Plate No. 1	strip of 6	4 strips
Plate No. 2	strip of 6	3 strips
Plate No. 2	strip of 18	1 strip

IM 418 9.3c Mail Wagon
Plate No. 1	strip of 5	10 strips
Plate No. 1	strip of 18	1 strip
Plate No. 2	strip of 5	10 strips
Plate No. 2	strip of 18	1 strip
Plate No. 3	strip of 5	1-2 strips
Plate No. 4	strip of 5	2-3 strips

IM 419 10c Tractor Trailer
Plate No. 1	strip of 6	6 strips
Plate No. 1	strip of 7	2 strips
Plate No. 1	strip of 18	1 strip

IM 420 10.1c Oil Wagon (black precancel)
Plate No. 1	strip of 6	15 strips
Plate No. 1	strip of 18	1 strip

IM 420A 10.1c Oil Wagon (red precancel)
Plate No. 3	strip of 6	250 strips
Plate No. 3	strip of 18	1 strip

IM 421 10.9c Hansom Cab
Plate No. 1	strip of 6	10 strips
Plate No. 2	strip of 6	10 strips

IM 423 12.5c Pushcart
Plate No. 1	strip of 6	30 strips
Plate No. 1	strip of 18	1 strip

IM 424 13.2c Coal Car
Plate No. 1	strip of 6	30 strips
Plate No. 2	strip of 6	5 strips
Plate No. 2	strip of 18	1 strip

IM 425 14c Iceboat
Plate No. 1	strip of 6	25 strips
Plate No. 2	strip of 6	25 strips

IM 425A 15c Tugboat
Plate No. 2	strip of 6	5-10 strips
Plate No. 2	strip of 18	1 strip

IM 426 16.7c Popcorn Wagon
Plate No. 1	strip of 6	10 strips

IM 427 17c Electric Auto
Plate No. 1	strip of 6	8-10 strips
Plate No. 2	strip of 6	8-10 strips
Plate No. 3	strip of 6	8-10 strips
Plate No. 3	strip of 18	1 strip
Plate No. 4	strip of 6	8-10 strips
Plate No. 4	strip of 18	1 strip
Plate No. 5	strip of 6	*1 strip*

IM 427 17c Electric Auto, continued
Plate No. 5	strip of 18	1 strip
Plate No. 7	strip of 18	1 strip
Plate No. 7	strip of 6	1 strip

IM 428 17c Electric Auto (precancelled)
Plate No. 3	strip of 6	6 strips
Plate No. 4	strip of 6	5 strips

IM 429 17c Dog Sled
Plate No. 2	strip of 5 or 6	4 strips

IM 429A 17.5c Racing Car
Plate No. 1	strip of 6	3 strips
Plate No. 1	strip of 5	*1 strip*

IM 430 18c Surrey
Plate No. 1	strip of 6	1 strip
Plate No. 2	strip of 6	3 strips
Plate No. 8	strip of 6	1 strip
Plate No. 9	strip of 6	15 strips
Plate No. 10	strip of 6	15 strips
Plate No. 13	strip of 4	1 strip

IM 432 20c Fire Pumper
Plate No. 1	strip of 4	1 strip
Plate No. 1	strip of 5	2 strips
Plate No. 2	strip of 2	1 strip
Plate No. 3	strip of 2	1 strip
Plate No. 4	strip of 6	1 strip
Plate No. 5	strip of 4	1 strip
Plate No. 5	strip of 6	4 strips
Plate No. 9	strip of 6	10-15 strips
Plate No. 10	strip of 6	10-15 strips
Plate No. 15	strip of 6	7-10 strips
Plate No. 16	strip of 4	1 strip
Plate No. 16	strip of 5	3-7 strips

IM 433 20c Cable Car
Plate No. 2	strip of 6	20 strips
Plate No. 2	strip of 18	1 strip

IM 433A 20c Cog Railway
Plate No. 1	strip of 6	25+ strips
Plate No. 1	strip of 18	1 strip

IM 434 21c Railroad Mail Car
Plate No. 1	strip of 6	50 strips
Plate No. 1	strip of 18	1 strip

IM 435 23c Lunch Wagon
Plate No. 2	strip of 6	20 strips
Plate No. 2	strip of 18	1 strip
Plate No. 3	strip of 6	15 strips
Plate No. 3	strip of 18	1 strip

IM 436 25c Bread Wagon
Plate No. 1	strip of 6	9 strips
Plate No. 1	strip of 7	1 strip
Plate No. 2	strip of 6	50-75 strips
Plate No. 2	strip of 18	1 strip
Plate No. 3	strip of 6	50-75 strips
Plate No. 3	strip of 18	1 strip
Plate No. 4	strip of 6	50-75 strips
Plate No. 4	strip of 18	1 strip
Plate No. 5	strip of 6	9 strips
Plate No. 5	strip of 5	1-2 strips

IM 438 32c Ferryboat
Plate No. 2	strip of 6	*4 strips*
Plate No. 2	strip of 18	1 strip
Plate No. 3	strip of 2	*2 strips*
Plate No. 5	strip of 1	*1 strip*

IM 439 $1 Seaplane
Plate No. 1	strip of 22	1 strip

FLAG COILS

IM 401 18c Flag
Plate No. 2	strip of 2	30 strips
Plate No. 2	strip of 3	*1-2 strips*
Plate No. 2	strip of 4	3 strips
Plate No. 3	strip of 4	1 strip
Plate No. 4	strip of 6	6 strips
Plate No. 5	strip of 6	75 strips

IM 407 20c Flag
Plate No. 1	strip of 2	1 strip
Plate No. 1	strip of 3	1 strip
Plate No. 2	strip of 5	10-15 strips
Plate No. 2	strip of 18	1 strip
Plate No. 3	strip of 5	10 strips
Plate No. 4	strip of 6	25 strips
Plate No. 4	strip of 18	1 strip
Plate No. 5	strip of 6	20 strips
Plate No. 6	strip of 6 or 7	6 strips
Plate No. 8	strip of 6 or 7	100 strips
Plate No. 8	strip of 18	2 strips
Plate No. 9	strip of 6	75 strips
Plate No. 9	strip of 18	1 strip
Plate No. 10	strip of 6	75 strips
Plate No. 10	strip of 18	2 strips
Plate No. 11	strip of 6	5 strips
Plate No. 11	strip of 18	1 strip
Plate No. 12	strip of 6 or 7	10 strips
Plate No. 13	strip of 6	10 strips
Plate No. 13	strip of 18	1 strip
Plate No. 14	strip of 6	7-10 strips
Plate No. 14	strip of 18	1 strip

IM 478 22c Flag
Plate No. 1	strip of 6	10 strips
Plate No. 1	strip of 18	2 strips
Plate No. 2	strip of 5	50 strips
Plate No. 2	strip of 18	1 strip
Plate No. 3	strip of 5	10 strips
Plate No. 3	strip of 18	1 strip
Plate No. 4	strip of 5	15 strips
Plate No. 4	strip of 18	1 strip
Plate No. 5	strip of 5	15 strips
Plate No. 5	strip of 18	2 strips
Plate No. 6	strip of 6	9 strips
Plate No. 7	strip of 6	8 strips
Plate No. 7	strip of 18	1 strip
Plate No. 8	strip of 6	25 strips
Plate No. 8	strip of 18	1 strip
Plate No. 10	strip of 6	15 strips
Plate No. 11	strip of 6	11 strips
Plate No. 11	strip of 18	1 strip
Plate No. 12	strip of 6	20 strips
Plate No. 12	strip of 18	1 strip
Plate No. 13	strip of 18	1 strip
Plate No. 15	strip of 6	9 strips

IM 478 22c Flag, continued
Plate No. 17	strip of 5 or 6	6 strips
Plate No. 17	strip of 18	1 strip
Plate No. 18	strip of 6	20 strips
Plate No. 18	strip of 18	2 strips
Plate No. 19	strip of 6	20 strips
Plate No. 19	strip of 18	1 strip
Plate No. 20	strip of 6	7-10 strips
Plate No. 20	strip of 18	1 strip
Plate No. 22	strip of 6	20 strips
Plate No. 22	strip of 18	2 strips

IM 493 25c Flag (block tagging)
Plate No. 2	strip of 6	10-15 strips
Plate No. 2	strip of 18	2 strips
Plate No. 3	strip of 6	10-15 strips
Plate No. 3	strip of 18	1 strip
Plate No. 4	strip of 6	8 strips
Plate No. 5	strip of 6	15 strips
Plate No. 5	strip of 18	2 strips
Plate No. 7	strip of 6	20-25 strips
Plate No. 8	strip of 6	10-15 strips
Plate No. 9	strip of 6	10-15 strips

IM 494 25c Flag (phosphor tagging)
Plate No. 2	strip of 6	50-75 strips
Plate No. 2	strip of 18	2 strips
Plate No. 3	strip of 6	30 strips
Plate No. 5	strip of 6	10 strips
Plate No. 5	strip of 18	1 strip
Plate No. 6	strip of 6	9 strips
Plate No. 6	strip of 18	1 strip
Plate No. 7	strip of 5 or 6	15 strips
Plate No. 7	strip of 18	1 strip
Plate No. 8	strip of 5 or 6	10 strips
Plate No. 8	strip of 18	1 strip
Plate No. 9	strip of 5 or 6	30 strips
Plate No. 9	strip of 18	1 strip
Plate No. 10	strip of 5 or 6	25 strips
Plate No. 10	strip of 18	2 strips
Plate No. 11	strip of 6	20 strips
Plate No. 11	strip of 18	1 strip
Plate No. 13	strip of 6	4 strips
Plate No. 13	strip of 18	1 strip
Plate No. 14	strip of 6	15-20 strips
Plate No. 14	strip of 18	2 strips
Plate No. 15	strip of 6	5 strips
Plate No. 15	strip of 18	1 strip

IM 512 29c Flag & Rushmore
Plate No. 1	strip of 6	10-15 strips
Plate No. 1	strip of 18	2 strips
Plate No. 2	strip of 6	9 strips
Plate No. 2	strip of 18	1 strip
Plate No. 3	strip of 6	20-30 strips
Plate No. 3	strip of 18	2 strips
Plate No. 4	strip of 6	30-50 strips
Plate No. 4	strip of 18	1 strip
Plate No. 6	strip of 6	6 strips
Plate No. 6	strip of 18	2 strips
Plate No. 7	strip of 6	30-50 strips
Plate No. 7	strip of 18	1 strip
Plate No. 9	strip of 6	2-4 strip
Plate No. 9	strip of 18	1 strip

IM 533 29c Flag & White House
Plate No. 1	strip of 6 or 7	10 strips
Plate No. 1	strip of 18	2 strips
Plate No. 2	strip of 6 or 7	10 strips
Plate No. 2	strip of 18	3 strips
Plate No. 3	strip of 6	6 strips
Plate No. 3	strip of 18	1 strip
Plate No. 4	strip of 6	20-30 strips
Plate No. 4	strip of 18	1 strip
Plate No. 5	strip of 6 or 7	10 strips
Plate No. 5	strip of 18	2 strips
Plate No. 6	strip of 6	9 strips
Plate No. 6	strip of 18	2 strips
Plate No. 7	strip of 6	10-15 strips
Plate No. 7	strip of 18	2 strips
Plate No. 8	strip of 6	10-15 strips
Plate No. 8	strip of 18	1 strip
Plate No. 9	strip of 6	15-20 strips
Plate No. 9	strip of 18	3 strips
Plate No. 10	strip of 6	n/a
Plate No. 10	strip of 18	1 strip
Plate No. 11	strip of 18	1 strip
Plate No. 12	strip of 7	4 strips
Plate No. 12	strip of 18	1 strip
Plate No. 13	strip of 7	3 strips
Plate No. 13	strip of 18	1 strip

IM 557 32c Flag & Porch (water activated)
Plate No. 11111	strip of 6	50-100 strips
Plate No. 11111	strip of 18	1 strip
Plate No. 22222	strip of 6	50-100 strips
Plate No. 22222	strip of 18	1 strip
Plate No. 33333	strip of 6	*12-16 strips*
Plate No. 33333	strip of 18	1 strip
Plate No. 44444	strip of 6	*16-50 strips*
Plate No. 44444	strip of 18	1 strip
Plate No. 45444	strip of 6	*4 strips*
Plate No. 45444	strip of 18	1 strip
Plate No. 66646	strip of 6	*4 strips*
Plate No. 66646	strip of 18	1 strip
Plate No. 66666	strip of 6	10-15 strips
Plate No. 66666	strip of 18	1 strip
Plate No. 77767	strip of 6	*50-100 strips*
Plate No. 77767	strip of 18	1 strip
Plate No. 78767	strip of 6	*50-100 strips*
Plate No. 18767	strip of 18	1 strip
Plate No. 91161	strip of 6	n/a
Plate No. 91161	strip of 18	1 strip
Plate No. 99969	strip of 6	*2 strips*
Plate No. 99969	strip of 6	1 strips

IM 558 32c Flag & Porch (self-adhesive)
Plate No. 11111	strip of 6	*3 strips*
Plate No. 11111	strip of 18	1 strip
Plate No. 23222	strip of 6	*7-8 strips*
Plate No. 44444	strip of 6	*3 strips*
Plate No. 44444	strip of 18	1 strip
Plate No. 45444	strip of 6	n/a
Plate No. 45444	strip of 18	1 strip
Plate No. 55555	strip of 6	n/a
Plate No. 55555	strip of 18	1 strip
Plate No. 66666	strip of 6	*3-4 strips*
Plate No. 78777	strip of 6	*3 strips*
Plate No. 78777	strip of 18	1 strip
Plate No. 88888	strip of 6	*3-4 strips*
Plate No. 88888	strip of 18	1 strip
Plate No. 89898	strip of 6	*3-4 strips*

IM 558 32c Flag & Porch (self-adhesive), continued
Plate No. 89898	strip of 18	1 strip
Plate No. 99999	strip of 6	n/a
Plate No. 99999	strip of 18	1 strip
Plate No. 11111A	strip of 6	n/a
Plate No. 11111A	strip of 18	1 strip
Plate No. 13231A	strip of 6	3-4 strips
Plate No. 13311A	strip of 6	n/a
Plate No. 22222A	strip of 6	3-4 strips
Plate No. 23221A	strip of 6	3-4 strips
Plate No. 44444A	strip of 6	3 strips
Plate No. 44444A	strip of 18	1 strip
Plate No. 55555A	strip of 6	3-4 strips
Plate No. 66666A	strip of 6	3-4 strips
Plate No. 88888A	strip of 6	3-4 strips

IM 600 33c Flag Over City (self-adhesive)
Plate No. 1111	strip of 6	2 strips
Plate No. 6666	strip of 6	new, 3-4 strips
Plate No. 7777	strip of 6	new, 3-4 strips
Plate No. 8888	strip of 6	new, 3-4 strips
Plate No. 9999	strip of 6	new, 3-4 strips
Plate No. 2222A	strip of 6	new, 3-4 strips

NON-DENOMINATED COILS

IM 477 D (22c) Non-denominated
Plate No. 1	strip of 5 or 6	15 strips
Plate No. 1	strip of 18	1 strip
Plate No. 2	strip of 5 or 6	8-10 strips
Plate No. 2	strip of 18	1 strip

IM 492 E (25c) Non-denominated
Plate No. 1111	strip of 5 or 6	20 strips
Plate No. 1111	strip of 18	1 strip
Plate No. 1211	strip of 5 or 6	6 strips
Plate No. 1211	strip of 18	1 strip
Plate No. 2222	strip of 5 or 6	8 strips
Plate No. 2222	strip of 18	1 strip

IM 510 F (29c) Non-denominated
Plate No. 1111	strip of 6	50 strips
Plate No. 1111	strip of 18	1 strip
Plate No. 1222	strip of 6	12 strips
Plate No. 1222	strip of 18	1 strip
Plate No. 2211	strip of 6	4 strips
Plate No. 2211	strip of 18	1 strip
Plate No. 2222	strip of 6	50 strips
Plate No. 2222	strip of 18	1 strip

IM 529 (10c) Bulk Rate (ABN)
Plate No. A43335	strip of 6	3 strips

IM 530 (10c) Bulk Rate (BEP)
Plate No. 11111	strip of 6	100 strips
Plate No. 11111	strip of 18	3 strips
Plate No. 22221	strip of 6	20 strips
Plate No. 22221	strip of 18	3 strips
Plate No. 22222	strip of 6	n/a

IM 551 (32c) G & Flag (BEP)
Plate No. 1111	strip of 6	9-12 strips
Plate No. 1111	strip of 18	1 strip

IM 566 (5c) Western Butte
Plate No. S111	strip of 6	6-10 strips
Plate No. S111	strip of 18	1 strip

IM 568 (5c) Mountain
Plate No. S111	strip of 6	9 strips
Plate No. S111	strip of 20	1 strip

IM 596 (33c) H & Hat
Plate No. 1111	strip of 6	new, 4 strips
Plate No. 1131	strip of 6	new, 4 strips
Plate No. 2222	strip of 6	new, 8 strips
Plate No. 3333	strip of 6	new, 4 strips

OTHER COILS

IM 485 18c Washington (precancelled)
Plate No. 3333	strip of 6	5 strips

IM 486 18c Washington (no precancel)
Plate No. 1112	strip of 6	2 strips

IM 524 19c Fishing Boat
Plate No. A1112	strip of 3	1 strip
Plate No. A1112	strip of 5	1 strip
Plate No. A1112	strip of 5 (# at end)	4 strips
Plate No. A7767	strip of 6	10 strips

IM 451 20c Consumer Education
Plate No. 1	strip of 2	10 strips
Plate No. 1	strip of 6	5-10 strips
Plate No. 1	strip of 18	1 strip
Plate No. 2	strip of 6	5-10 strips
Plate No. 2	strip of 18	1 strip
Plate No. 3	strip of 6	4 strips
Plate No. 4	strip of 6	4 strips

IM 594 20c Ring-necked Pheasant
Plate No. 1111	strip of 6	new, 6-8 strips

IM 537 23c Chrome U.S.A.
Plate No. 1111	strip of 6	100 strips
Plate No. 1111	strip of 18	1 strip

IM 495 25c Honeybee
Plate No. 1	strip of 6	50-75 strips
Plate No. 2	strip of 6	50-75 strips
Plate No. 2	strip of 18	1 strip

IM 565A 32c Yellow Rose
Plate No. 1112	strip of 6	3-4 strips
Plate No. 1122	strip of 6	3-4 strips
Plate No. 2223	strip of 6	n/a
Plate No. 4455	strip of 6	3 strips
Plate No. 5555	strip of 6	3-4 strips
Plate No. 5556	strip of 6	3-4 strips
Plate No. 5566	strip of 6	3-4 strips
Plate No. 5566	strip of 22	1 strip
Plate No. 5666	strip of 6	3-4 strips
Plate No. 6666	strip of 6	3-4 strips
Plate No. 7777	strip of 6	3-4 strips

OFFICIAL MAIL

IMO 3 20c Official Mail
Plate No. 1	strip of 3	1 strip
Plate No. 1	strip of 8 w/splice	1 strip

EFOs & OTHER UNUSUAL STAMPS

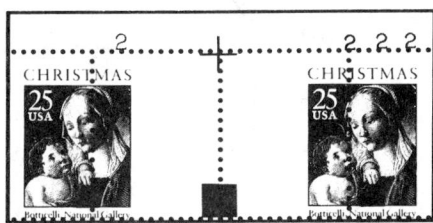

Tens of thousands of stamps exist with irregularities, such as misaligned perforations or color(s), paper folds or creases, over- or under inking, or other factors, that make them unusual in appearance. They are commonly referred to as EFOs (errors, freaks, and oddities). They are far too numerous to list or price individually. Even a reasonably modest discussion of EFOs could easily fill a book by itself. What follows is a generalized overview of the most commonly encountered types together with a few representative illustrations and some basic price guidelines.

Because so many EFOs are unique, and because no reliable population statistics exist for the rest, rarity is often not the primary factor in pricing. Visual appeal and topical appeal are most often the key elements in EFO pricing. The element of scarcity comes more into play in pricing non-unique EFOs, where a definite quantity is known. The best way to get a handle on EFO prices is to check dealer price lists for comparables, study prices realized from public auctions, and talk to EFO dealers and collectors.

EFO collecting is one of the most fascinating areas of philately. A growing number of collectors finds their peculiar appearance irresistible. And in a day and age where the Postal Service is flooding the market with hundreds of new issues whose primary—and often sole—purpose is to boost revenue, many find it appealing to collect the very items that the postal service goes to such great lengths to keep from the public—errors. There is something magical about owning the uncommon and the offbeat, about owning something few others own or choose to appreciate.

To the uninitiated the distinction between major errors and EFOs is not always clear or logical. Over the years, the way in which major errors were distinguished from other types of errors focused on how they were produced, major errors generally considered to be the result of a complete omission of one of the steps of production (e.g. perforations or color), the unintentional reversal of a sheet passing through the printing press (i.e. an invert), or the use of the wrong color ink to print a stamp. EFOs were generally considered to be the result of random flukes in production, e.g. misperfs, foldovers, misregistrations of color, smears, under- or overinking, odd shades resulting from ink-fountain contamination, etc., and not deemed as important or as valuable as major errors.

Before the 1960s major errors surfaced rarely—only a handful of inverts, a couple of color-omitted stamps, and precious few imperfs during the previous hundred years. Discovery of a new major error became a celebrated event, collectors prized them for their rarity and value, and stamp catalogues accorded them individual catalogue listings. By contrast, EFOs—although never common—turned up much more frequently, but were not accorded individual catalogue listings due to the randomness of their physical appearance and the sheer impossibility of trying to classify and describe each one of them. For years mainstream philately largely ignored EFOs, regarding them as little more than curiosities.

Since the late 1960s, hundreds of new imperforates and color-omitted errors have been discovered. The newfound abundance of major errors spawned a phenomenal rise in the popularity of error collecting and all types of error material—major errors and EFOs. EFOs have come into their own, now seriously studied, collected and appreciated by error enthusiasts.

Traditionally dividing line between a major error and an EFO focused on how an error was created, an approach that sometimes left gray areas. For example, until recently some did not regard imperforates resulting from foldovers to be major errors because they were created in the same random fashion as freaks. More and more, the tendency is to classify errors by their physical appearance rather than by how they were created, which cannot always be known with certainty. Nevertheless, gray areas still exist. It seems that in the taxonomy of errors, there is always room for question about which phylum, class, order, family, genus or species an item belongs. Differences of opinion regarding nomenclature also exist, i.e. what should properly be called an error, a variety, a freak, and so forth. The foregoing is mentioned for the benefit of those new to the hobby, who may find all this confusing and difficult to understand at first. In the final analysis, definitions and classification should never be allowed to stand in the way of appreciating an error for what it is—something unusual, intriguing, and exquisite in its own right. And many EFOs are arguably as eye-arresting and fascinating as major errors. Beauty—as the saying goes—truly lies in the eye of the beholder.

MISPERFS

Misperfs (misperforated; also known as misplaced perforations; also used to refer to misplaced die cuts) and perforation shifts occur when stamps are misaligned with perforating or die cutting equipment or when part of a sheet of stamps (typically, a corner) has been folded over during production (see **foldovers**). They can occur on any perforated or die cut stamp: sheet stamps, coil stamps, and booklet panes. Misperforated commemorative stamps are generally priced higher than misperforated definitive stamps, and misperforated sheet definitives are generally (but not always) priced higher than misperforated coil stamps. Too many misperfs exist to list individually or attempt to price. Value is generally a function of topical appeal and degree of misperforation. Usually, the more visually striking (the more severe or unusual the misplacement of perforations) and topically popular an item, the greater its relative value.

Misperfs range from barely misaligned to dramatically misaligned, as illustrated by the two coil stamps above. The 20-cent flag coil is only slightly misperfed; the 22-cent flag coil is perforated nearly down the center of the stamp. Misperfed coils are most commonly collected in pairs or strips. Misperfed modern coil pairs, such as those illustrated, range in retail price from $2 to $5 for slightly misperfed to $10 to $20 per pair for those perforated down the center. Occasionally an older or scarcer item sells for more.

Misperfed commemorative stamps are generally scarcer than misperfed coils. Slightly misperfed modern commemoratives, such as the First Man on the Moon commemorative illustrated above, usually range in retail price from $15 to $25 per stamp depending on age and topic. The illustrated stamp trades nearer the high end of the range because aerospace is a popular topic. A similar perf shift on a less popular topic might sell more toward the lower end of the price range. Pairs and blocks are priced proportionately. Older (pre-1940) or rarer misperfs also sell for more.

Some stamps exist misperfed only slightly, shifting a legend or denomination from top to bottom or from one side to another, resulting in an outwardly normal appearing "change of design." This effect is illustrated by the Thomas Gallaudet stamp shown above. The stamp on the far right is normal; the stamp on the far left is a changed design by virtue of the inscription moving to the opposite side of the stamp as a result of the perforation shift.

The Kennedy stamps of the Prominent Americans series illustrate another type of change of design. A normal 13-cent stamp is seen on the left; a "3-cent" variety is seen on the right, created by a very slight perforation shift. In most cases, a stamp with such a slight perforation shift would be unsalable, however, this "changed design" possesses eye-appeal and retails for about $10.

Misperfed "change of design" stamps are generally worth more than other slightly misperfed items in which no change of design occurs.

The Perry commemorative above is an example of a modest misperforation that yields a nice effect—you can read part of the design at top that normally appears at the bottom of the stamp. Again, pricing is a function of degree of misperforation and visual effect. This stamp has a retail value of $10 to $20.

Dramatically misperfed modern commemoratives such as the one illustrated above usually range in retail price from about $20 to $40 per stamp. Occasionally a rare or expensive item will command a price of as much as $125 or more per stamp.

Stamps with drastically angled misperfs, such as the illustrated 2-cent Liberty series definitive, whose appearance is striking (it almost makes you dizzy to look at it), retail for considerably more, as much as $75 to $100 per stamp.

Misperfs are sometimes collected as singles, however, multiples often reveal the misperforation more dramatically, as illustrated above by the block of Love stamps. Its perforations slant as a result of having gone through the perforator at a slight angle. The illustrated block sold at public auction for $66, or about $11 per stamp. Slightly angled misperfs tend to sell at prices similar to those for non-angled slight misperfs.

FOLDOVERS

As the name implies, foldovers occur when part of a sheet of stamps (most often a corner) is inadvertently folded during production, then subsequently trimmed, resulting in an odd shaped piece, often with an unusual perforation pattern (commonly known as crazy perfs). A foldover can occur prior to printing and perforating, or it can occur after printing but prior to perforating. Foldovers often contain extra portions of selvage (known as appendages) that normally would have been trimmed off. Foldovers are occasionally responsible for creating a major error such as the imperforate error **IMA 6A** or the color omitted error **CO 1**. Major errors resulting from foldovers are rare. Usually a foldover results in an EFO. Each foldover is unique.

Foldovers are often collected in multiples, which are usually more visually striking and better illustrate an error. The 2-cent Liberty block appearing above is a good example of a foldover resulting in crazy perfs. Its retail value is $125 to $150. As with other EFOs, the range of value for crazy-perf foldovers varies and is a function of topical appeal and appearance.

Foldovers resulting in crazy perfs typically range in value from $10 to $150, with many retailing in the $20 to $50 range, such as the example illustrated above. Older examples and eye arresting examples sell for more, occasionally hundreds of dollars.

MISCUTS

Miscuts occur when the production sheets of stamps become misaligned with cutting equipment. Miscuts often occur on imperforate coil stamps, and mention is made of them in the listings for imperforate stamps. Dramatically miscut imperforate coil stamps usually sell for a premium. Slightly miscut imperforate coils do not. Miscuts also occur on perforated coil stamps. Generally, the more dramatic the miscut, the greater its value. Miscut pre-1981 coil stamps often occur with partial plate numbers or marginal markings. The greater the amount of partial number or marginal marking showing, the more valuable the item. Miscuts also occur on sheet stamps, and they occur on booklet panes, yielding portions of adjoining stamps or in some cases selvage or gutters. Miscuts often occur in combination with misperfs, yielding uncommonly large selvage, or in some cases, gutters and portions of adjoining panes. Slightly miscut perforated coils (showing 15- to 25 percent of the adjoining stamp) typically retail in the $15 to $25 a pair range; those drastically miscut (half each of two stamps), retail in the $50 to $75 a pair range.

Most collectors prefer to collect miscut booklets in the form of intact panes. Miscut booklet panes that result from a simple shift often sell in the $15 to $50, depending upon the severity of the miscut. Slight miscuts sell toward the lower end of the range, dramatic miscuts toward the high end. The 5-cent Washington illustrated above is an example.

COLOR SHIFTS

Occasionally, dramatic and visually striking color shifts, such as the honeybee coil illustrated above, sell for as much as $100 to $200. As with other EFOs, there are no hard and fast rules; price is a function of eye-appeal and demand.

GUTTER PAIRS & GUTTER SNIPES

Postage stamps are usually printed in press sheets yielding either four, six or more finished panes of stamps when trimmed apart. The spaces between panes on a press sheet are known as gutters. Gutter pairs and gutter snipes occur when press sheets are miscut so that a pane contains a portion of an adjacent pane, including the gutter separating the two. Gutter pairs and gutter snipes can also result from pre-trimming foldovers.

Color shifts (also known as misaligned color or misregistered color) occur when one or more of the plates used to print multicolored stamps is out of register with the others, or when sheets are improperly fed on one or more of multiple passes through a press. Refer to sections on **lithography** and **photogravure** in the introduction for information on multicolor printing. Color shifts range from mundane to dramatic. Value is generally a function of topical appeal and appearance. Usually, the more visually striking (the more pronounced the misregistration of color) and topically popular an item, the greater its value. On rare occasions, color shifts occur in combination with misperfs. And on occasion, a color shift is mistaken for a misperf.

Color shifts generally range in retail price from $10 to $25 per stamp. Those with slight shifts sell toward the lower end of the range. Those with more dramatic shifts, such as the owl stamps illustrated above, sell toward the higher end of the range. Stamps with minute or barely discernable color shifts generally command little or no premium.

To be considered a full gutter pair, the pair must contain at least one complete stamp on either side of the gutter. Gutter pairs on issues available from the postal service in configurations that normally contain gutters (such as certain of the Farley sheets and modern uncut press sheets) are not considered errors. Pairs (or multiples) with full gutters between are rare and usually retail for hundreds of dollars, typically in the range of $250 to $750. The illustrated 3-cent Presidential is one of the more common full gutter pairs. It retails in the $125 to $150 range.

Items with less than a complete stamp on either side are known as gutter snipes and sell for considerably less, the price determined by the size of the incomplete stamp and the issue. The illustrated $5 postage due is much rarer than the 3-cent Win the War stamp. Some slight gutter snipes can be purchased for less than $25. Those with larger portions of stamps showing sell for more, usually in the $50 to $125. The illustrated $5 postage due pair retail in the $75 to $100 range. The Win the War pair, $45 to $60. Again, it's a matter of eye-appeal, and prices range broadly across the spectrum. Stamps showing only perforations from an adjoining pane (and no part of an adjoining stamp) are also called gutter snipes and typically sell for a dollar or so per stamp.

OPEN CREASES

Pre-production open creases result from paper bunching or folding over on itself prior to receiving a printed impression. Such stamps should normally be left in the largest multiple possible. Typically, the folded or creased portion of the affected stamp can be gently pulled apart revealing an unprinted (or open) area. The determining factors of value are: the size of the opening, the underlying catalogue value of the stamp, and the age of the stamp. Generally, the larger and more pronounced the crease, the greater its value. Ironically, open creases are more common on pre-1940 stamps than on later issues, and prices reflect this situation. Many open creased stamps fall in the $40 to $100 price range. However, a fair number sell for more than $100, especially mint examples and stamps with high underlying catalogue value, which can boost the price to as much as $1,000 or more. Mint examples sell for more than used examples of the same stamp. Of those illustrated above, the one on the left would be expected to sell for $100 to $125, while the one on the right would fetch $125 to $150.

ALBINOS & BLANK STAMPS

Albinos and blank stamps result from the omission of all printed colors. An albino stamp is generally understood to have a blind, intaglio plate impression embossed on its surface, which is often enough to permit identification of the stamp in the absence of its colors. A blank stamp results when all colors are omitted from a stamp printed by lithography or photogravure and no intaglio blind impression occurs. Blank stamps are usually impossible to identify unless attached to a normally (or partially) printed stamp of the same design. Blank stamps and albinos are collected in pairs or strips containing both normal (or partially normal) stamps and stamps with all color omitted. Blank stamps and albinos usually retail in the $75 to $300 range.

Albino impressions are much more common on stamped envelopes, where color is omitted but the embossed part of the design remains. Pre-1960 albino stamped envelopes typically sell for $2 to $10 each. Recently issued albino stamped envelopes are much scarcer and sell for more, especially used copies.

MISCELLANEOUS

Smears, blobs and blotches are caused by excess ink, by cleaning solvent or other chemicals on a printing plate at some point during production. Solvent smears are usually collected in blocks, strips, or panes large enough to show the entire smear pattern.

Minor overinking smears (such as the one on the left) command only a nominal premium; heavily smeared stamps (such as the one on the right) usually sell in the $5 to $15 per stamp price range. Again, price is a function of eye-appeal. Ink blobs and blotches on stamps usually sell for more than smears. Again, it's a matter of eye appeal.

Underinked stamps (sometimes known as dry prints) are caused by too little ink being applied to a plate during printing. The stamp on the left is normal; the one on the right is underinked. Those sufficiently underinked to be considered collectible typically retail from $3 to $15 per stamp depending on severity of the effect. The illustrated 2-cent Presidential retails about mid-range, $7.50 or so.

The two examples above are severely underinked and retail in the $10 to $15 per stamp range. Slightly underinked stamps have little value. On occasion, truly startling examples sell for as much as $50.

Offsets. The most pronounced examples are caused by a printing plate leaving a fully inked impression on an underlying roller when the press skips a sheet of paper. Subsequent sheets then receive normally inked impressions on the top side, as well as a reversed impression on the gummed side, where it has come in contact with the roller. The illustrated examples were created in this fashion. The first sheet going through after a skipped sheet receives the most vivid impression. Subsequent impressions fade as ink on the roller is exhausted, until after a few sheets there is no evidence that a skip ever occurred. Generally, the more bold and pronounced the offset, the greater its value. As with other EFOs, the price of offsets varies with the intensity of the offset image and topical appeal. Prices for roller offsets typically range from $25 to $100 per stamp, and can range higher depending on the item.

Offsets are occasionally simulated by normally printed stamps sticking together due to high humidity. When pulled apart, they can give the appearance of an offset, however, they are not true offsets and have no philatelic value.

Imperforate Margins. Occasionally stamps occur with perforations omitted between the design and the margin. They should not be confused with stamps issued with natural straight edges. Although not considered major errors because the omission of perforations does not occur between stamps, imperforate margined stamps are, nevertheless, collectible. Usually, they're worth only a fraction of the value of an imperforate error.

Partial or Blind Perforations. Blind perfs are incompletely or partially impressed (or ground) perforations (or die cuts), often barely indented into the paper, giving a stamp the appearance of being imperforate. They are usually worth little, unless the perforations are so slightly impressed as to be barely noticeable. Occasionally, blind perfs are shifted into a stamp's design making their presence even more subtle and giving the item the appearance of being imperforate. Such dramatically blind-perfed stamps usually range in price from $5 to $20.

Plate Varieties. This term applies to a large class of small flaws that trace to the platemaking process or from damage to the plate during printing, which result in individualized flaws unique to one stamp or on an issued pane. Plate varieties occur more frequently on older engraved stamps than on modern engraved or photogravure stamps. Gripper cracks and double transfers are examples of plate varieties. Retail values tend to be modest, typically three to five times the retail value of a normal example.

Design errors, as opposed to production errors, typically exist on all stamps of an issue. Design errors consist of things such as the wrong number of stars on a flag or the misspelling of a name. Because all stamps of the issue contain the error, no premium is attached to the "error."

The Postal Service rarely attempts to correct design errors once issued. The 1994 Legends of the West issue, a se-tenant pane of twenty designs, which initially included the wrong portrait of Bill Pickett, is an exception. When the Pickett design error was discovered, the Postal Service ordered all post offices to return stocks of the error pane. The discovery and recall were made before the scheduled first day of issue, however, several panes reached public hands before the recall.

The Postal Service reprinted the pane with the correct portrait of Bill Pickett and released it in due course. Subsequently, it sold 150,000 panes containing the design error (the incorrect portrait of Bill Pickett, known as the "recalled" pane) by lottery. The recalled error pane is more valuable than the regular pane, only by virtue of the fact that it was released in limited quantity—150,000 panes—and because many collectors regard it as essential to completing a general collection of U.S. stamps.

Error collectors generally do not consider design errors to fall within the scope of the error collecting field. In philatelic vernacular, the term "error" almost always refers to a production error: imperforate, color omitted, invert, EFO, and so forth.

Errors?
We buy the unusual.

Collections wanted for purchase or auction.
US ★ Worldwide ★ Errors ★ Revenues ★ Washington-Franklins

Consignments always welcome!

Call Bob Dumaine
1-800-231-5926

Fax us a copy of your error! 281-496-1445

Sam Houston Philatelics

P. O. Box 820087, Houston, TX 77282 ♦ 281-493-6386 ♦ www.shduck.com

WANTED
U.S. FREAKS
AND ERRORS

ALWAYS BUYING

Imperfs, missing colors, color shifts, perf shifts, offsets, foldovers, miscuts or anything unusual!!!!!

Phone or ship what you have by insured or registered mail with your price or for my offer.

ALWAYS SELLING
A FULL RANGE OF MAJOR
AND MINOR ERRORS
AVAILABLE

I think you'll find them an excellent addition to any collection, even the most advanced. Many eye catching showpieces are available for a few dollars each. Why not see for yourself - request a selection of the odd and unusual in U.S. on approval. (References please.)

Errors
My specialty for more than 30 years.

MARVIN FREY
516-826-1852

2199 Legion St.
Bellmore, NY 11710

America's #1 EFO Source:

United States Major Errors

Whether you're buying or selling...

We have over 50 years experience in the unique Errors, Freaks and Oddities area of philately. Depend on us as your #1 source with our huge stock of these rare and elusive issues. And when it comes time to sell your holdings of EFO's, *always* contact us first! Phone, write, fax or e-mail us with description of your material for our top guaranteed offer, or to request our **free comprehensive price list.**

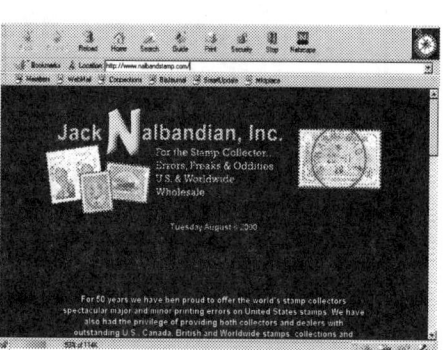

Visit our always-changing Internet website today. It's full of wonderful offers and resources.

www.nalbandstamp.com

Jack Nalbandian, Inc.

Life Member

Post Office Box 71
East Greenwich RI 02818
Phone: (401) 885-5020
Fax: (401) 885-3040
E-Mail: nalbandianj@earthlink.net

William S. Langs

Buying & Selling
United States
Major Errors

**ALWAYS BUYING U.S. ESSAYS, PROOFS,
POSTAGE LOTS, U.S. STAMPS & ACCUMULATIONS.**

William S. Langs

Send $1.25 for our price
list Essays and Proofs;
55¢ for our list of Major
Errors. Postage stamps
accepted at face value.

P.O. Box 46
New Milford, NJ 07646
Telephone (201) 262-5220
Fax (201) 262-4367

**ALL UNITED STATES & FOREIGN COLLECTIONS,
ACCUMULATIONS AND POSTAGE LOTS WANTED.**

FOUNDED 1978

Errors, Freaks, Oddities Collectors' Club

While various groups provide some information on EFOs, the EFOCC is the only club that covers the topic from A to Z. The EFOCC publishes a quarterly journal (The EFO Collector) that has articles, a mail auction, member ads and literature reviews. The EFOCC also offers members access to an exhibit critique service, an heir's assistance program and a sales circuit for buying and selling error stamps among members.

We want to hear about and publish your EFO finds and questions. Sent them to:

To join the EFOCC, send $16 ($30 overseas) with your name, address, and special interests to:

Editor, The EFO Collector
P.O. Box 1126
Kingsland, GA 31548-1126

Secretary EFOCC
CWO Jim McDevitt
955 S. Grove Blvd. #65
Kingsland, GA 31548
912-729-1573

Overseas memberships include airmail delivery of the EFO Collector. Life memberships, U.S. and Canada are $210; overseas, $440. For a sample copy of the EFO Collector, send $3 to the secretary.

EzStamp
The Millennium Edition

EzStamp $79.99
Includes 53 Countries to end of 1999

On CD ROM

NO SCANNING REQUIRED! COLOR IMAGES PRE-SUPPLIED

EzStamp is Simply the BEST & easiest way to track & inventory your collection! Includes data, images & values using the MINKUS Numbering System.

The #1 Stamp Program!

Join the thousands of other satisfied EzStamp users & see for yourself how easy it is to track your collection.

FREE DEMO VERSION FROM OUR WEBSITE

- Over 12,800 separate entries in our USA database. Includes Current pricing for Mint & Used singles, Plate Blocks, Mint Sheets, PNC's & FDC. Annual Updates. • The most complete US database available! IMPORT your cross-reference files so you can update your data by other numbering systems (ie. Scott™). ALL DATABASES COMPLETE TO THE END OF 1999 WITH FULL COLOR IMAGES!
- Easily create WANT lists, Inventory Reports, & custom reports with the Report Generator
- Thumbnail viewer to **visually search through the databases** & quickly find your stamps. Nothing could be easier!
- **Search** for any stamp by Image Viewer (just click on the image you want), Key Word or Topic, Year of issue, Minkus # or Denomination
- Built in **help** with easy to use manual. Right click help also available.
- Easily **backup** your valuable data with our ZIP compression backup function. • With over 53,500 full color images available on our CD's, EzStamp is the most comprehensive program available. More images, more databases & the most complete. EzStamp - the undisputed leader.
- Up to date, current pricing for Mint & Used singles, Plate Blocks, Mint Sheets & FDC. Annual Updates.
- **Complete to end of 1999:** Includes ISRAEL, USA, UN, CANADA, USA Revenues, Canal Zone, Confederate States, GB, JERSEY, GUERNSEY, ALDERNEY, ISLE of MAN, SCOTLAND, WALES & MONMOUTHSHIRE, NORTHERN IRELAND, AAT GERMANY, BERLIN, SAAR, 20 German States, IRELAND, JAMAICA. Also available are PRC, CHINA & RUSSIA for $39.99 or ITALY, VATICAN, SAN MARINO, GREECE, CYPRUS, NETHERLANDS, ICJ, Fr. & Spanish ANDORRA, GREENLAND & ICELAND for $39.99
- More countries, more features than any other stamp software. EzStamp is simply the best!

AlbumGen

AlbumGen $49.99 Easy to use!

On CD ROM

- Place rectangles, triangles, circles, diamonds, lines & text anywhere on the page, quickly & easily.
- Easy alignment tools, page & print previews.
- Import Images & data DIRECTLY from EzStamp including stamp sizes & cat # with one mouse click.
- With EzStamp & AlbumGen together, you can generate an entire country's album automatically. AlbumGen will draw & place the stamps on the page for you automatically. Then modify it to your liking if needed.
- Create unlimited number of pages & albums & print them on your own paper.
- Can give pages & objects different border styles to add your own personal touch.
- Built in search tools so you can find any item in your albums.
- Great for TOPICAL albums & EXHIBIT display pages.
- Design your albums YOUR WAY, anytime.
- Requires Win 95/98 or NT

FREE DEMO version to try before you buy from our website

AlbumGen is ..	$ 49.99
EzStamp is	$ 79.99
CHINA/RUSSIA CD add	$ 39.99
ITALY/VATICAN CD add	$ 39.99

Please add + $4 s/h in North America.

We accept VISA / MC, CHQ or Money Orders payable to SoftPro 2010 Inc.

ORDERS / Inquiries call, email or write to

SoftPro 2010 Inc.

18 Leverhume Cres., Scarborough Email : mariost@home.com
Ontario , M1E 1K4 , CANADA or marios@msn.com
Tel/Fax: (416) 261 - 7763
Website: http://www.members.home.net/mariost

Windows is a registered trademark of Microsoft Corporation. MINKUS is a trademark of KRAUSE Publications Inc. ©1994 -2000 SoftPro 2010 Inc. EzStamp for Windows is Copyright Protected Under International Laws. ALL RIGHTS RESERVED. Once opened or installed , SOFTWARE IS NON-RETURNABLE.

BOOKS YOU WILL TREASURE

**2001 Krause-Minkus Standard Catalog
of U.S. Stamps**
4th Edition
edited by Maurice D. Wozniak
You'll find over 8,000 stamps listed plus many new varieties in this up-to-date edition, which features more price listings and photos that the previous edition. New stamps issued during 2000 are featured, and U.S. and territories listings are more complete than ever. Individual sections include airmail, special delivery, postage due, parcel post, revenue, Confederate states, U.S. Possessions issues, encased postage, postal stationery and seldom-seen Test Stamps.
Softcover • 8-1/2 x 11 • 672 pages
5,600+ b&w photos
Item# SCM04 • $24.95

**Krause-Minkus Standard Catalog™
of Israel Stamps**
edited by Maurice D. Wozniak
Key information on every Israeli postage stamp - regular, commemorative and airmail - issue is available in this one convenient source. More than 1,500 stamps are listed and priced for used and unused stamps in the most collectible grades. Crisp, clean black and white photos of all stamps are available to aid in identification. Stamps are listed in easy-to-follow chronological order, with an accompanying table of tabs for specialty collectors.
Softcover • 6 x 9 • 104 pages
Item# ISR1 • $14.95

**Krause-Minkus Standard Catalog™
of Australia Stamps**
edited by Maurice D. Wozniak
Find information on every postage stamp from Australia and its territories - regular, commemorative and airmail - since 1902 in this volume. Features more than 1,900 stamps in used and unused prices in the most collectible grades. Crisp black and white photos aid in stamp identification, and stamps are listed in easy-to-follow chronological order. Handy, small size format makes it easy to carry and reference at shows.
Softcover • 6 x 9 • 104 pages
Item# AUS1 • $14.95

All About Stamps
An Illustrated Encyclopedia of Philatelic Terms
by Wayne L. Youngblood

What's a cinderella stamp? Omnibus issue? Or a socked-on-the-nose cancel? You'll find the answers to these and many other stamp collecting questions in All About Stamps, An Illustrated Dictionary of Philatelic Terms. Whether you're an advanced or beginning collector, you'll appreciate quick, clean definitions for almost every English philatelic term. Extremely well illustrated with hundreds of crisp, clear photos, this handy reference gives you the essence of the hobby without the clutter of country identifiers and confusing, outdated text.

Softcover • 6 x 9 • 192 pages
300+ b&w photos
Item# ABS • $14.95

Krause-Minkus Standard Catalog™ of Canadian & United Nations Stamps
edited by Maurice D. Wozniak

This new 2nd Edition features more than 7,000 updated and revised prices, and 3,800 listings of all Canadian and UN stamps through 1999 - a 20 percent increase over the first edition. The collector-friendly format lists all stamps chronologically in the two most-collected grades of condition. Features detailed stamp stories, histories, an introduction to stamp collecting, tips on how to use the catalog, as well as special sections covering postcards and stationery.

Softcover • 8-1/2 x 11 • 200 pages
2,500 b&w photos
Item# KMCU2 • $19.95

January 2001

2001 Krause-Minkus Stamps & Prices
A Mini-Catalog of United States Stamps
edited by Maurice D. Wozniak

This new guide features more than 4,000 U.S. postage issues, priced used and unused in the most collectible formats. All regular and commemorative U.S. Postal issues are covered and numerous photos and keys make stamp identification fast and easy. It is inexpensive, easy to carry and reference when at shows, and features extra space for cross-referencing with other catalog systems.

Softcover • 6 x 9 • 200 pages
Item# STP1 • $14.95

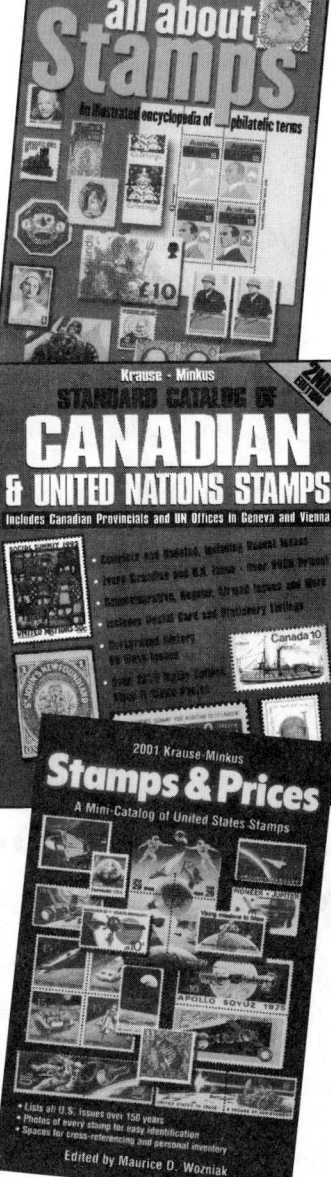

To place a credit card order or for a FREE all-product catalog, call
800-258-0929   Offer STBR
M-F, 7 am - 8 pm • Sat, 8 am - 2 pm, CST
Krause Publications, Offer STBR, P.O. Box 5009, Iola, WI 54945-5009
www.krausebooks.com

Shipping and Handling: $3.25 1st book; $2 ea. add'l. Foreign orders $20.95 1st item, $5.95 each add'l.
Sales tax: CA, IA, IL, PA, TN, VA, WA, WI residents please add appropriate sales tax.
Satisfaction Guarantee: If for any reason you are not completely satisfied with your purchase, simply return it within 14 days and receive a full refund, less shipping.

The Error Discovery of The Year?

(when you find out how much more you could have gotten for your EFOs by selling them to Gary Posner, Inc.)

When you sell your individual errors or a collection, there is only one value that <u>really</u> counts: <u>the best possible price</u> you can get. And that's what you will get from Gary Posner, Inc.

> And when you seek outstanding singles and plate blocks, including EFOs, through our vast stock and our "Premium Quality" want list service, we'll locate the stamps you want and send you color copies so you can see for yourself before you buy.

Bob Prager

Buying or Selling EFOs, One Number is All You Need

Gary Posner

800-323-4279
Gary Posner, Inc.

1405 Avenue Z, PMB #535, Brooklyn, NY 11235

Phone 800-323-4279 • FAX 718-241-2801

email: garyposnerinc@aol.com,

web site: www.garyposnerinc.com

Your Bi-Weekly Marketplace to the World Of Stamp Collecting

FEATURED IN EVERY ISSUE

- Timely News Stories
- Fascinating Features
- Informative Columns
- Lively Letters and Editorials
- Comprehensive Show Calendar
- New Issues Listings
- Special Stamp Pricing
- Large Classified Ad Marketplace
- Full-Color Photos & Illustrations

TAKE ADVANTAGE OF THIS OFFER AND HAVE A LOOK FOR YOURSELF

1 yr (26 issues) of Stamp Collector Only $25.98

Credit Card Customers Call

800-258-0929

Offer ABA1GG

M-F, 7 am - 8 pm • Sat, 8 am - 2 pm, CST

Mail orders on a 3x5 card to:

Krause Publications, Offer ABA1GG • 700 E State St., Iola, WI 54990-0001

Check out and order on our secure web site: www.coincollecting.net

EXPERT INFORMATION AT YOUR FINGERTIPS

2001 Brookman Stamp Price Guide
edited by David S. Macdonald
Updated annually, this 2001 edition includes over 10,000 price changes for U.S., United Nations and Canadian stamps, First Day Covers, souvenir cards and most areas of postal collectibles from 1847 to 2000. User friendly, this guide features a subject index, identifier and how to collect articles.
8-1/2 x 11 • 350 pages
4,000+ b&w photos
Softcover • **Item# BRP01** • **$17.95**
Spiral • **Item# BRS01** • **$22.95**

The Duck Stamp Story
Art-Conservation-History
by Eric Jay Dolin and Bob Dumaine

Now you can learn the history about the duck stamp program and find out the value of the stamps and artwork that have made this one of the best conservation programs in history. It also takes a look at what went into creating a program that has grown into one of the richest art contests ever. This is a must for anyone interested in wildlife conservation, stamp and art collecting or waterfowl hunting.
8-1/4 x 10-7/8 • 208 pages • Color throughout
Softcover •**Item# DUCK** • **$29.95**
Hardcover • **Item# DUCKH** • **$49.95**

Political Campaign Stamps
by Mark Warda
This impressive volume contains almost 2,000 listings and up-to-date pricing for stamps and labels from presidential campaigns, prohibition, woman suffrage, and anti-war, "win the war," and anti-communism movements.
Softcover • 8-1/2 x 11 • 224 pages
2,600 b&w photos • 8-page color section
Item# PCS • **$19.95**

To place a credit card order or for a FREE all-product catalog, call
800-258-0929 Offer STBR
M-F, 7 am - 8 pm • Sat, 8 am - 2 pm, CST
Krause Publications, Offer STBR, P.O. Box 5009, Iola, WI 54945-5009
www.krausebooks.com

Shipping and Handling: $3.25 1st book; $2 ea. add'l. Foreign orders $20.95 1st item, $5.95 each add'l.
Sales tax: CA, IA, IL, PA, TN, VA, WI residents please add appropriate sales tax.
Satisfaction Guarantee: If for any reason you are not completely satisfied with your purchase, simply return it within 14 days and receive a full refund, less shipping.

Sources

Buddhist Service Book, Buddhist Churhes of America, (1967)

Dharma School Service Book, Buddhist Churches of America (1983).

Jodo Shinshu – A Guide, Hongwanji International Center, Kyoto, Japan, (2004).

Jodo Shinshu Service Book, Hongwanji International Center, Kyoto, Japan, (2013).

Senshin Buddhist Temple Service Book, M. Kodani, editor (2001).

Services and Observances, San Fernando Valley Hongwanji Buddhist Temple, www.sfvhbt.org.

Shin Buddhist Handbook, Buddhist Churches of America (1972).

Traditions of Jōdo Shinshū Hongwanji-ha, M. Kodani and R. Hamada, Senshin Buddhist Temple, Pure Land Publications (1995).